Also edited by the RCC Pilotage Foundation
North Brittany Pilot
The Atlantic Crossing Guide

North Biscay Pilot

Brest to La Gironde

K Adlard Coles and A N Black
Revised by the RCC Pilotage Foundation
Edited by Lt. Col. C. A. Biddle
Third Edition

ADLARD COLES LIMITED
8 Grafton Street, London W1

Adlard Coles Ltd
William Collins Sons & Co. Ltd
8 Grafton Street, London W1X 3LA

Partly based on
Biscay Harbours and Anchorages, Vols I and II,
by K. Adlard Coles, first published in 1959 and 1960

As North Biscay Pilot
Revised by Professor A. N. Black
Second edition 1977
Reprinted with amendments 1978
Third edition 1982
Revised by the RCC Pilotage Foundation
Reprinted with amendments 1985
Reprinted with amendments 1987

Distributed in the United States of America
by Sheridan House, Inc.

Copyright © RCC Pilotage Foundation 1982, 1985

ISBN 0-229-11661-2

Printed in Great Britain by BAS Printers Limited, Over Wallop, Hampshire

The RCC Pilotage Foundation

In 1976 an American member of the Royal Cruising Club, Dr Fred Ellis, indicated that he wished to make a gift to the Club in memory of his father, the late Robert H Ellis MD, of his friends Peter Pye and John Ives who were both prominent members and as a mark of his esteem for Roger Pinckney, a past Commodore of the Club. An independent charity known as the RCC Pilotage Foundation was formed and, with the approval of Dr Ellis, the funds provided by him were transferred to the Foundation.

At the request of K Adlard Coles, the Foundation undertook the 1980 revision of the North Brittany Pilot and was then asked by Professor A N Black to revise the North Biscay Pilot. The RCC Pilotage Foundation gratefully acknowledges the gifts by the authors of the copyright of both these famous pilot books. It is the intention of the Foundation and the publishers to revise them at appropriate intervals so that the valuable work of the original authors will be kept up-to-date for the benefit of cruising yachtsmen. The Foundation has also undertaken a new book, The Atlantic Crossing Guide, and other projects will follow.

The Foundation is deeply indebted to Christopher Biddle for the enormous amount of meticulous work and many miles of travelling in France by land and sea that have gone into the preparation of this edition of the North Biscay Pilot.

The history of pilotage books on the Biscay coast for yachtsmen is a long one. The first was Frank Cowper's *Sailing Tours—Falmouth to the Loire*, one of a set of volumes he published at the end of the nineteenth century. Anyone who can lay hands on a copy will find in it a fascinating contrast to the situation described in the present volume. He was surprised to find a French naval vessel in almost every port he visited, but eventually realised that the French navy had hit on the only reasonable explanation for his eccentric behaviour—that he was a spy. Then came H. J. Hanson's great work, the *Cruising Association Handbook* but, as this covered the British Isles and much of north western Europe, the space devoted to this coast in the earlier editions was necessarily limited.

After the World War II, the race programme of the Royal Ocean Racing Club normally ended with a race to a port in the Bay of Biscay. Most owners and crew members had then to make fast passages to get back to work as quickly as possible. Only a few, of whom Adlard Coles was one, were able to finish the season with a comparatively unhurried cruise home. This enabled him, often accompanied by his wife alone, to make a thorough exploration of this coast and he realised the need for a detailed pilotage book.

The result was two volumes of *Biscay Harbours and Anchorages*, published in 1959 and 1960. The careful preparation of these volumes, with the selection of just that information which yachtsmen required, encouraged many British yachtsmen to visit this excellent cruising ground. After about ten years *Biscay Harbours* was in need of up-dating due to the many changes which had occurred in that time. As Adlard Coles himself was not able to find the time for the work involved, I undertook the task. Robin Brandon was then preparing his *South Biscay Pilot*, so the name was changed to the *North Biscay Pilot*, to avoid confusion, and the work was published as a single volume. Despite the change in name and format, the layout, and indeed much of the text, that had proved so successful was maintained.

An up-dated reprint was published in 1977, with much new information. It could not fairly be called a new edition, because it was not preceded by the check of all the ports which this would have implied. It is increasingly difficult for one author to find the time to do all the work involved in a complete revision. Now that the introduction of the IALA buoyage system has made a full new edition necessary Adlard Coles and I have gladly handed the responsibility for this to the RCC Pilotage Foundation. The Foundation will be able to use the resources of the Club, of which Adlard Coles and I are both members, to maintain the usefulness of a book which it has given us much pleasure to produce in our more active cruising days.

A. N. Black

Acknowledgements

The charts in this book, as in the previous edition, are almost all based on the official French charts, with the kind permission of the Directeur du Service Hydrographique et Océanographique de la Marine. Exceptions are based on Admiralty Chart 3427 with the permission of the Hydrographer of the Navy, and ECM Chart 347, with that of Editions Cartographiques Maritimes.

The revision of the book in 1980 and 1981 coincided with the introduction into these waters of the IALA system of buoyage, which is not yet quite complete as it goes to press, and not yet fully incorporated in French or British charts; in a few cases therefore a French published intention has had to be accepted as a *fait accompli*. Without exception the charts of the 1978 edition have required amendment or redrawing to take into account the new buoyage, the revised Admiralty light abbreviations, the progress of marina development, and such results of development as the silting of the Vilaine estuary. As it was desirable that the chart amendments should harmonise with the style of the originals, it was fortunate that my son John could combine the necessary draughtsmanship with knowledge of the sea, and thanks are due to him for hours of careful work.

Many of the photographs of the previous edition were out of date and some 70 have been replaced. With very few exceptions these have been contributed by Royal Cruising Club members, and carry no individual acknowledgement; this does not indicate any lack of gratitude.

It would have been presumptuous to attempt to improve on the work of K Adlard Coles and Professor Black except when changes have made revision unavoidable; those who have used previous editions of the Pilot know how much is owed to them. It would be difficult to list all the sources from which information has been obtained; still more the individuals who have contributed. To all are due the thanks of the RCC Pilotage Foundation and its editor.

C. A. Biddle 1982

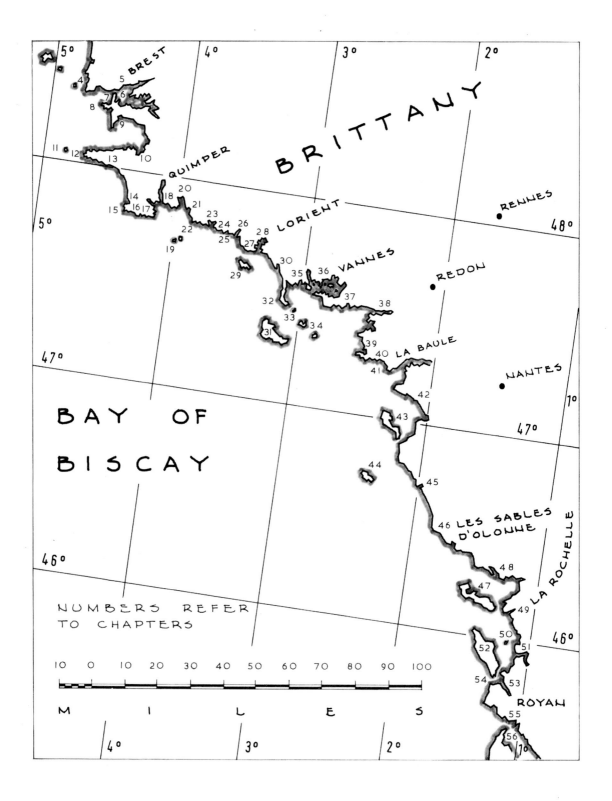

5°

BREST

5°

4

5

6

7

8

9

11

12

13

10

QUIMPER

BRITTANY

RENNES

48°

14

18

20

15

16 17

21

22

23

24

26

28

LORIENT

25

27

19

29

30

35

36

VANNES

REDON

37

32

38

33

34

31

39

40 LA BAULE

41

42

NANTES

1°

43

47°

BAY OF

BISCAY

44

45

47°

46 LES SABLES
D'OLONNE

LA ROCHELLE

48

47

49

46°

50

52

51

NUMBERS REFER
TO CHAPTERS

54

53

ROYAN

46°

10   0   10   20   30   40   50   60   70   80   90   100

55

M   I   L   E   S

56

4°

3°

2°

1°

Contents

9

Late corrections

This book has been corrected up to Admiralty Notices to Mariners 10 Nov 84; as it went to press, the following further changes were noted:

1 Cruising in South Brittany and Biscay

A small yacht heading for the Bay of Biscay will pass Ushant, usually passing inside through the Chenal du Four. After she has rounded Pointe de St Mathieu, the Rade de Brest lies to the east, providing in itself a magnificent cruising ground. Next comes the Baie de Douarnenez, a fine big bay, having however only two secure harbours.

Bound south, a vessel will next pass through the Raz de Sein. Here, as in the Chenal du Four, the tidal streams are strong and in bad weather the seas are dangerous, but once through the channel the Bay of Biscay is entered. The tidal streams are weaker and the weather becomes progressively warmer the further south one sails. Between Penmarc'h and La Rochelle there are three granite islands, Ile de Groix, Belle Ile and Ile d'Yeu, each of which has a harbour and minor anchorages. To the north and east of these islands, the mainland coast offers the variety of harbours and anchorages which makes it so attractive to the cruising man. There are anchorages in deep water and shallow, fishing harbours, busy ports, sophisticated holiday resorts, yachting centres, estuaries and rivers with peaceful reaches.

The first busy sailing area to be reached is the large bay from Loctudy to Concarneau, sheltered by the Iles de Glénan with their enormous and famous sailing school. Thence some passage-making leads to Quiberon Bay, another sheltered area, very popular with French yachtsmen. Here, between the yachting centres of La Trinité and Le Croisic, there lie all the anchorages in the Morbihan ('the little sea'), Penerf and the beautiful river La Vilaine. To seaward there are the little islands of Houat and Hoëdic, and to the west Belle Ile with the crowded harbour of Le Palais and another, less active, at Sauzon. In this area one could spend a month exploring and sailing in shelter even in bad weather.

Shallow draft yachts which do not wish to make the passage down Channel and through the rough waters of Four and Sein can come through the Breton Canals. The usual exit from these is to La Vilaine, but it is also possible to go on to Nantes and come down the Loire. The real canal enthusiast, if his draft is small enough, can turn aside at Redon, where he is almost at sea, and after another hundred locks, emerge at Lorient.

Beyond Le Croisic is the Loire, the southern boundary of Brittany. The coastal scene changes, rock reluctantly, but never entirely, giving place to sandy shores. The character of the harbours changes too; there are not so many harbours in which a yacht can lie afloat and come and go freely at any state of the tide. For this reason the best time for cruising in this region is when the tides are taking off from springs to neaps. It is then possible to leave near the morning high water and arrive in time for the evening one. On this part of the coast there are two large islands, Noirmoutier and Ile d'Yeu. Noirmoutier offers interesting anchorages, and one marina. Port Joinville is the only good harbour on Ile d'Yeu.

Another passage leads to the area round Ile de Ré and La Rochelle. La Rochelle is a historic city with two fine old towers guarding the entrance to one harbour and a vast new marina. Ile de Ré is low and sandy. St Martin, the capital, has a secure harbour with a wet dock. This area is the end of the popular cruising ground, but a few ports down to the entrance to the

Gironde have been included for the benefit of those using the Canal du Midi, which connects with the Mediterranean.

The cruising area which this book covers is a fascinating and varied one. For many British yachtsmen, the difficulty lies in the time taken to get there and return within the span of a summer holiday. A good plan is to work the yacht down Channel in weekends before the real holiday begins. Then make a direct passage from there to the South Brittany coast. The English Channel is fairly wide here, say 120 miles to Ushant, and it is about the same distance on to Belle Ile.

Ushant is not a nice landfall in bad weather and in fog it is horrid; in thick weather it is better to keep offshore, outside all the dangers. However in summer really bad weather is uncommon.

Winds. Winds in the north of Biscay are variable, but westerly winds (SW to NW) are most frequent in the summer months, especially in July and August. In spring, early summer and late autumn, winds between N and E are also common. There is some indication that the climate is changing; the strong westerlies of the last few decades seem to be dying away. The Bay of Biscay has a reputation for gales, but in summer from May to September winds of force 7 and over are recorded only about once in 25 days. Most summer gales are associated with depressions passing to the northward, with backing winds followed by a veer to the W or NW. At intervals of several years, very severe short storms may occur, which may be missed by the forecasters. Beware of a sudden fall in the barometer in muggy, thundery weather, with poor visibility.

Land and sea breezes near the coast are common in settled summer weather. Especially in the southern part of the area they result in the 'Vent Solaire'. After a noonday calm a westerly sea breeze sets in. This goes round to NW and by evening to N, and finally about midnight, or a little later, it settles in the NE, when it sometimes blows very freshly, causing quite a rough sea, and continues until 0800.

Another feature of this part of the Bay of Biscay is that if a NE wind starts to veer to S in the morning, and only goes as far as S and then backs to the NE, the NE wind may be accompanied by strong squalls.

Visibility. Fog, mist or haze is quite frequent during the summer. There is visibility of under 5 miles on about one day in five, but real fog, reducing visibility to less than $\frac{1}{2}$ mile, averages only one day in twenty. The coast is so well marked by beacons and towers that navigation in poor visibility is possible, but thick fog is very unpleasant if it occurs when one is sailing in narrow tidal waters.

Currents and Tides. When navigating in light weather and fog, the tidal streams are of great significance. Small-scale tidal charts only show the main streams, but in coastal waters there are local variations and eddies. The local set can be estimated by examination of pot buoys, which are numerous on this coast.

Swell. Swell is a factor which sometimes has to be reckoned with on the NW and W coasts of France. It appears to run higher in some parts than others, and is notable in the vicinity of Ushant and NE of Le Four. In the Bay of Biscay itself swell seems to be less frequent as the weather is better, and the swell ranges from gentle undulations to waves of considerable height, though it is rarely so uncomfortable as between Ile Vierge and Ushant, where the strong tidal streams are an added complication.

A large swell will break heavily on bars and in shallow water, with the result that the approaches to some of the harbours, such as Bélon, Le Pouldu and Etel, are dangerous even in fine weather if there is a ground swell. Swell can break intermittently and dangerously on rocks rising from deep water, even when there is apparently a safe depth over them.

Another characteristic of swell is that when it enters a narrowing inlet it tends to increase in height and steepness. It funnels up the entrance and will surge into anchorages which one would expect to be sheltered from the direction of the swell. For this reason, anchorages open to the Atlantic, such as those on the west side of Ile de Groix, Belle Ile and Ile d'Yeu should be used only with caution, in settled weather, with an offshore wind and in the absence of swell. Furthermore, if ground swell manifests itself in calm weather (and it can arrive with little warning, originating in disturbances far out in the ocean), a vessel should leave the open anchorage before it builds up to possibly formidable dimensions, when no anchor will hold. French fishermen take swell seriously, and none should know better. The French weather forecasts for shipping include forecasts of swell (la houle).

Type of Yacht—Draft and Drying Out. The North Biscay coast suits all types of yacht, large or small, deep-keeled or shallow draft.

For large yachts there are plenty of deep-water anchorages and most of the shallower harbours can be entered near high water, and the yacht can dry out against a quay. Before doing so it is best to make local enquiries, as the bottom in parts of some harbours is rough or rocky. To ensure taking the bottom with the yacht at the correct angle against the quay, which need not be great, it is usual to put all movable weights on the landward side of the yacht. In addition it is a wise precaution to shackle the main halyard to a bollard on the quayside and set it up as the tide falls. By this means the mast is stayed to the quay and the yacht cannot fall outwards, but do not forget to release the halyard when the tide rises. Good fenders are needed, as quay walls are often very rough; they should be hard and not squashy or they will be squeezed flat and the yacht will lean heavily inwards.

The yacht *Cohoe III*, in which Adlard Coles carried out his many surveys, had a draft of 1.8m (6 ft). She has a fairly long straight keel, which is an advantage when drying out alongside a quay. Yachts with very cut-away forefoots rest bow down at a considerable angle, which is not necessarily dangerous, but decidedly uncomfortable. The modern racing yacht with short fin keel and separate skeg does not usually lie comfortably against a quay.

French fishing vessels and most small French yachts are equipped with legs. Not only can they dry out against a quay more safely, but they can dry out anywhere in any sheltered anchorage if the bottom is smooth and hard. Legs are a great asset to cruising on the Biscay coast. Best of all is a bilge-keel yacht that can take the ground. She can explore many parts that are impossible for keel yachts, and can often find a snug berth inside the local moorings while her deep-keeled sister is rolling farther out.

Where reference is made in the text to a 'yacht which can take the ground', it is implied that she does not need the outside support of a quay wall.

A very large number of French yachtsmen sail dinghies or small yachts that are launched from trailers and the launching facilities are good nearly everywhere. It is quite easy, therefore, to trail a boat out and spend a happy holiday on this coast exploring its nooks and crannies, rocks and sands.

Navigating among Rocks. The coast of Brittany and North Biscay is famous for its rocks, which to a stranger may cause some apprehension. This will be especially the case if he is accustomed to mud pilotage, as on the east coast of England. He will soon come to realise that although it is much more important to avoid hitting the bottom, the large number of landmarks, natural and man-made, make it easy to know exactly where one is: if one knows exactly where one is, one has no reason to run aground. It is usually easy, by sliding a ruler over the chart, to find your own transits to keep out of trouble.

Beacons and towers are permanent, although occasionally damaged by gales, but complete reliance should not be placed on buoys, which may drag their moorings during gales, though in practice I have never found one out of position. Many of the rocks and shoals shown on the charts are not dangerous to moderate draft yachts, except in bad weather, when they cause the seas to break. Much depends upon the state of the tide. A useful tip is to estimate the rise of tide at the time when a harbour is to be approached, and then to put a pencilled circle on the chart round each rock or shoal which will not have a safe depth of water over it, remembering that tides do not always rise exactly as predicted. It is often surprising to find how few they are, so that pilotage is simplified by concentrating on the ones which are dangerous.

A common feature of a rocky coast is the extension of a pronounced headland in the form of a reef continuing seaward under water. For this reason, when approaching an inlet between two promontories, never cut across one of the promontories to the entrance, unless the chart indicates clear water. Approach from seaward with the middle of the inlet well open, allowing for the probable extension of the promontory under water.

If there is a big swell the seas will probably break over sunken rocks which are dangerous, and it may be necessary to avoid rocks which are covered by water of a depth equal to several times the yacht's draft. In strong streams the presence of rocks may be indicated by rips, or in smooth water by circles of oily-looking water. Even in deep water an uneven bottom causes a disturbance on the surface if the current is strong, so the oily circles do not always denote danger. In parts of Brittany the water is very clear, and if a member of the crew stands forward he can often see underwater rocks.

Rocks can be dangerous in light weather to yachts not equipped with reliable auxiliary power. In such circumstances the danger is greater than in rough conditions, if the tide is setting towards them. There is a theory that if a yacht is drifting becalmed, the stream will set her safely past rocks on one side or the other. This may be true of steep isolated above-water rocks, but it is certainly not true of underwater ledges. Great care must be exercised when navigating in calm weather near rocks; a good kedge with a very long warp must be ready for use.

Some harbours, such as the Ile de Sein and St Guénolé, have many rocks in the approaches. These present no great difficulty to the experienced cruising man, but as a mistake could have serious consequences, a newcomer to these coasts may prefer to limit his cruising on the first occasion to the better known and more easily accessible harbours. The more difficult anchorages should only be attempted in settled weather with clear visibility and preferably at neaps. The transits and landmarks should be identified with certainty *before* the yacht enters the danger area of rocks.

It is a good idea to check the yacht's position regularly by reference to natural features. New beacons can be built, or one mistaken for another, the large white building can be rendered inconspicuous by a larger whiter building, but nobody replaces or removes headlands or islands. Above all keep the identifications going well ahead of the yacht; not only does this give more time if things do not 'add up', but minor headlands may be quite prominent when looked at along the coast, but insignificant and unidentifiable when seen from directly offshore.

Harbours. In artificial harbours formed by breakwaters, it is inadvisable to cross close off the end of a breakwater, as these are often built on rocks, or have rocks at their bases. When entering a strange harbour it is best to approach about midway between the jetties with the inner harbour open; see page 19.

Unless using a mooring or a berth at a marina there is generally no need to seek out the authorities on entering a port. They will often visit a yacht after she is berthed. Stay away from areas assigned to the fishing fleets.

Mooring. It may be worth mentioning some methods of mooring which are commoner in France than in England. The first is lying close packed, side by side, with a mooring or anchor ahead and the stern pulled in to a quay or pontoon. If it is necessary to lay out an anchor ahead, one must note the direction in which the chains of those already berthed lead, and lay the anchor accordingly. Sometimes there is a line of buoys to which to secure the bow. Sometimes the pick-up rope for the bow mooring is led back to the pontoon; this can be tricky, as one has to back into the pontoon before getting the mooring on board, unless one sends out a dinghy.

Another unfamiliar method of mooring uses a big-ship buoy. Each new arrival takes a bow rope to the buoy and a cluster forms. When this is full a second circle is sometimes formed, by anchoring and taking a line to the buoy.

Both of these methods call for a good supply of fenders. Both methods, and also more familiar methods, are made less comfortable than they might be because French yachtsmen hardly ever use springs in circumstances in which the English regard their use as normal. I have, indeed, been positively asked not to use them by my neighbour when we were moored head and stern to buoys.

Provisions. Ordinary provisions can be bought in all towns, and even in small villages there are shops which supply necessities, and are nearly always open. Very small communities sometimes rely on a travelling shop, which is less convenient. Milk should be bought pasteurised, or it will not keep long. '*Sterilisé*' is similar to 'long life'. Groceries are expensive, and it is wise to stock up with non-perishables before starting the cruise. Meat is good, but very expensive; sea food, such as crabs and prawns, is good and usually cheap, though lobsters, alas, command their price anywhere. Mackerel can be caught, though less easily than in the English Channel; they seem more sluggish and will not come if the yacht is travelling fast. French bread is delicious, but does not keep. Where there is a baker it will be available early, but there may be delay where it comes by van from a central bakery to a 'depot de pain'.

In the text, under *Facilities*, 'all shops' implies at least bread, grocer, butcher, cooked meats and usually ironmonger and 'droguerie' (paraffin, paints etc) as well.

Water. There is a tradition that French water is suspect. The installation of central piped water supply almost everywhere has changed this and brought other changes, too. The water towers, which have appeared in great numbers, are conspicuous marks for the navigator, but piped supplies everywhere mean that the taps in the streets, which used to be so convenient, have now gone.

The availability of convenient watering points is given in the text under the heading *Facilities*. Only rarely is the absence of a watering point specifically mentioned; if water is not mentioned under this heading it should be assumed that water may be difficult to find, except by courtesy from shops or cafés.

Fuel. It is no longer permitted for yachtsmen to buy the tax-free fuel available to fishermen, or the red-tinted diesel oil sold for domestic heating as 'fuel oil domestique' (FOD). It is, however, now exceptional for the numerous marinas not to offer both petrol and diesel oil from quayside pumps, though not all will operate outside the French holiday season. Where there is no marina, fuel may also be available from pumps, though the presence of a pump does not guarantee this: it may be for fishermens' supply only. In some ports it may be necessary to fill by can from roadside garages.

Petrol (essence) comes in 2 grades, 'super' and 'normal'. Prices are (1984) rather above those in UK, with a rather higher differential between grades. Diesel (gasoil, pronounced 'gazwahl') is cheaper than in UK.

Formalities. British yachts must complete and deposit Part I of Customs Form C1328 (revised 1981 edition) before departing from British waters for abroad. Parts II and III must be retained on board and dealt with on return.

When in France all visiting yachts must carry a Certificate of Registry on board. Very heavy fines may be imposed on defaulters. The British certificate can be that of the Board of Trade, or the Small Ships Register, administered by the RYA, Victoria Way, Woking, Surrey GU21 1EQ. The status of yachts registered elsewhere should be established in advance.

16

Personal passports should be carried by all members of the ship's company. In practice they are likely to be required only for cashing cheques, for independent return to the UK by public transport and, in the case of the owner, for dealing with the Customs. The green card (Passeport du navire étranger) is needed to obtain duty free stores (although at some ports it is not asked for). To obtain it, report to the Customs with the ship's Certificate of Registry and the owner's personal passport. Although it is not otherwise necessary to report to Customs, doing so can be taken as legally equivalent to a formal declaration that the vessel is healthy and is not engaged in importing goods, being chartered, or otherwise infringing the regulations.

Few officials, except in marinas, speak English. To enforce the ownership regulations Customs visit yachts, even under way. A 'fiche' from them will simplify later visits. It is forbidden for one skipper to hand over to another in French waters, except between part-owners or immediate members of a family, including 'habitual concubines'. These regulations are intended to stop chartering in French waters by non-French organisations.

The French search and rescue organisations (CROSSCO, N of Pte du Raz; CROSSA, S of Pte du Raz) operate an excellent passage surveillance service. Some harbour masters require a form to be completed showing 'where from' and 'where to'. This information is passed on to CROSSCO/CROSSA. It is important that, if a yacht does not go where she has said she is going, the information should be reported quickly. Otherwise a futile search may be instituted.

Yacht Clubs. There are yacht clubs and sailing schools in most French harbours; they are invariably hospitable to visitors. Assistance or advice is always given readily, and showers are often available.

Laying up. In order to spend more time on the Biscay coast, it may be convenient to take a holiday late in the summer and to leave the yacht in France for the winter. By taking an early holiday in the following year, the cruise can be continued and the yacht brought home again in time for the remainder of the season. When laying up the green card must be deposited with the local Customs Office.

Chart Datum

Datum in the sailing directions and in the plans reproduced in this book is the same as on French charts; soundings are reduced to the approximate level of the lowest predicted tides. This level is referred to as LAT (lowest astronomical tide). Although the actual lowest predicted tide can only occur near the equinox and will not, therefore, affect most yachtsmen, predicted tides nearly down to LAT can occur at any time. At such times exceptional meteorological conditions could result in tides falling below chart datum.

This datum is of the utmost importance when navigating in the Bay of Biscay, for it means, especially in Brittany, that at *mean low water springs* there may be 0.6m (2 ft) more water than is shown on the chart, and at *mean low water neaps* even greater depth. The height of MLWS and MLWN above datum is shown at the head of each chapter and under each plan, so that the appropriate figure can be added to the soundings shown on the plan or given in the text. British charts of the French coast adopt the same datum as the French charts on which they are based.

In view of the current change of the British tide tables and charts to metric depths and heights, metric units have been used on the plans; where tidal values have been up-dated in chapter headings, heights in feet are no longer given as well. A conversion table is given on page 26.

Heights.

In the plans and sailing instructions in this book the French method of measurement has been followed which differs in some respects from British practice.

Rocks that uncover and drying patches. The heights are given above chart datum, being shown in underlined figures. In the text the word 'dries' is used. This is the same as British practice. On modern French charts, but not in this book, these figures are in italic.

Rocks that never cover. The heights are given above chart datum, being shown in underlined figures. In the text the word 'high' is used. British practice is to give these heights above MHWS. On older French charts these rocks are marked with the symbol 'T' over them; this must not be misread as representing a beacon. This convention is not used in this book.

Land heights. Heights on land, not underlined, are above mean tide level. British practice is to give these heights above MHWS.

Lighthouses. The elevation of the lights—not the actual heights of the structures—is given above MHWS. This is the same as British practice.

Sailing Directions

The description of each port is set out in the same form, so that the reader will come to know where to look for the information he wants. It is written from the point of view of the master of a sailing yacht of normal size. If there is more than 3m (10 ft) of water, the channel is described as deep, on the assumption that users of the book will not have a greater draft than this. Low bridges are treated as blocking navigation; although many motor yachts will be able to pass them unhindered, the upper reaches beyond them have not been inspected.

Beacons. There are many kinds of beacon and it is hard to find a descriptive terminology. British charts use 'Bn.' or 'Bn. Tr.' to cover this wide range. The scheme which has been followed as far as possible in this book can be set out thus:

Description on French charts	Appearance	Description in this book
Balise	A wood or iron pole beacon usually on ground which covers and uncovers, *or*	*Beacon*
	A modern version of the above, made of concrete, usually about 1m (3 ft) in diameter, on a wider base. They resemble thin tourelles, *or*	*Concrete beacon*
	A built up beacon on shore, often of iron or masonry in the shape of a pillar.	*Masonry beacon*
Tourelle	A stone or concrete beacon, usually on ground which covers with the tide. Cylindrical or slightly tapered in shape.	*Tower*
Amer	A built up beacon on shore which may be of any shape, often painted white.	*Masonry beacon*
Mur blanchi	A wall painted white (sometimes specially built as a beacon).	*Wall beacon*
Pyramide	A slender conical beacon painted white (not a mathematical pyramid).	*Pyramid*

Beacons, concrete beacons and towers are commonly painted to conform with the buoyage systems (cardinal or lateral) and have the appropriate topmarks; the others are not. The word 'tower' is also used in a less restricted sense on occasion; there should be no confusion, since when it refers to a *tourelle* it will be followed by a note on the colour. The heads of breakwaters, forming a harbour entrance, are often marked with white paint, with a black or green triangle or red square indicating the side on which to pass them.

Buoys. French buoyage has always been magnificent. It is perhaps unfortunate that the new edition of this book must be prepared during the period of transition to the Combined Cardinal and Lateral System (IALA Buoyage System A). This simplified system, already adopted in UK waters, is illustrated both in day and night use on the back endpapers of this book.

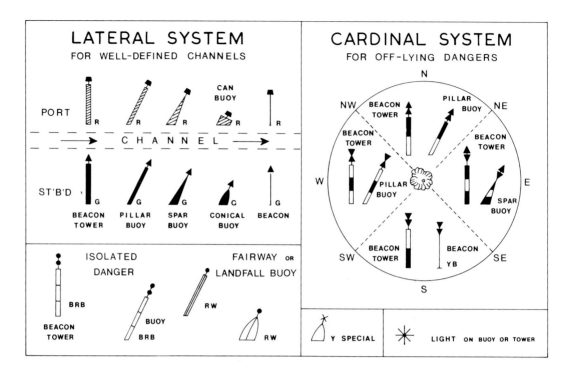

For the cardinal system, the change from that previously in use in French waters lies only in colour. The topmarks, in four arrangements of two cones, are unchanged. The N and S cardinal marks are straightforward, with both cones pointing up or down to the side on which one should pass. The cones point apart for E, and together for W; these arbitrary arrangements may be remembered, since *West* has a *Waist*. The colours are in bands of black and yellow; easy to recall, if it is remembered that the cones indicate the position of the black band or bands: at the top for N, at the bottom for S. For E, the points apart show top and bottom black bands, separated by yellow; for W, a central black band separating yellow above and below. Cardinal lights are all quick or very quick flashing white, memorable from a clock face: 3 flashes at 3 o'clock for E, 6 for S, 9 for W and continuous, which may be thought of as 12 for N. An additional long flash is added at the end of each sequence of 6 quick flashes for cardinal south.

Lateral marks follow the older system, the channel being marked as an entrance without regard to the direction of the flood tide. Port hand marks are generally unchanged, but starboard hand marks, formerly black, now become green and their lights are also green. Transition marks to indicate the changeover from lateral to cardinal or vice versa are no longer used, nor are middle ground marks; wrecks no longer rate special treatment and are marked by lateral or cardinal warnings in the same way as any other obstacle to navigation. The only other marks are:

Isolated Danger: for small dangers surrounded by navigable water; marks in black and red, with two black sphere topmarks.

Fairway or Landfall: in red and white vertical stripes, with white lights, one red sphere topmark; to show navigable water.

Special: in yellow, with yellow lights and St. Andrew's cross topmark: for such purposes as delineating restricted areas.

The French describe their buoys as 'pylone' (pillar) 'espar' (spar), 'cylindrique' (can) or 'conique' (conical). The conventional signs used in this book for these shapes are shown on page 20. The pillar buoy is tall and thin, of lattice construction; from a distance it may resemble a small lighthouse. The spar buoy is also thin, with a central solid spindle, generally smaller than the pillar buoy and used for less important marks. The new Admiralty charts and the chartlets used in this book distinguish pillar buoys from spars, but the distinction should not be too much relied on, since buoys designated to be pillars in the IALA change schedule are sometimes being replaced by spars instead.

Can and conical buoys are less conspicuous and are used for port and starboard lateral marks inshore only.

Bearings. Bearings are expressed in degrees true, but in the text magnetic bearings in points are occasionally given to indicate an approximate direction of a course or object. Variation is at present 8°W in the north and $5\frac{1}{2}$°W in the south of the area.

Lights

The descriptions of all the lights to be used in entering a port are collected into one tabulation to assist in identification. The heights are given in metres (m) only, as the descriptions are already sufficiently complex. The range of visibility is given in miles (M). Where a light has sectors the limits of the sectors are shown only on the plan and the range given refers to the light of maximum range (white, or intensified sector).

The light from a lighthouse may become invisible at a long range for one of two reasons; the light may not be sufficiently bright, or it may disappear below the horizon (geographical range). The geographical range normally quoted, and copied into this book, is for a height of eye of 4.5m (15 ft). From a typical yachting height of eye of say 1.5m (5 ft) the actual visible range is about 2 miles less than the quoted geographical range.

The distance at which a light is bright enough to be seen varies with the haze in the atmosphere; the term nominal range is used for this distance when the meteorological visibility is 10 miles, though a light may of course be seen at a greater distance. It is this nominal range that is now quoted in Admiralty and French light lists.

In the text, where the nominal range exceeds the geographical range, it is shown in *bold* type as an indication of the brightness of the light; the geographical range being shown in italic type thus: **23** *15*M. Where the nominal range is less than the geographical range it is shown in roman type; the geographical range is not then of interest, and only the nominal range is shown, thus: 10M. Such lights are relatively weak and may be difficult to identify amongst other lights on the shore.

The characteristics referred to in the text are for 1981, and are liable to alterations which will be shown on chart corrections and in the current List of Lights (for shore lights) and Pilot (for buoys).

Although the general practice is for coloured sectors to indicate dangers and white sectors the clear passages, this is not universal, and it should not be assumed that the white sectors indicate deep water over the whole sector at all distances from the light. Generally, if a light shows a white safe sector with red and green sectors on each side, the green sector is to starboard and the red to port, at least in the principal channel. To return to the white sector, show your green to a green light, your red to a red light, a variant on 'green to green or red to red, perfect safety'. This rule is not universal and should be checked for each light. Also narrow intensified sectors usually, but not always, fall within the safe width of the channel.

The French make considerable use of rhythmic lights, such as:

	Fl (2 + 1), on French charts	F. 2é. 1é.
or	Oc (1 + 2), ,,	F. 10. 20.
or	Oc (1 + 3), ,,	F. 10. 30.

The description of the flashing lights is clear enough, but I find the description of the occulting lights confusing. What one sees is a continuous sequence of long and short lights, rather than the sequence of occultations quoted in the descriptions above. The two occulting rhythms given above are the only ones in use, virtually always with a 12 second period. Oc (1 + 2) shows as a continuous sequence of 2 long dashes of 4 sec each followed by a short of 1 sec. Similarly Oc (1 + 3) shows as 2 long dashes of 3 sec followed by 2 shorts of 1 sec. These lights are given their standard description on the plans, but in the text they are quoted as Oc (−−·) and Oc (−−··) for the benefit of those who share my confusion. Lights are often 'Directional'; that is, they show brightly over a very narrow sector, sometimes faintly outside the sector.

Radiobeacons. The descriptions of the radiobeacons are given with the lights; they comprise:

1. The call sign.
2. The frequency in kHz (formerly called kc/s).
3. The period of transmission and the cycle time; thus '1/6 min' means that the beacon has a cycle time of 6 min, during which it transmits for 1 min and is silent for 5 min.
4. The beginning of the first transmission in each hour, if transmission is not continuous; thus 'H + 1 min' means that transmission begins at 1 min past each hour; if the cycle time is 6 min, transmission will also begin at 7, 13, 19, etc. min past each hour.

Plans
Each plan has been subdivided along the right hand and bottom margins into tenths of a minute of latitude and longitude. The use of identical units on each plan should give an immediate impression of the scale of each plan; the right hand margin serves as a scale of cables. One division on each edge is numbered so that reference to other charts, notices to mariners, etc. is easily made.

Among the conventions used on the plans are the following. The shore line, above which the sea never rises, is a thick black line. The drying line, at chart datum below which the sea never falls, is a thin line. The drying area between these is stippled. Where it is desirable to indicate the sides of a channel and these are not one of the standard contours, they are shown dotted. The danger line is shown dashed; this is usually the 3m (10 ft) contour, but occasionally a deeper contour is used.

In showing the sectors of lights, white sectors are denoted by solid arrows, red by dotted arrows, green by double dotted arrows and obscured by double solid arrows. Leading lights, other than fixed lights, are nearly always synchronised, so as to show simultaneously. This helps recognition and makes them easier to follow. On the plans space is sometimes saved by writing the characteristic of pairs of leading lights, if they are identical in colour as well, once only against the line joining them.

Tides

Tidal Streams. The Biscay currents and tidal streams offshore are weak, but inshore they are sometimes strong, notably in the Chenal du Four, Raz de Sein, Passage de la Teignouse and the Morbihan. As is to be expected the streams tend to be faster off headlands. Small scale tidal maps, based on the French publications, are provided in the end papers of this book for reference, but for practical use it is better to use either the Admiralty *Pocket Tidal Stream Atlas*, *France*, *West Coast*, or the French *Courants de Marée de la Côte Ouest de France*, which are on a larger scale.

The rates and even the directions of tidal streams may be affected by the wind, especially if it blows hard for a long time from one direction. In rivers and estuaries they may be affected by flood water from the land. They often run perpendicular to the coastline.

Tidal heights. The Admiralty Tide Tables give the most accurate predictions of tidal heights, but few yachtsmen carry them and the calculations are tedious.

Special tables (see page 280) have been prepared for this volume which give adequate accuracy, while being very much simpler to use. They are based on the principle that HW and LW heights can be found by taking the mean tide level (MTL) of the port and adding or subtracting the half-range of the tide for the day at that port.

The appropriate half-range is found by adding two index numbers: one, for the day's tide (small near neaps, large near springs) and one for the port (small for a port with a small tidal range, and larger for one with a greater range). The index number for the day's tide is given in the tables in terms of the height of HW at Brest, the standard port used on this coast. The index number for each port is given, with the MTL, at the head of each chapter, and under each plan. Detailed instructions, and an example of the calculations, follow.

From the Nautical Almanac take the time and height of HW Brest. From the chapter heading for the port take the time of local HW as compared with Brest, the port Index and the mean tide level (MTL).

1. Calculate the time of local high water.
2. Calculate the interval between local H W and the time when the tidal height is required.

3. Along the top of the tide table, pages 280–1, find the column with the nearest height of HW Brest (in feet or metres).

4. Note the corresponding tide Index, add the port Index, and locate the column headed by the total. Another way of putting this is that the port Index tells you how many columns to move to the right.

5. Run down this column to the correct interval from local HW, calculated in 2. above, and read off the correction to the MTL. The answer will be in metres (even if you started with Brest HW in feet).

Example: Required the height of tide at La Trinité on 16 August 1980 at 1330 French double summer time = 1130 GMT.

    From the Almanac: Brest HW is at 0707 GMT, height 6.5m.

    From chapter 35: La Trinité; HW —0015 Brest, Index 1, MTL 3.0m.

    Working: Local HW is at 0707–0015 = 0652 GMT.

    Interval from HW = 1130–0652 = 4h 38.

The table on page 281 has a column for 6.5m, giving a tide index of 9; where there is no column for the particular tide height, use the nearest column. Adding the port index of 1 to 9 gives a total of 10. In the column headed 10 for interval 4h 40 (the nearest to 4h 38) the correction to MTL is − 1.0. Tide height will then be 3.0–1.0, or 2.0, which, in this case, agrees with the figure reached by more laborious calculation from the Admiralty tide tables. There may well be differences of 0.1 or 0.2m from the more accurate tables, but this simplified system with no interpolation is good enough for practical purposes.

    The first 5 lines of the tables on pages 280–1 suffice to find HW and LW heights. Look up in the Almanac the height of HW Brest. Line 3 gives the corresponding tidal index, to which add the port index, taken from the chapter heading or below the plan. Corresponding to this total index, the fifth line (interval for oh oo) gives the half-range. Look up the MTL for the port, and add/subtract this half-range for HW/LW.

Weather forecasts

Forecasts broadcast by the French coastal stations are more detailed than those broadcast by the B.B.C. and the English coastal stations. The form of the forecast is: the general situation followed first for the next 12 hr for each area general weather type, wind direction and speed in knots, state of sea (*calme* to 0.1m = 6 in., *belle* to 0.5m = 1½ ft, *peu agitée* to 1.25m = 4 ft, *agitée* to 2.5m = 8 ft, *forte* to 4m = 13 ft, *très forte* to 6m = 20 ft, *grosse* to 9m = 30 ft, *très grosse* to 14m = 45 ft, *énorme* the rest), swell (if necessary), visibility in miles; secondly for each area for the following 12 hr similar information in rather less detail; and finally the outlook. The forecasts are read slowly and repeated, so they are not hard to follow with even limited French. Some less familiar words: *brume* = fog, *coup de vent* = gale, *averses* = showers, *houle* = swell, *suroit* = south west, *noroit* = north west, *sudé* = south east, *nordé* = north east.

    There are also forecasts broadcast by the national stations, including a special one for yachtsmen, during the summer only, on long wave.

    The sea areas covered by this book are Ouest Bretagne (Brest to Quiberon), Nord Gascogne

(Quiberon to La Rochelle) and Sud Gascogne (south of La Rochelle). The broadcasts are detailed below. The times are occasionally changed but are given on a leaflet issued annually and obtainable from harbour masters and marinas.

Coastal Stations
Times are French Standard Time; add one hour for French Summer Time.
Brest–Le Conquet 1673 kHz, 179m; 0833, 1733, 2253. (areas Ouest Bretagne, Nord Gascogne, repeated by Quimperlé 1876 kHz, 159m; 0833, 1733.)
St Nazaire 1722 kHz, 174m; 0903, 1903. (areas Ouest Bretagne, Nord Gascogne, Sud Gascogne.)
Bordeaux-Arcachon 1820 kHz, 165m; 0803, 1803. (area Sud Gascogne.)
These bulletins are followed by notices about floating dangers, extinguished lights etc.
Gale warnings are broadcast at H+03 and H+33 from Le Conquet, 1806 kHz, OH+7 St Nazaire 1687 kHz and EH+7 Bordeaux on 1862 kHz, where EH/OH are even/odd hours of GMT.

VHF Stations
The following VHF stations transmit local forecasts at 0733 and 1233 French clock time (GMT+2 during French summer time):

Ouessant	Channel 82
Le Conquet	Channel 26
Pont l'Abbé	Channel 27
Belle Ile	Channel 87
St Nazaire	Channel 23
St Gilles Croix de Vie	Channel 27
La Rochelle	Channel 21
Royan	Channel 23

Yachtsmen's Forecast
France-Inter 164 kHz, 1829m. Forecasts are given at the end of bulletins, starting at the advertised time; now 0825, 1950 French clock time.

Severe passages
With some trepidation a few passages marked as SEVERE have been included for the benefit of those who may wish to use them in suitable conditions. They are strictly only for those with some local knowledge and reliable auxiliary power, in fine weather and good visibility, at the correct time of tide. They are generally narrow and beset by fierce tides which could quickly lead to disaster. It is hoped that they will not be a challenge to the foolhardy, who must keep clear of them. One is tempted to add that the French impose heavy fines on fool-hardy yachtsmen, but presumably anyone who is prepared to risk his yacht and the lives of himself and his crew is not going to be daunted by the prospect of tangling with the French police.

Corrections

The editors would be glad to receive any corrections, information or suggestions which readers may consider would improve the book, as new impressions will be required from time to time. Letters should be addressed to the Editor, North Biscay Pilot, care of the publishers. The more precise the information the better, but even partial or doubtful information is helpful, if it made clear what the doubts are.

Conversion tables

An approximate method of converting metres to feet is to multiply by 10 and divide by 3. The answer will be too great, but only by one part in 60, which can usually be neglected.

Feet	Metres	Metres	Feet	Naut. Miles	Kilo- metres	Gallons	Litres	Pounds	Kilo- grams
1	0.3	1	3.3	1	1.9	1	4.5	1	0.4
2	0.6	2	6.6	2	3.7	2	9.1	2	0.9
3	0.9	3	9.8	3	5.6	3	13.6	3	1.4
4	1.2	4	13.1	4	7.4	4	18.2	4	1.8
5	1.5	5	16.4	5	9.3	5	22.7	5	2.3
6	1.8	6	19.7	6	11.1	6	27.3	6	2.7
7	2.1	7	23.0	7	13.0	7	31.8	7	3.2
8	2.4	8	26.2	8	14.8	8	36.4	8	3.6
9	2.7	9	29.5	9	16.7	9	40.9	9	4.1
10	3.0	10	32.8	10	18.5	10	45.5	10	4.5
20	6.1	20	65.6	20	37.1	20	90.9	20	9.1
30	9.1	30	98.4	30	55.6	30	136.4	30	13.6
40	12.2	40	131.2	40	74.1	40	181.8	40	18.2
50	15.2	50	164.0	50	92.6	50	227.3	50	22.7
100	30.5	100	328.1	100	185.3	100	454.6	100	45.4

Port signals

The French authorities use two systems of signals to control the traffic into harbours. These are best explained by means of diagrams, which are based, by permission of the Service Hydrographique de la Marine, on those appearing in *Instructions Nautiques*.

Figure 1 shows the International port signals used in large ports. *Figure 2* shows the simplified system used in smaller harbours. Supplementary signals are sometimes used, in particular flag P of the International Code (Blue Peter) is often used to indicate open dock gates.

The traffic signals are not usually hoisted for yachts, and they should therefore be regarded more as a signal to keep out of the way of large vessels.

Charts

For the British yachtsman cruising in the Bay of Biscay the appropriate Admiralty charts are recommended. These cover the area well and are prepared with the conventions, abbreviations, soundings and compass roses with which he is familiar. General coverage is on a scale of ½ in to the mile, although from Brest to the Loire there is coverage on a scale of 1 in or

IN GRAVE EMERGENCY

DAY   NIGHT

Entrance prohibited

IN NORMAL CIRCUMSTANCES

Entrance prohibited

Entrance & departure prohibited

Departure prohibited

SIMPLIFIED SYSTEM

	DAY		NIGHT
Entrance prohibited	■	Red flag	R
Departure prohibited	□	Green flag	G
Entrance & departure prohibited	■□	Red & green flags	R G

Figure. 2 SIMPLIFIED PORT SIGNALS

Figure. 1. PORT SIGNALS

larger. They are particularly useful for passage making, and in addition some areas, such as the Rade de Brest and the Morbihan, are covered on a scale suitable for detailed exploration in yachts. They are obtainable, corrected to date of sale, from Admiralty chart agents, which means, in effect, that they must be obtained before leaving English waters. They can be kept corrected from Admiralty Notices to Mariners, published weekly and obtainable free (but not post free) from chart agents, or from the quarterly small craft summaries. A list of charts is given on pages 30 and 31.

Messrs Imray, Laurie, Norie & Wilson publish two coloured charts, Nos. C35 and C36, covering the coast from L'Aberwrac'h to the Raz. They include large scale insets of harbours. Monthly bulletins of corrections may be obtained from the publishers.

The most complete coverage is naturally by the official French charts. The general coverage is on a scale of $1\frac{1}{2}$ in to the mile, with generous overlaps between adjacent charts, but there are also large scale plans of many areas, such as the Glénan islands, which are of great interest to the exploring yachtsman, but are not covered by large scale British charts.

French official charts have no compass roses, so some form of protractor is needed. The Hurst Plotter, Douglas Protractor, the Sestrel Course Setting and Compass Conversion Protractor and the Harries Direct Course Finder provide solutions with a variety of compromise between cost and convenience. Although modern French charts are very easy to read, the older ones are very finely engraved, and a chart magnifier is helpful in reading them.

Editions Cartographiques Maritimes (ECM) publish a series of four-colour charts intended for yachtsmen. The standard scale is 1:50,000 with large-scale inserts. These charts show very clearly all features in which yachtsmen are interested, have legends which are also in English, and bulletins of corrections are available.

French official charts can be obtained from J. D. Potter, 145 Minories, London E.C.3; they should be ordered about two months in advance as delivery is sometimes very slow. They can also be ordered direct from Bureau des Cessions au Public, Service Hydrographique de la Marine, 29283 Brest Cedex. They may also be obtained, while cruising, at the authorised agents in the principal ports. These agents keep local charts in stock, but do not correct them after receipt. They usually require two or three days' notice to obtain ones of more distant parts. The French hydrographic office publish weekly notices to mariners, but they are very expensive. However they also publish, each April, primarily for yachtsmen, a summary of notices issued during the last 12 months affecting the French coast and adjacent waters. This summary entitled *Recueil des Corrections de Cartes, 198–* is not expensive, and enables one to correct one's French charts in time for a summer cruise.

Full lists of the abbreviations and conventional signs in use on French and British charts can be obtained but a short list of the more useful ones, arranged in parallel columns to serve as a glossary, is given on page 29.

Lights and Beacons

F.	Fixed	F.*f.*	*Feu fixe*
Oc	Occulting	F.*o.*	*Feu à occultations*
Iso.	Isophase	F.*i.*	*Feu isophase*
Fl.	Flashing	F.*é.*	*Feu à éclats.*
Q	Quick Flashing	F.*sc.*	*Feu scintillant*
VQ	Very Quick	F.*sc.rap*	*Feu scintillant rapide*
IQ	Interrupted Quick Flashing	F.*sc.d*	*Feu scintillant discontinu*
Alt.	Alternating	F. alt.	*Feu alternatif*
Oc (2)	Group Occulting (e.g. 2)	F. 2*o.*	*Feu à occultations groupées*
Fl. (2+1)	Group flashing (e.g. 2 flashes, then 1)	F. 2*é.*1*é.*	*Feu à éclats diversement groupés*
Dir.	Directional light	F.*d.*	*Feu de direction*
obsc^d	Obscured		*Masqué*
occas^l	Occasional	*occas.*	*Occasionel*
	Sector	S., Sect.	*Secteur*
dest^d	Destroyed	*détr.*	*Détruit*
vert^l	Vertical	V.	*Vertical*
hor^l	Horizontal	Hor.	*Horizontal*
Bn.	Beacon	*Bal.*	*Balise*
Tr.	Tower	*T*	*Tour*
Bn. Tr.	Beacon Tower	*T^{lle}*	*Tourelle*
Ro. Bn., R.C.	Radiobeacon	R.C., R.D.	*Radiophare Circulaire, Directionnel*

Colours (On French charts the colours of lights are in *italic*, but of the buoys, beacons themselves in Roman)

B.	Black		n.	*Noir*
Bu.	Blue formerly Bl	*bl.*		*Bleu*
G.	Green	*v.*	v.	*Vert*
Y.	Orange formerly Or	*org.*		*Orangé*
R.	Red	*r.*	r.	*Rouge*
W.	White	*b.*	b.	*Blanc*
Y.	Yellow		j.	*Jaune*
W.	Whitewashed		bli	*Blanchi*
Cheq.	Chequered			*à damier*
Vi.	Violet			

Fog Signals

Fog Sig.	Fog Signal Station	*S^{al} br.*	*Station de signaux de brume*
Whis.	Whistle	*Sif.*	*Sifflet*
	Bell	*Cl.*	*Cloche*
	Siren	*Sir.*	*Sirène de brume*
Dia.	Diaphone		*Diaphone*
Reed.	Reedhorn		*Trompette*

Buildings and Miscellaneous

Cas.	Castle	*Ch^{au}*	*Château*
Cem^y	Cemetery	*Cim^{re}*	*Cimetière*
Ch.	Chapel	*Ch^{lle}*	*Chapelle*
Ch^y	Chimney	*Ch^{ee}*	*Cheminée*
Ch.	Church	*Egl., Cl^{er}*	*Eglise, Clocher*
Conspic.	Conspicuous	*Rem.*	*Remarquable*
Fm.	Farm		*Ferme*
F.S.	Flagstaff (signals)	*M^t S^x*	*Mât de Signaux*
F.S.	Flagstaff	*M^t P^{on}*	*Mât de Pavillon*
	Gable		*Pignon*
Ho.	House	*M^{on}*	*Maison*
L.B.	Lifeboat	*St^{on} de sauv.*	*Station de sauvetage*
Mon^t	Monument	*Mon^t*	*Monument*
P.A.	Position Approximate	P.A.	*Position Approchée*
	Seamark	*S^{et}*	*Amer*
	Summit		*Sommet*
Water T^r	Water Tower	*Ch^{au} d'eau*	*Château d'eau*
	Windmill	*M^{in}*	*Moulin à vent*
W^k	Wreck	*Ep.*	*Epave*

Admiralty Charts

No.	Name	Scale, 1 in	No.	Name	Scale, 1 in
1104	Bay of Biscay	1 000 000	304	Lorient Harbour	10 000
2643	Raz de Sein to Goulven, including Brest and Ushant	145 000	2353	Rade de Croisic to Presqu'île de Quiberon	73 100
20	Ile d'Ouessant to St Nazaire	290 000	2358	Morbihan including Rivière de Crac'h ..	25 100
2694	The Channels between Ushant and the Mainland	46 400	2359	Entrée du Morbihan, Rivière d'Aurray	10 000
3345	Chenal du Four	18 200	3216	Approaches to La Loire	50 000
2690	Cap de la Chèvre to Pointe de Corsen including Rade de Brest	46 300	2989	Entrance to La Loire, and Approaches to St Nazaire	15 000
3427	Rade de Brest	29 200	2985	La Loire, St Nazaire to Nantes	30 000
3428	Port de Brest	12 000	2647	Les Sables d'Olonne to Bourgneuf	142 500
798	Baie de Douarnenez	46 900		St Gilles sur Vie; Port Joinville ..	29 200
	Douarnenez	15 000	2648	Pointe de la Coubre to Les Sables d'Olonne ..	150 000
2351	Anse de Benodet to chaussée de Sein	72 400		Port of Les Sables d'Olonne	25 000
	Port d'Audierne	24 000	2641	Pertuis Breton	50 000
2645	Ile de Groix to Raz de Sein	140 000	2746	Pertuis d'Antioche, with the Approaches to La Rochelle and Rochefort	50 000
2352	Presqu'île de Quiberon to Anse de Benodet ..	72 500	2743	La Rochelle; La Pallice	15 000
3641	Loctudy to Concarneau	20 000	2748	La Charente, Fouras to Rochefort	20 000
3640	Anse de Benodet	20 000	2910	Entrance to La Gironde	75 000
2646	Bourgneuf to Ile de Groix	140 000	2664	Pointe d'Arcachon to Pointe de la Coubre ..	150 000

Charts by Editions Cartographiques Maritimes (ECM)

No.	Name	Scale, 1 in	No.	Name	Scale, 1 in
540	Argentan, Camaret	50 000	546	La Trinité, Le Croisic	50 000
541	Morgat, Ile de Sein	50 000	547	Le Croisic, Pornic	50 000
542	Brest, Douarnenez	50 000	549	Pornic, St Gilles, Ile d'Yeu	50 000
543	Audierne, Trévignon	50 000	1022	St Gilles, La Rochelle	100 000
243	Iles de Glénan	25 000	551	Ile de Ré, La Rochelle	50 000
544	Concarneau, Lorient, Ile de Groix	50 000	522	La Rochelle, Ile d'Oleron	50 000
545	Lorient, La Trinité, Belle Ile	50 000	553	Royan, Gironde entrance	50 000

French Official Charts

As there is complete coverage of this coast by British charts on a scale of 1 in 150 000, no French charts on a smaller scale than this are listed. The list is divided into groups according to scale. A number of charts in the list have British counterparts, with the same scale and coverage, eg 6470, 3165. Some of the names have been abbreviated. When a new French chart is issued, replacing a similar one of the same area, it is given a new number, unlike British charts, where the old number is re-used. The dates given in the second column indicate the edition, or the date of the most recent 'grandes corrections' incorporated. These dates are from the official 1984 list or subsequent information. Charts with a prefix 'P' are also available in the 'P' series, folded on thin, water-resisting paper.

Scale 115 000 to 125 000, about ⅔ inch to the mile.

P5316	79	De l'île d'Ouessant à la Pointe de Penmarc'h; abords de Brest
6791	80	Du Cap de la Chèvre aus îles de Glénan
P6790	84	De Bénodet au Croisic
P6789	81	De Belle Ile à l'île d'Yeu
P6902	84	De l'île d'Yeu à la Pointe de Chassiron
P6788	80	De l'île de Ré à la Pointe de Grave

Scale 45 000 to 50 000, about 1½ inch to the mile.

5287	79	De Porsal à la Pointe St Mathieu; Chenal du Four et Ouessant
6609	83	De la Pointe St Mathieu à Audierne; Goulet de Brest
6099	77	Baie de Douarnenez
6593	83	De l'Ile de Molène au Cap de la Chèvre; Entrée de la Rade de Brest
6594	82	Du Cap de la Chèvre à Audierne; chaussée et Raz de Sein
6377	76	D'Audierne à la Pointe de Penmarc'h
P5368	80	De la Pointe de Penmarc'h à la Pointe de Trévignon; îles de Glenan
P5479	81	De la Pointe de Trévignon à Lorient; île de Groix
P5560	80	De Lorient à Belle Ile et à Quiberon
P5420	81	De Quiberon à Penerf; Baie de Quiberon et Morbihan
P 135	81	Belle Ile; entrée de la Baie de Quiberon
P5482	82	De la Pointe du Grand Mont au Croisic
P6825	81	Du Croisic à l'Herbaudière
6854	81	Cours de la Loire; de St Nazaire à Nantes
5039	73	De la Pointe St Gildas à Fromentine, Bourgneuf, l'Herbaudière
6853	81	Du Goulet de Fromentine à l'île d'Yeu
6523	74	De St Gilles-Croix de Vie aux Sables d'Olonne; île d'Yeu est
6522	73	Des Sables d'Olonne à la Pointe du Grouin du Cou
P6521	80	Du Grouin du Cou à La Rochelle; Pertuis Breton; île de Ré
P6333	80	De l'île de Ré à l'île d'Oléron; Pertuis d'Antioche
P6334	82	De La Rochelle à Rochefort; Pertuis d'Antioche
P6335	82	De l'île d'Oléron à Cordouan; Pertuis de Maumusson
P6336	83	De la Coubre à la Négade; embouchure de la Gironde
6139	82	La Gironde. Du Verdon à Pauillac; Port de Pauillac
6140	82	La Gironde, la Garonne et la Dordogne à Libourne; Port de Blaye

Scale 20 000 to 30 000, about 3 inches to the mile

5721	79	De la Pointe de Kermorvan à l'île d'Iock; Chenal du Four
5567	50	De l'île de Molène à l'île d'Ouessant; passage du Fromveur

5159	79	De la Pointe St Mathieu à Molène; chaussée des Pierres Noires
6678	77	Accès à la Rade de Brest
6542	79	Rade de Brest
5252	77	Raz de Sein
P6647	80	Iles de Glénan—Partie Nord
P6648	80	Iles de Glénan—Partie Sud
P6679	80	Course de l'Odet de Bénodet à Quimper
5912	82	Ile de Groix
5911	43	Belle Ile—Rade du Palais
5352	81	Baie de Quiberon
P3165	82	Golfe de Morbihan
5418	82	Port de Penerf et Anse de Suscinio—Passe de Penerf
6890	82	Ile d'Yeu
6912	82	Coureau d'Oléron—Du Pertuis de Maumusson au Viaduc d'Oléron
6913	82	Coureau d'Oléron—Du Viaduc d'Oléron à la rade des Trousses
6914	82	Embouchure de la Charente. Accès Nord au Coureau d'Oléron

Scale 7 500 to 17 000, 4 to 10 inches to the mile

6427	81	Partie Ouest de la Rade de Brest
6426	81	Port de Brest
6676	77	Abords et Port de Morgat
6677	77	Abords et Port de Douarnenez
5937	62	Port d'Audierne
P6645	80	Pointe de Penmarc'h—Abords de St Guénolé
P6646	81	Abords et Ports de Guilvinec et de Lesconil
P6649	82	Anse de Bénodet—Ports de Bénodet et de Loctudy
P6650	80	Abords et Port de Concarneau—Baie de la Forêt
6470	82	Passes et Rade de Lorient
5554	81	Entrée du Morbihan, rivière d'Auray
2381	78	Entrée de la Vilaine
6826	80	Rade et Port du Croisic
6797	81	Abords de St Nazaire
6493	81	Cours de la Loire; de St Nazaire à Paimboeuf
6260	82	Cours de la Loire; de Paimboeuf à l'île Bernard
6261	80	Cours de la Loire; de l'île Bernard au Pellerin
5992	80	Cours de la Loire; du Pellerin à Nantes
6613	82	St Gilles sur Vie—Port Joinville (île d'Yeu)
6551	81	Rade et Port des Sables d'Olonne
6668	82	Rade de St Martin et ses environs (île de Ré)
6468	83	Baie de La Rochelle
4333	77	Cours de la Charente
6141	82	Embouchure de la Gironde. Rades de Royan et de Verdon
4610	82	Cours de la Garonne—Du Bec d'Ambès à Bordeaux

It is of interest, and sometimes actually of value to the navigator, to know the meanings of some of the commoner Breton words which appear in place names. Those who have cruised on the Celtic fringes of Britain will recognise some of them; the Irish *inish* corresponds to the Breton *inis*, and those who have cruised in West Highland waters will know the meanings of *glas* and *du*. I have no pretensions to a knowledge of Breton, but set down here the results of a few investigations.

The pronunciation is, or should be, more like English than French, with the final consonants sounded. The letters *c'h* represent the final sound of Scottish *loch* or Irish *lough* (but not English *lock*); there is indeed a word *loc'h*, meaning a lake or pool; *ch* is pronounced as in *shall*. The French books and charts do not always distinguish between these, and there may be some errors in this book in consequence. In France, as in England, mobility and the radio/TV are killing regional differences and *Raz* is now usually pronounced *Rah*; *Penmarc'h*, pronounced *Penmargh* a generation ago is now often *Painmar* and *Bénodet* has gone from *Benodette* to *Bainoday* and collected an accent in the process. The most misleading example of this process is *porz*, which means an anchorage, possibly quite exposed and/or lacking all shore facilities, not a port. This gets frenchified into *port*, and the French word *port* does mean a port, and not an anchorage which is *anse* or *rade*.

A Breton glossary is hard to use, because initial letters are often mutated into others, following complicated rules, depending on the preceding word. I have tried to meet this by suggesting, after the relevant letters, other(s) from which the initial might have come. Thus suppose that one wants to find the meaning of *I. ar Gazek* (which is quite likely since *The Mare* seems to be the commonest name given to an islet). There is no word *gazek* in the glossary, but after *G* it says 'try K'; *kazek* means a mare; it mutates into *gazek* after *ar*. Mutations of final letters also occur, but these do not usually cause difficulty in finding a word.

al, an, ar	the	*breiz*	Brittany
arvor	seaside	*bri, brienn*	cliff
aven	river	C (try K)	
B (try P)		D (try T)	
bann, benn	hilltop	*daou*	two
baz	shoal	*don, doun*	deep
beg	point, cape	*du*	black
beniget	cut, slit	*enez*	island
benven	above-water rock	*er*	a, an, the
bian, bihan	small	G (try K)	
bir	needle, point	*garv*	rough
bras, braz	large	*gavr*	goat
bre, brenn	small hill	*glas*	green

gromil, gromilli	roaring	*men*	rock
gwenn	white, pure	*mor*	sea
hir	long	*nevez*	new
hoc'h, houc'h	pig	*penn*	head, point
inis	island	*plou, plo*	parish
karn	cairn	*porz porzig*	anchorage
karreg	rock	*poul*	pool, anchorage
kastel	castle	*raz*	strait, tide race
kazek	mare	*roc'h*	rock
ker	house, hamlet	*ros*	wooded knoll
kern	summit	*ruz*	red
koad	wood	*ster*	river, inlet
kornog	shoal	*teven tevenneg*	cliff, dune
koz	old	*toull*	hole, deep place
kreiz	middle	*trez treaz*	sand, beach
kriben	crest	V (try B, M)	
lan, lann	monastery	W (try Gw)	
marc'h	horse	*yoc'h*	group of rocks
melen	yellow		

The port of registration of fishing vessels may be identified by the letters on their bows, as follows:

AD	Audierne	LO	Lorient
AY	Auray	LS	Les Sables d'Olonne
BR	Brest	MN	Marennes
BX	Bordeaux	NA	Nantes
CC	Concarneau	NO	Noirmoutier
CM	Camaret	SN	Saint Nazaire
DZ	Douarnenez	VA	Vannes
GV	Le Guilvinec	YE	Ile d'Yeu
IO	Ile d'Oléron		

4 Chenal du Four

Charts: 3345, 2694, 2643.
High water: −0005 Brest, Index 4, MTL 4.2m.
MHWS 7.1m; MLWS 1.3m; MHWN 5.5m; MLWN 2.9m
Tidal streams: The N stream begins about −0600 Brest, spring rates: 1 knot at 1 mile north of Les Plâtresses, 2¼ knots at St Pierre buoy (SW of Corsen), 5¼ knots at La Vinotière. The S stream begins about HW Brest, spring rates: 1 knot at 1 mile north of Les Plâtresses, 2½ knots at St Pierre buoy, 5 knots at La Vinotière. At Les Vieux Moines the stream is rotatory clockwise, spring rates: at −0100 Brest, N 1¼ knots; at +0200 Brest, SSE 3½ knots; at +0500 Brest, SW ¾ knot; at −0600 Brest, WNW 1½ knots. The streams are considerably affected by the wind.
Depths: The main channel is deep.

The Chenal du Four is the channel ordinarily used by small vessels bound coastwise for Bay of Biscay ports; it saves distance and avoids the larger seas and heavy steamer traffic outside Ushant. Those unfamiliar with the channel may think it presents special difficulties in navigation, but it is a wide, well-marked route, and anyone who has piloted his boat along the north coast of France as far as Ushant will find the Chenal du Four rather easier than some of the coastline that he has already passed. The difficulties lie rather in the facts that the strong tides and exposure to the Atlantic swell often result in steep seas, and the visibility is frequently poor. There are two other channels, the Chenal de la Helle, which is farther west and is also described here, and the Passage du Fromveur, SE of Ushant, noted for the strength of the tidal streams, which attain 9 knots at extreme springs. In rough weather the Chenal de la Helle is to be preferred to the Chenal du Four.

The roughest seas do not occur in the Chenal du Four, but in the approaches. Eastward,

Le Four lighthouse bearing about NE. Shoal water extends up to 1½ cables W of the lighthouse.

La Grande Vinotière light tower (red octagonal). Pointe de St Mathieu in the background bearing 155°; Les Vieux Moines tower to the right.

between Ile Vierge and Le Four lighthouse, northerly winds often bring a considerable swell, and a strong weather-going stream over an irregular bottom produces steep seas. With westerly winds some distant shelter is found as the Chenal du Four is approached and the vessel comes under the lee first of Ushant and then of the inner islands and shoals. The seas drop as soon as the tide turns fair.

With a leading wind one will naturally arrange to pass the channel when the tide is favourable, but if the wind is ahead it is desirable to try and make the passage through the narrow part, where the tides run hard, near slack water. Coming from the north it is unfortunate that the tide turns in the Four Channel before it does in the English Channel, so that starting from l'Aberwrac'h, say, on the first of the SW tide, most of the tide in the Four Channel will have run to waste before one gets there. But one can cross the Iroise on the foul tide without difficulty, and reach the Raz de Sein as the tide turns fair again.

In fog or thick weather navigation is tricky in the Chenal du Four. If the outer marks have been sighted, and the visibility is sufficient to enable the towers and buoys to be seen at a reasonable distance, pilotage is possible even if the distant landmarks and lighthouses are hidden in the mist. With poor visibility, however, it is better to remain either in harbour or out at sea. A VHF-equipped yacht can be talked through even in nil visibility by the English-speaking radar station on Pointe St Mathieu, who listen on channel 16 and work on channel 12.

Coasting southward from Le Four lighthouse a fair offing should be given to Les Liniou

Pointe de Kermorvan and the town of Le Conquet, bearing about E.

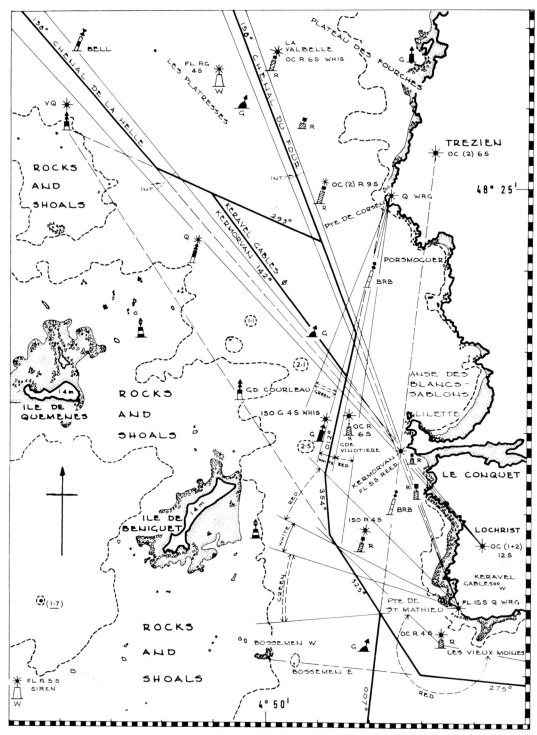

CHENAL DU FOUR
MLWS 1.3m; MLWN 2.9m; −0005 Brest, Index 4, MTL 4.2m
Based on French Chart No. 5287 with corrections.
Depth in metres; right hand margin in cables

and the Plateau des Fourches. The Chenal du Four may then be entered NE of Les Plâtresses tower (white), with the lighthouses of St Mathieu (white circular red top) and Kermovan (white square tower) in transit, bearing 158°. The remaining transits and marks are shown on the plan on page 36. This plan has been simplified by the omission of soundings, other than the 3m (10 ft) line, which shows the shoal areas. Except in certain parts, the area free from danger in normal weather is considerable; when it is rough the orthodox channel should be adhered to, as the overfalls are worse over an irregular bottom, such as the 3.7m (13 ft) patch SE of the Grande Vinotière.

If a vessel bound south is late on the tide she can avoid the worst of the tide by standing into the bay towards the Anse des Blancs Sablons, and again into the bay south of Le Conquet, but care must be taken to avoid the dangers.

Chenal de la Helle. Bring Kermorvan lighthouse to bear 138°, between the first and second houses from the right of five similar houses forming Le Conquet radio station. In good weather steer on this until Corsen lighthouse bears 012°, when steer 192° on this stern bearing. This transit leads across the Basse St Pierre (4.5m, 15 ft), marked by a buoy (stbd), which the transit leaves to port. In bad weather the shoal can be avoided, either by bringing the two white painted gables (resembling pyramids) of Keravel (near St Mathieu lighthouse) in transit with Kermorvan, bearing 142°, or more simply, by leaving the buoy to starboard.

By night: The transits are shown on the plan. Bound south steer with Kermorvan and St Mathieu in transit, bearing 158°. Note that in a narrow sector each side of this transit St Mathieu shows a fixed white directional light as well as the flashing light which shows all round. For the Chenal de la Helle steer with Kermorvan in transit with Lochrist, bearing 138°. To avoid the Basse St Pierre, if necessary, leave this alignment when the Stiff light comes in transit with Le Faix, bearing 293°, and steer 113° on this stern transit to join the Four channel alignment.

In any case, when Corsen light turns white steer in this sector, with the light astern, until the auxiliary light on St Mathieu opens red. Then steer 174°, entering the red sector of Corsen, but being careful not to leave the red sector of Corsen until the Tournant buoy is

Les Vieux Moines light tower (red octagonal). Pointe de St Mathieu in the background, bearing 030°, with Lochrist lighthouse on the left.

abeam, when the auxiliary light on St Mathieu will turn white and the light on Les Vieux Moines will open. Then steer 145°, making sure that Kermorvan is brought in transit with Trézien, bearing 007° astern, before the green sector of the St Mathieu auxiliary light is left. If proceeding south, steer nothing to west of the 007° alignment; if going east or SE steer to leave Les Vieux Moines to port.

Bound north, follow the above directions in reverse. The lights are:

Chenal du Four:
Kermorvan; Fl W 5s, 20m **23**, *13*M. Reed 1 min.
St Mathieu; Fl W 15s, 56m, **27**, *19*M,
    also Dir FW, 54m, **28**, *19*M.
    Radiobeacon, call SM, 289.6 kHz, 1/6 min, begins H + 2 min.
    auxiliary light, see below.
La Valbelle by; Oc R 6s, 8m, 5M, Whistle.
Les Plâtresses; Fl RG 4s, 17m, 6M.
Basse St Paul by; Oc (2) R 9s, 7m, 5M.
Chenal de la Helle:
Kermorvan, see above.
Lochrist; Dir Oc (— —·) W 12s, 49m, **22**, *18*M.
Le Faix; Q W 16m, 9M.
Le Stiff; Fl (2) R 20s, 85m, **25**, *23*M.
Les Pourceaux NE by; Q W 7m, 8M.
Both channels:
Corsen; Q WRG 33m, 12M.
La Grande Vinotière; Oc R 6s, 15m, 5M.
Le Rouget by; Iso G 4s, 7m, 5M Whistle.
St Mathieu auxiliary; Q WRG 26m, 14M.
    main light, see above.
Tournant by; Iso R 4s, 7m, 5M.
Les Vieux Moines; Oc R 4s, 16m, 5M.
Trézien; Dir Oc (2) W 6s, 84m, 21M.

Anchorages
The following temporary anchorages are available under suitable conditions:

Anse de Porsmoguer. Good holding ground in sand in the pretty bay, with depths shoaling from 6m (20 ft) to zero. It is sheltered from N and E and popular for bathing. The village is about ½ mile to the north, but there are no shops there.

Anse des Blancs Sablons. This wide sandy bay is free from dangers except off the headlands on each side. There is anchorage anywhere, in from 9 to 1m (30 to 3 ft) on a sandy shelving bottom which dries out nearly ¼ mile from the shore, except on the west side, where there is 3m (10 ft) close to the rocks off Kermorvan. This peninsula protects the anchorage from the W and SW, and the land shelters it from E and S. Yachts can work into this bay inshore against a foul tide, anchor there and slip round L'Ilette (off Kermorvan) when the stream becomes fair; note that there is a rock 1 cable east of this islet which is awash at chart datum. There is little stream in the bay, but often some swell. No facilities.

Le Conquet. There is good anchorage in this inlet south of Pointe de Kermorvan. Leave the red La Louve tower to port and go as far in as draft and tide permit. For a full description see North Brittany Pilot, published by Adlard Coles Limited.

Anse de Bertheaume. This is a convenient bay, about 3 miles east of Pointe de St Mathieu, in which to wait before making the passage of Chenal du Four. It is sheltered from N and W, but exposed to the S and E. The Château de Bertheaume, on the SW corner of the bay, is itself fairly clean and can be passed at $\frac{1}{2}$ cable; but 2 cables to the NE is Le Chat, an area of rocks nearly 1 cable across, with heads drying 6.6 and 7.2m (22 and 24 ft). These are a particular hazard when they are covered, near HW springs. Anchor in one of the two bays immediately north of Le Chat, going as far in as possible for shelter. Farther north and east the bottom of the bay is foul, with rocks. Village and simple shops one mile. Keep well to the south of the local moorings.

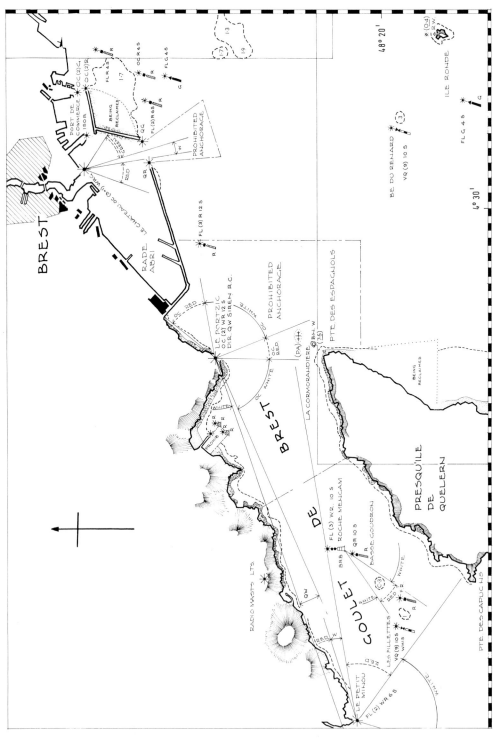

GOULET DE BREST   MLWS 1.4m; MLWN 3.00m; 0000 Brest, Index 5, MTL 4.4m
Based on French Chart Nos. 3799 and 6427 with corrections (No. 6542 supersedes)   Depths in metres; right hand margin in cables

5 Brest

Charts: 2690, 3427, 3428, 2643.

High water: Standard port, Index 5, MTL 4.4m.

MHWS 7.5m (24.5 ft); MLWS 1.4m (4.5 ft); MHWN 5.9m (19.5 ft); MLWN 3.0m (10 ft)

Tidal streams: Goulet de Brest. On the northern side the flood begins at −0535 Brest and runs E. On the southern side the flood begins at −0605 Brest, direction ENE, and attains 4 knots NE off Pointe des Espagnols. The ebb begins on the northern side at −0030 Brest, on the southern side at HW Brest. Within about 100m of the southern shore there are ENE and E eddies, which begin about +0100 Brest and continue until the flood begins. These eddies cause tide rips where they meet the main ebb from the Rade off Pointe des Espagnols. In the southern entrance to the harbour the N stream begins at −6000 Brest, 1½ knots springs. The S stream begins at +0030 Brest, 1 knot springs. There is an eddy off the long breakwater which begins off the SW corner at −0330 Brest, and extends over the next 1½ hr until it sets along the whole breakwater, at 2 knots springs, in a WSW direction contrary to the main stream ¼ mile to the south. In the eastern entrance to the Port de Commerce the E stream begins at −0500 Brest, weak, the W at −0100 Brest, 1 knot springs.

Depths: There is plenty of water at all states of the tide in the approach fairways and in the harbour, but in approaching the eastern entrance near LW the buoyed fairway should be used.

Many yachts bound south stop the night at Camaret but avoid making the detour eastward to visit Brest. Though yachts are not very welcome in Brest itself, there is a large marina two miles to the east, and the Rade de Brest, dealt with in the next chapter, offers an excellent cruising ground reminiscent of the Clyde.

Approach

The outer approach to Brest (Avant Goulet de Brest) is made with the twin lighthouses of Le Petit Minou (two adjacent white towers) in transit with the grey octagonal tower of Pointe du Portzic, bearing 068°. These lighthouses are on the north side of the Goulet de Brest. If the visibility is not good they may not be seen at first, but if the steep coastline east of Pointe St Mathieu is followed round, leaving to port Les Vieux Moines tower, Le Coq buoy (port), Charles Martel whistle buoy (port) and Basse Beuzec buoy (port), the lighthouses of Le Petit Minou will normally come into sight.

The outer approach from the SW, through the Chenal du Toulinguet, is described in chapter 8.

On approaching Le Petit Minou, bear to starboard to pass up the Goulet on the northern side, between the north shore and the mid-channel shoals of Plateau des Fillettes (YBY pillar whistle buoy), Kerviniou (R buoy), Basse Goudron (R buoy) and Roche Mengam (tower, BRB horizontal bands), which are left to starboard. After passing Pointe du Portzic steer for the harbour entrance. Alternatively, if approaching from the SW, or on the ebb, use the south side between the central shoals and the Presqu'île de Quélern, making use of the eddy along the shore on the ebb.

By night: The approach is as by day, except that there are no lights for the passage on the south side of the Goulet, and some light would be needed for this. There is a white sector

Pointe des Espagnols and La Coromandière rock and beacon, bearing about 215°.

on le Petit Minou light, from 252° to 260°, which leads through the eastern part of the Goulet, and a red sector on Roche Mengam, from 034° to 054°, which covers the shoals to the SW of it. The light on Terre Plein du Château leads through the southern entrance to the harbour.

The lights are:

Le Petit Minou; Fl (2) WR 6s, 32m, **20**, *16M except from* 066° to 070° when it is Q W 30m, *23*, *15*M, Siren, 1 min. Also F Dir Fog detector light.

Le Portzic; Oc (2) WR 12s, 56m, 19M, *except from* 065° to 071° when it is Q W, 54m, **23**, *19*M, Siren (2) 1 min. Radiobeacon call PZ, 298.8 kHz, continuous, 5M.

Basse du Charles Martel by; Q R 7m, 7M, Whistle.

Les Fillettes by; VQ (9) 10s, 7 m, 8M.

Kerviniou by; Oc (2) R 6s.

Basse Goudron by; Q R.

Roche Mengam; Fl (3) WR 12s, 11m, 11M.

Penoupèle by; Fl (3) R 12s.

South Entrance:

Le Château; Oc (——··) WRG 12s, 20m, 10M.

West mole head; Q R 10m, 7M.

East mole head; Q G 10m, 7M.

Passage to Port de Commerce:

South side; Fl G 4s, 10m, 6M.

North side; Iso R 4s, 10m, 9M.

Eastern entrance to Port de Commerce:

3 Port hand buoys: No. 2, Fl (2) R 6s; No. 4, Oc R 4s; No. 6, Fl R 4s.

South side entrance; Oc (2) R 6s, 8m, 4M.

North side entrance; Oc (2) G 6s, 8m, 9M.

42

Mooring

If there is room, yachts are still tolerated in the W basin of the Port de Commerce. Arrival must be reported to the Bureau du Port on the western side of the Port de Commerce, but there are no other formalities, nor is any charge made. There is much commercial shipping and movement here and yachts must be manned to move if required. The Anse du Moulin Blanc two miles E is much preferable.

Facilities

All ordinary food shops, chandlers and sailmakers are close to the berth. The principal shopping area is on rising ground, at some little distance to the north. Here there are shops of all kinds, and restaurants and hotels of all grades. Shipyard and marine engineer. Bonded stores can be obtained from Fournier, close to the berth, who can also arrange for the delivery of fuel by lorry alongside. Water by hose can also be had by arrangement, but a man has to come to connect the hose; there is a tap for small quantities on the head of the jetty. Baths at the Foyer de Gens de Mer.

There are good railway connections and a twice daily air service to Paris (not on Sunday). Bus connections to all local parts. Besides being a major naval base it is an important commercial town. It has been largely rebuilt since the war, and although it has not the attraction of the smaller ports, it is a pleasant place, with all facilities at hand, and convenient for changing crews.

The Port de Commerce at Brest, seen just below the tall monument, bearing about 340°. Yachts are now crowded out.

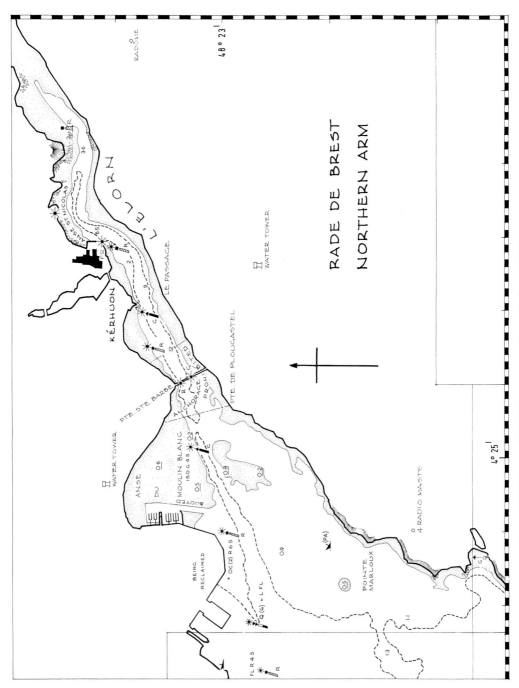

RADE DE BREST, NORTHERN ARM   MLWS 1.4m; MLWN 3.0m; 0000 Brest, Index 5, MTL 4.4m
Based on French Chart No. 3799 with corrections (No. 6542 supersedes)   Depths in metres; right hand margin in cables

Charts: 2690, 3427, 2643.
High water: Standard port, Index 5, MTL 4.4m.
MHWS 7.5m (24.5 ft); MLWS 1.4m (4.5 ft); MHWN 5.9m (19.5 ft); MLWN 3.0m (10 ft)
Tidal streams: For the Goulet de Brest, see Chapter 5. The flood, beginning −0605 Brest, in the south of the Goulet continues ENE to the Elorn and E towards Pointe Marloux. For the first half hour the ebb is still running out of the estuary of the Aulne and there are tide rips where the two streams meet off Pointe des Espagnols. Half an hour later, at −0530 Brest, the flood stream divides off Pointe des Espagnols, one branch setting, as before, E and ENE, with an eddy setting towards Pointe Marloux. The other branch sets S into the Baie de Roscanvel and SE towards the Aulne at 2¾ knots springs. The ebb stream from the Elorn begins at HW Brest and from the Aulne about 10 minutes earlier.
Depths: Given under the individual headings for the anchorages.

The Rade de Brest provides an excellent cruising ground, with many anchorages and beautiful creeks. In bad weather it can be rough, especially with wind against tide, for there is often a fetch of 5 miles, but as it is sheltered on all sides it is free from the swell of the open sea. It makes an ideal place for a family cruise, or for filling in if caught by bad weather between the Four and the Raz.

Parts of the Rade are used for naval exercises, mining grounds etc. There are a few areas, shown on the plans, where anchorage, or even passage, is prohibited. The Rade is entered through the Goulet de Brest, which is described in the previous chapter.

The northern arm of the Rade extends some 10 miles in an ENE direction. Eastward of the port of Brest the water shoals leaving a comparatively deep narrow channel leading under a high bridge to St Nicholas and the Elorn. A little way beyond the port of Brest, a new yacht harbour has been built in the Anse du Moulin Blanc and is already being extended.

The southern arm is the more attractive and is reminiscent of the Clyde, with hilly shores and higher hills in the background, naval activity in places, but plenty of yachtsmen's anchorages. This part is some 10 miles long and 2 to 4 miles across. It is deeply indented, offering many interesting anchorages. On the south side lie the bays of Roscanvel and Le Fret, both open only to the E and NE. There is also the less sheltered Anse du Poulmic, but this is rather too busy with naval affairs for most yachtsmen. On the north side it is prettier but shallower, offering anchorages in the Anse de l'Auberlac'h and the Baie de Daoulas. Eastwards there is the lovely Aulne with many anchorages, at the head of which is Port Launay, nestling in the hills, where the sea seems, and is, far away.

Approach
The approach, through the Goulet, has been described in the previous chapter, with the port of Brest itself.

Anchorages
Northern arm.
Anse du Moulin Blanc. Make the port hand buoy marking the entrance to the Elorn. Thence

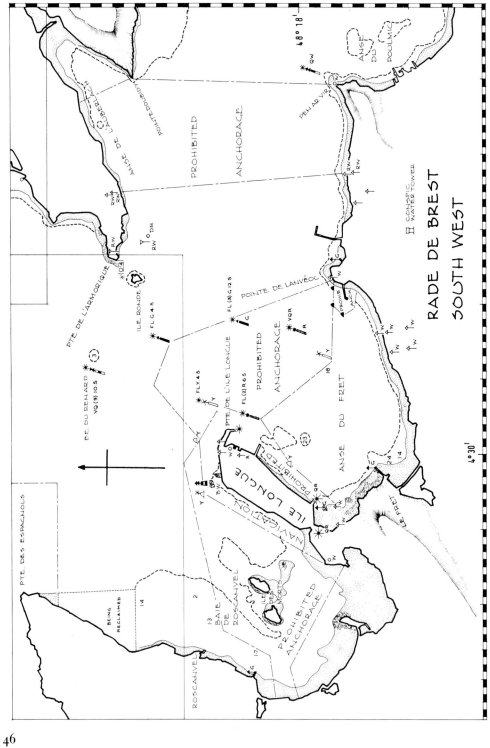

RADE DE BREST, SOUTH WEST   MLWS 1.4m   MLWN 3.0m; MTL, 4.4m; MHWN 3.0m; oooo Brest, Index 5, MTL 4.4m
Based on French Chart No. 3799 with corrections (No. 6542 supersedes)   Depth in metres; right hand margin in cables

steer about NNE for the ends of the breakwaters, leaving them to port; secure to a pontoon and enquire at the bureau for a berth to be allotted. The approach channel and harbour have been dredged to 1m; two light buoys mark the channel. Facilities include chandlers, showers, petrol and diesel from the quay (not at LW), water piped to the pontoons.

L'Elorn rivière. The channel is marked at its entrance by a buoy (port) and another (stbd) 1 mile farther up. Thence steer off Pointe Ste Barbe, where the river is spanned by a bridge. The channel passes under the northern arch. There is a clearance of 36m (118 ft) above datum. There is an anchorage 1 mile above the bridge at Le Passage, and also opposite off Kerhuon, where there is a slip, the end of which is marked by a beacon with an orange top; there are simple shops and a café in the village. There is also anchorage at St Jean, 3 miles up the river, up to which point there is a least depth of 3.3m (11 ft). Above the tower (port) 1 mile east of St Jean the river dries out. It is navigable at HW with 3m (10 ft) draft as far as Landerneau, where vessels can lie alongside the quay, with a hotel and all shops. The channel is buoyed with 3 lit and 15 ordinary buoys, but it is said to be difficult to follow, and should not be attempted by night.

Southern arm, southern side.
Roscanvel. The Baie de Roscanvel lies immediately east of Presqu'île de Quélern, and is formed between this peninsula and the smaller peninsula called Ile Longue, which separates it from the Anse du Fret. The bay is sheltered by land from all directions except N, NE and E.

An important feature of the bay is the tidal stream. The flood stream begins to run S into the bay at −0530 Brest, but 1 hr later the stream, running S down the east side of the bay, sweeps along the south shore and causes an eddy up the west side towards Pointe des Espagnols. By −0200 Brest the stream is weak in the inner part of the bay, but the north-going eddy on the west side attains 1 knot springs. The ebb stream is simpler. It runs from Pointe de l'Ile Longue towards Roscanvel and Pointe des Espagnols, leaving only a weak stream in the south of the bay.

Though the bay is attractive, it is best avoided because of the very strict security surrounding the naval base on Ile Longue.

There is a slip at Roscanvel, which is a small holiday village, with village store, cafés and a restaurant grouped round the village green. Anchor off the slip, clear of the local boats on moorings. The end of the slip dries at LW and there are obstructions to the east of it. Towards LW approach the slip from the south, and use the inside only. Further south anchorage is prohibited.

Le Fret. This is the second bay on the south after entering the Rade. The base at the northern end of Ile Longue is very conspicuous. The bay is pleasant enough, though less attractive than some other parts of the Rade. It is open to N and E, but very well sheltered from S and W. There are acoustic ranges in the bay, which are occasionally closed to navigation.

The anchorage lies off Le Fret village in the SW corner of the bay. The slip, with a beacon (stbd) at the end is used by the ferries and the buses which meet them, and must be

47

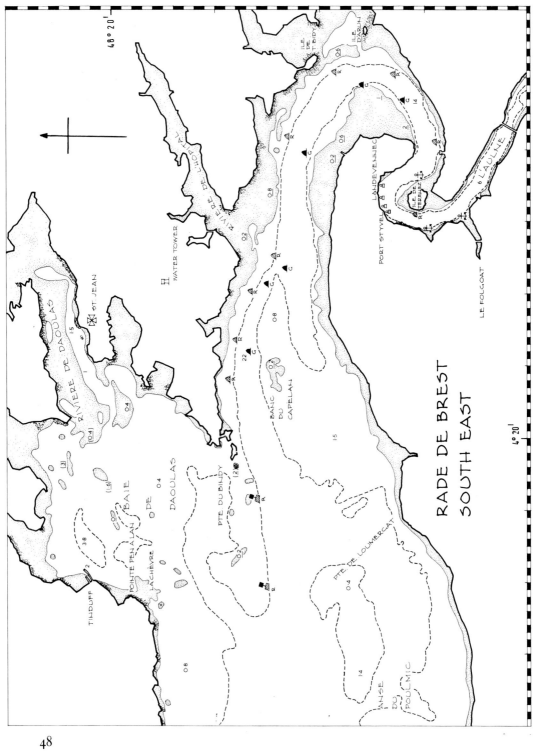

RADE DE BREST
SOUTH EAST

RADE DE BREST, SOUTH EAST   MLWS 1.4m; MLWN 3.0m; 0000 Brest, Index 5, MTL 4.4m
Based on French Chart No. 3799 with corrections (No. 6542 supersedes)   Depths in metres; right hand margin in cables

48

Anse du Moulin Blanc, one pontoon and floating breakwater. The central mole is on the right, the Elorn Bridge behind its end.

left clear. Anchor farther to the SE, clear of the moorings, and land at the slip by the village. There are several shops and a restaurant, but bread comes by van, rather late, as there is no local baker. Keep well clear of the prohibited area round Ile Longue, the French nuclear submarine base.

Lanvéoc. There is a slip, but there are complicated restrictions on passage and anchoring, and too much naval activity. Avoid it.

Anse du Poulmic. It is possible to anchor here, but there is a large naval establishment, and most people will prefer to go elsewhere.

Southern arm, northern side.
Anse de l'Auberlac'h. This bay to the east of Ile Ronde is clear of dangers. Anchor at the head of the bay off the jetty in the NW corner, clear of the local boats. There is good shelter from northerly winds; as a large number of small boats lie on permanent moorings it cannot be too dangerous in any winds in the summer, though doubtless uncomfortable if the wind is blowing into the bay. At night beware unlit red buoys in the centre of the bay which mark an experimental fish farm; similar care is necessary off Tinduff.

Tinduff. This is an inlet on the west side of the Baie de Daoulas, $\frac{1}{2}$ mile to the north of Pointe Pen a Lan. In the approach this point must be given a berth of over $\frac{1}{4}$ mile as there are shoals and La Chèvre rock which dries 3.1m (10 ft) off it, and another, which dries 4.1m (14 ft) closer inshore. The bay itself is shallow, but may be entered with sufficient rise of tide. There is deeper water, 2m (6 ft), off the end of the pier, which is sheltered from W and N, and the holding is good. There are no shops or facilities, other than two cafés.

The entrance to the Rivière de l'Hôpital, bearing about 040°.

Rivière de Daoulas. This runs into the NE corner of the Baie de Daoulas. The bay is shallow and can only be entered at sufficient rise of tide, but there is a long narrow pool, with depths up to 7m (23 ft), just inside the entrance of the river near the southern shore. This provides a good anchorage. There are two slips on the southern shore. Land at the second, off which the depth is 1.4m (4 ft); very limited provisions are available at the village store at St Jean, ¼ mile up the hill.

It is possible, but difficult, to go up the river to the town at spring tides, as the river dries 5m (16 ft).

Rivière de l'Hôpital. The pretty entrance of this small river is passed when sailing up the Aulne. There is much local sailing activity but the boats all dry out at low water. It would be possible to go in and land at tide time.

Rivière du Faou.. This river joins the Aulne east of Landévennec. The entrance lies between Ile de Tibidy and Ile d'Arun. There is a bar which dries 0.6m (2 ft) at the entrance, then a small pool with up to 1.3m (4 ft) north of Ile d'Arun, and above that the river dries. It is possible to go up to the substantial village of le Faou at springs, but it is not very attractive and the river dries at least 4.5m (15 ft) and is said to be silting.

L'Aulne rivière. This is a beautiful river which winds between steeply wooded hills on either side, and is quite comparable in charm with the Odet, though much less sophisticated. It is worth going out of the way to visit one of the quiet anchorages in this deeply sheltered river. The outer approach lies between Ile Ronde on the north and Ile Longue on the south.

The first port hand buoys are Nos 4 and 6 (R, can topmarks). Thereafter there are many buoys, all conical, but correctly painted R or G, on both sides of the channel, which lies between mud banks. At No. 12 buoy the channel turns SE towards Landévennec, turning E again after

50

Landévennec on the starboard bow, bearing about SE. The deep water lies on the left of the picture; the channel goes round by the yacht and the distant woods, and is well buoyed.

passing Nos 5 and 14. But if the tide is high enough to disregard the Banc du Capelan, which dries 0.3m (1 ft), a mid-channel course can be followed to No. 5 buoy, disregarding the outer buoys. Thence the buoyed channel should be followed. At No. 16 buoy a complete 's' bend begins, as shown on the plan; this curves round the headland of Landévennec, turning through S and W to NW and round again through SW to SE.

There are expanses of mud on the north and east sides of Landévennec, though at neaps one can anchor off the slip at Landévennec beside the moorings; for facilities, see below. The main channel lies about ½ mile off this headland until the inner river is entered on the south side of the headland, between thickly wooded hills on either side. The deep water is then on the north and west side, and a wide berth should be given to Ile de Térénez, marked by the last port hand buoy, No. 24. On the starboard side there are a number of large mooring buoys for naval vessels.

It is possible to anchor anywhere in these reaches of the river but the bottom is rocky and the tide runs hard. It is better to sound into one of the inlets to get out of the tide into shallow water with a muddy bottom. Some suggested places are shown on the plan, of which Le Folgoat is probably the best, with a restaurant on the other bank. At Port Styvel there is no port (see page 32), but one can land on the beach and walk up a path through the woods to Landévennec, where there are shops, a hotel and the famous abbey, now revived. It is possible to anchor here inside the naval buoys as the shore is very steep-to.

The river is navigable for a further 12 miles above this point. There is a suspension bridge with a clearance of 27m (88 ft) above the highest tides. Above this the river is crossed at various points by high-tension cables, of which the clearance is unknown, but sufficient to clear any normal mast. There is no chart, but a generally mid-channel course tending to the outside of the bends will serve until the river narrows, when keep in the middle. The upper reaches dry, but vessels of 2.7m (9 ft) draft can go up with the tide. Trégarvan, about 2 miles above the bridge, is a reasonable anchorage; there are several local boats and a slip. There is also a landing at Le Passage, 2 miles further up. After that there are no landings until the lock is reached, although at a number of places local boats are launched off the banks.

Above Trégarvan the scenery is less impressive but still very pretty. The lock at Guly Glas, 1 mile below Port Launay, is worked about 1 hr each side of HW. There is a grassy quay just above it, but it is easy to go on to Port Launay where there are plenty of quays and the usual shops. Port Launay consists of a line of houses with high tree-covered hills behind and is most attractive. The river is navigable above Port Launay to Châteaulin. The canal to Nantes is closed, but a substantial length has been re-opened for pleasure traffic. There are no facilities for masting. The throng of transport vehicles at Guly Glas lock at lunchtime indicates a popular restaurant, not a busy port.

The quay at Port Launay, looking upstream.

7 Camaret

Charts: 2690, 3427, 2643.
High water: −0005 Brest, Index 4, MTL 4.2m.
MHWS 7.0m; MLWS 1.4m; MHWN 5.4m; MLWN 2.8m
Tidal streams: in the bay of Camaret are weak.
Depths: There are depths of 3m (10 ft) in the shelter of the northern breakwater. Thence the depths shoal quickly and the greater part of the harbour dries. The area, shown on the plan, dredged to 2m is largely occupied by floating fishtanks.

After passing through Le Four channel, Camaret is the most convenient port of call for yachts bound south. It is a considerable centre of shell-fishing for vessels of all sizes, but the activity seems to be declining. The town is built along the edge of the harbour, and has figured in many wars. The old fort on Le Sillon, on the north side of the harbour, and La Tour Dorée were designed by Vauban and date from 1689. Five years after their construction, the defences repelled with heavy loss a combined attack by Dutch and English, and in 1791 won a victory against five English frigates.

Camaret: the harbour, looking south-east.

The pontoons inside the north mole.

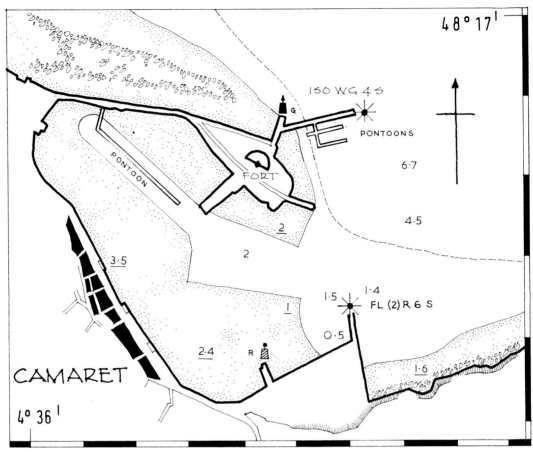

48° 17'

ISO WG 4 S

PONTOONS

6·7

4·5

PONTOON

FORT

2

2

3·5

1·5 1·4
FL (2) R 6 S

1

0·5

2·4 R

1·6

CAMARET

4° 36'

CAMARET MLWS 1.4m; MLWN 2.8m; −0005 Brest, Index 4, MTL 4.2m
Based on Admiralty chart No. 3427
Depths in metres, right hand margin in cables

   Most of the harbour dries out, but there is a dredged area with pontoon berths and there are others inside the northern mole, though it is a long way to the town.

Approach and entrance

The Anse de Camaret is entered between the Pointe de Grand Gouin on the west and Presqu'île de Quélern on the east, and the bay itself is clear of dangers. To the west the high cliffy coast between Pointe du Toulinguet and Pointe de Grand Gouin has no dangers more than 1 cable from the line of the shore and the above-water rocks. But SE of Pointe de Grand Gouin there is shallow water in the rocky corner of the bay, SW of a line from the point to the harbour entrance.

   The long breakwater with the lighthouse at its eastern end will be seen as soon as it is opened up to the SSE of Pointe de Grand Gouin. Leave this to starboard and enter the harbour.

By night: Approach in the white sector of the light on the northern breakwater, and round it at a reasonable distance. The lights are:
North mole; Iso WG 4s, 7m, **12**, *10*M.
South mole; Fl (2) R 6s, 9m, 5M.

Anchorage

The new pontoon in the inner harbour, dredged to 2m, is reserved for locals, except with permission from the harbour master of the outer marina, which will only be granted if that marina is full. The outer marina is exposed and is liable to damage in strong winds; it is also less convenient for the town.

Yachts which can take the ground could anchor in many parts of the harbour, but may not be permitted to do so. There is good hard standing off the quays in the middle of the SW side of the harbour, with a stern anchor off and a bow line to the quay.

There is a slip at the mole at the SE corner of the harbour where dinghies can land at all states of the tide, but it is quite a walk to the shops. There are plenty of slips for dinghy work nearer the town which can be used when the tide is up.

Facilities

All shops, restaurants, ship chandler, ship builder and a sailmaker. Water tap on the pontoons. There is communication with Brest two or three times a day by bus to Le Fret and connecting ferry.

Camaret harbour, looking north-west.

Charts: 2690, 2643.
Tidal streams: The S stream begins at +0015 Brest, the N at −0550 Brest, spring rates 3 knots. There is a cross tide at the northern end, the flood running to the E and the ebb to the W. To the south, between Les Tas de Pois and Cap de la Chèvre, the stream is weak, 1 knot springs, and runs almost continuously southwards.
Depths: As described here the channel has a least depth of 3.3m (11 ft), though with care a greater depth can be carried.

The Chenal du Toulinguet, which lies immediately west of the headland of that name, is a convenient passage for vessels bound south from Brest or Camaret, as it saves a long detour round the rocks and shoals outside.

On the east side of the channel there is La Louve tower (card W), on the rocks off the headland, and on the west side there is a rock named Le Pohen, which is steep-to and 12m (40 ft) high. The channel is over ¼ mile wide and carries a least depth of 3.3m (11 ft). No directions are necessary other than to keep near the middle of the fairway between Le Pohen rock and La Louve tower. If proceeding SSE towards Cap de la Chèvre, note that Le Bouc light tower was destroyed in 1980; now guarded by a cardinal W buoy 3 cables west.

By night: The passage is possible if there is enough light to see the rocks and La Louve tower at 100m. There are no lights for the narrows itself, and use must be made of two safe sectors. In the southern sector, Le Toulinguet light shows white, bearing less than 028°, and the Pointe de Petit Minou light shows open of Pointe du Toulinguet, bearing more than 010°. In the northern sector Le Toulinguet light shows white, bearing more than 090°, and the Pointe du Portzic light shows open of the Presqu'île de Quélern, bearing more than 040°. This last line passes very close to the rocks near La Louve tower, and it is desirable to keep Le Portzic light well open of Quélern.

From the south, enter in the southern safe sector and sail to its apex, with Le Toulinguet light just turning red and Le Petit Minou light just shutting in behind Pointe du Toulinguet. From this point La Louve tower bears about 350° and Le Pohen about 270°. Steer to make good about 310° to pass between them, and into the northern safe sector.

From the north, enter in the northern safe sector, keeping Le Portzic light well open of Quélern as La Louve tower is approached. Once the tower has been seen course can be shaped to pass through the channel, leaving the tower at least 1 cable to port, and out by

The lighthouse and semaphore on Pointe du Toulinguet, La Louve card W Tower on the left edge in front of the Pointe des Capucins.

Les Tas de Pois, bearing roughly SSE, and the coast north of them.

the southern safe sector. From the apex of the northern safe sector the course to steer is SW for 2 cables, thence SSE.

The lights are:

Le Toulinguet; Oc (3) WR 12s, 49m, 15M. Also F fog detector light.

Le Petit Minou; Fl (2) W 6s, 32m. Also F fog detector light.

Le Portzic; Oc (2) W 12s, 56m, 19M.

Both Le Portzic and Le Petit Minou lights have other sectors, given in full in chapter 5, but they are not of interest here.

Les Tas de Pois

There is no need to pass between these rocks, but as some may be interested to do so, in good weather only, the following notes may be helpful. There are five rocks, which may conveniently be numbered from seaward as follows:

1. Tas de Pois Ouest, 52m high.
2. La Fourche, 17m high.
3. Le Dentelé, 45m high.
4. Le Grand Tas de Pois, 66m high.
5. Le Tas de Pois de Terre, 59m high.

Between Nos 1 and 2 is the widest channel. A mid-channel course is clean. A rock dries 1.2m (4 ft) about 50m NE of No. 1, and there is a rock drying 0.2m (1 ft) very close to No. 2. Near LW it is, therefore, necessary to keep mid-channel, if anything closer to No. 2.

Between Nos 2 and 3 the channel is narrow but clean.

Between Nos 3 and 4 keep closer to No. 3; there is a rock drying 0.6m (2 ft) close NW of No. 4.

Between Nos 4 and 5 passage is only possible near HW; a rock dries 3.2m (11 ft) right in the middle of the narrow channel. Between No. 5 and the land there is no passage.

Anchorage

There is a snug anchorage in the Anse de Pen Hir, just inside Les Tas de Pois, in all winds but S or SE. There are no facilities ashore.

57

Charts: 798, 2690, 2643.
High water: −0010 Brest, Index 4, MTL 4.3m.
MHWS 7.1m (23.5 ft); MLWS 1.4m (4.5 ft); MHWN 5.6m (18.5 ft); MLWN 2.9m (9.5 ft)
Tidal Streams: Inside the Baie de Douarnenez the streams are very weak.
Depths: The old harbour dries; depths in the new harbour are 1.8–2.0m.

Morgat is situated in the NW corner of the Baie de Douarnenez. It is a pretty, sandy bay, sheltered from the N and W by the land, and by the Pointe de Morgat on the SW, almost round to S. The village is a pleasant holiday resort with good beaches and the new harbour makes it a popular port of call. It is more conveniently situated than Douarnenez as it is not so far east, and is nearer the Four channel and the Raz.

MORGAT   MLWS 1.4m; MLWN 2.9m; −0010 Brest, Index 4, MTL 4.3m
Based on French Chart No. 5186 with corrections   Depths in metres; right hand margin in cables

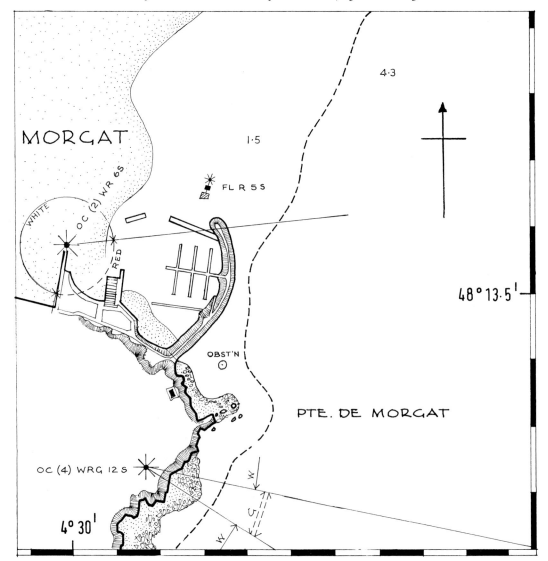

Approach

Cap de la Chèvre, 3½ miles to the south of Morgat, has fangs of rock extending seawards on all sides, especially to the SW, where the bottom is irregular as far as the Basse Vieille whistle buoy. In westerly winds the approach from Cap de la Chèvre provides pleasant sailing, completely sheltered by the land. The cliffs are bold and their tops are covered with grass and heather; many sandy beaches lie at their feet.

Pointe de Morgat, a bold headland with a lighthouse on top (see photograph), hides the village and anchorage until it has been rounded. Two conspicuous above-water rocks at its foot can be passed closely, say within ¼ cable. The breakwater of the new harbour lies just to the north of them but there is a concrete obstruction in the intervening bay.

Approaching from the east, the only outlying dangers are the group of rocks, Les Verrès and La Pierre Profonde, which lie about 2 miles ESE of Pointe de Morgat. They are not marked, but they can be seen in daylight as they are respectively 16m (52 ft) and 11m (36 ft) high. There is a wreck 1 cable NE of Les Verrès, and Le Taureau 3 cables N of La Pierre Profonde and 5 cables W of Les Verrès, dries. Apart from these hazards it is only necessary to give the group a berth of ¾ cable.

By night: The dangers south of Cap de la Chèvre can be cleared by keeping in one of the two white sectors of Pointe du Millier light until Pointe de Morgat light turns from red to white. Then steer in the white sector of Pointe de Morgat light. On close approach keep clear of the coast with a course not less than 035°, crossing the green sector of Pointe de Morgat light. The light on the old harbour breakwater will open red, seen over the new breakwater; when it turns from red to white, alter course to leave to port the harbour entrance buoy. The lights are:

Point du Millier; Oc (2) WRG 6s, 34m, 15M.
Basse Vieille by; Fl (2) W 6s, 8m, 10M, Whistle.
Pointe de Morgat: Oc (4) WRG 12s, 77m, 15M.
Morgat, old breakwater; Oc (2) WR 6s, 8m, 10M.
Morgat by; Fl R 5s.

The Pointe de Morgat, now heavily wooded, with the lighthouse on the top of the cliffs, bearing about WNW. The outer mole of the new harbour now occupies the right hand edge of this picture.

The pontoons in the marina.

Mooring

The yacht harbour has pontoons and mooring buoys; anchoring is not permitted inside the breakwater, which comprises a short and a long row of floating concrete caissons with the entrance between the rows marked by R and G paint and fixed lights. Six rows of pontoons in harbour. Visiting yachts berth on inner side of outer row. Twenty-seven places in 1987: water and electricity laid on.

Facilities

All shops, hotels and restaurants. Good bathing beaches nearby.

Morgat harbour, looking north-east, before the new wave-breaker was installed.

10 Douarnenez

Charts: 798, 2643.
High water: −0010 Brest, Index 4, MTL 4.2m.
MHWS 7.0m; MLWS 1.4m; MHWN 5.5m; MLWN 2.9m.
Tidal streams: Tidal streams inside the Baie de Douarnenez are very weak.
Depths: In Rosmeur the depths vary, but there is a considerable area with 3 to 5.5m (10 to 18 ft). In the Rade du Guet the depths shoal from 4 to 0.4m (13 to 1 ft). In the marina at Tréboul the dredged depth is 1.5m (5 ft). Port Rhu dries 3m (10 ft).

Douarnenez is an important fishing harbour situated in the SE corner of the bay of the same name. It is off the beaten track of yachts bound south or north, as it lies 17 miles to the east of Pointe du Raz, but the detour is worth while. Although not so picturesque as some others, it is an interesting town with all facilities, and the harbour provides protection in all weathers.

Approach
The only considerations in the approach are Basse Veur, with 4.2m (14 ft) over it, and Basse Neuve, with 1.6m (5 ft) over it. Except near LW or when a sea is running these can be ignored. To clear them keep Pointe du Millier lighthouse (5 miles west of Douarnenez) open of Pointe de la Jument (3 miles west) until Ploaré church, at the back of the town, comes open to the left of Douarnenez church and Ile Tristan lighthouse; the two churches and the lighthouse are almost in one line. The town is easy to locate from seaward, with Ile Tristan in the foreground, the two churches and the harbour mole to the eastward.

By night: Navigate on Ile Tristan light until the lights on the moles are picked up, when steer round them to the anchorage. Ile Tristan light has a red sector covering Basse Veur and

The approach to Douarnenez from the NW. The lighthouse on Ile Tristan is exactly in transit with the right hand of the two churches, bearing 148°. The fishing harbour is on the left, and the Rivière de Pouldavid on the right.

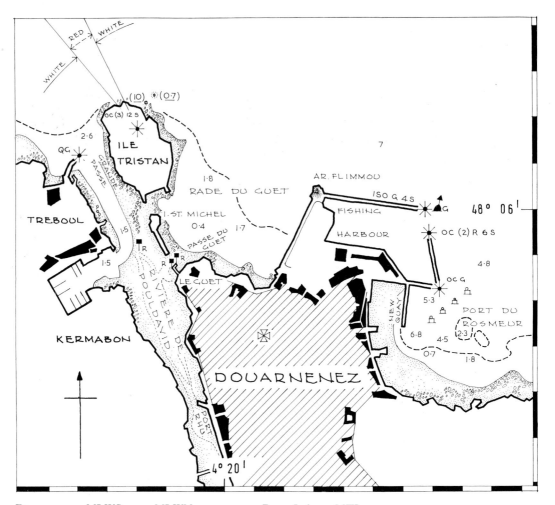

DOUARNENEZ   MLWS 1.4m; MLWN 2.9m; −0010 Brest, Index 4, MTL 4.2m
Based on French Chart No. 6128 with corrections   Depth in metres; right hand margin in cables

Basse Neuve. The lights are:
Ile Tristan; Oc (3) WR 12s, 35m, 13M.
Tréboul jetty head; QG.
Fishing harbour:
North mole head; Iso G 4s, 8m, 6M.
Entrance, south side; Oc (2) R 6s, 6m, 8M.
SE corner; Oc G 4s.

Anchorage and mooring
There are several anchorages or harbours at Douarnenez. As the vessel approaches the first
to be seen is the Rivière de Pouldavid on the west side between the land and Ile Tristan.

62

The Port de Rosmeur, looking WSW, with the SE corner of the fishing harbour on the right.

The river has been dredged and there is a dredged area with a yacht harbour at Tréboul on the west side and there are quays at Port Rhu farther up on the east side. Next there is the Rade du Guet, an anchorage, not much used, in the bay between the east side of Ile Tristan and the main fishing harbour. To the SE of the fishing harbour is the Port de Rosmeur. The following descriptions start with Port de Rosmeur and work back westwards.

Port de Rosmeur. This lies to the east of the town; it is protected by land on the W and S and by the breakwater on the N. Though open to the E the land there is only 1 or 2 miles away. There are three large mooring buoys which tend to be occupied by decaying fishing vessels, but there is plenty of room to anchor clear of these in depths of from 1 to 5m (3 to 16 ft). The depths vary rather irregularly and once the 3m (10 ft) line is crossed they shoal quickly in places.

Fishing harbour. Yachts may not use this harbour.

Rade du Guet. This lies between Ile Tristan and the mole leading to Ar Flimmou. It is sheltered except from winds from NW to NE, to which it is completely exposed. In offshore

The Port de Rosmeur, looking NE from the quay.

The Rivière de Pouldavid, looking seaward over Port Rhu at low water on a tide rather greater than mean tide (Index 11). The channel to Tréboul has now been dredged.

winds it is a good anchorage with a convenient dinghy landing at the slip in Passe du Guet. It is quieter than Port de Rosmeur. The depths decrease steadily towards the SW from 3m (10 ft). Go as far in as draft and tide permit to get as much shelter as possible. The Passe du Guet, leading from the anchorage into the river, dries 3.5m (12 ft), the best water being on the southern side near the beacons marking the slip.

Rivière de Pouldavid. This is entered through the Grande Passe, west of Ile Tristan. There are rocks close under the island shore, and the best water is nearer the jetty head on the west side. The river has a depth of about 1.5m (5 ft), and is crossed by power lines with a clearance of 25m (80 ft) above the highest tides. The river can also be entered through the Passe du Guet. Buoys in the entrance channel belong to the Centre Nautique.

Tréboul. An area has been dredged to 1.5m (5 ft) in the inlet off Tréboul. The outer quays are for commercial use, but the inner part has been developed as a yacht harbour with pontoons to which yachts moor, connected by gangways to the shore. There is a small visitors' pontoon to starboard at the entrance and moorings may be available in the river off the entrance.

Port Rhu. This is the commercial port. There is a short spur into the river above which are the quays. The bottom dries 3m (10 ft) for the most part, but 3.5m (12 ft) near the root of the spur.

Facilities
All the facilities of a substantial town, including shipyard and marine engineer. There are restaurants on and near the quays at Rosmeur, but most of the shops are some way up the hill in the town. Water tap near the dinghy slip at Rosmeur. There are also shops near the yacht harbour at Tréboul, where petrol and diesel can be obtained by hose. Water on the pontoons and a yacht club with showers.

64

Charts: 798, 2351, 2643, 2645.
High water: −0010 Brest, Index 3, MTL 3.8m
MHWS 6.4m; MLWS 1.2m; MHWN 5.0m; MLWN 2.6m
Tidal streams: Between Ile de Sein and Tévennec the NW stream begins +0535 Brest, SE stream begins −0045 Brest, spring rates 3 knots. To the north of Nerroth the flood begins NNW at −0600 Brest, turning steadily to W by HW Brest. The ebb begins at +0200, running S.
Depths: The approach is deep until Nerroth is reached; thence the channel has 0.8m (2 ft). In the anchorage there is 1.8m (6 ft).

On even the largest scale British chart, No. 798, the Ile de Sein appears to be so surrounded by reefs and rocks that it looks unapproachable, especially when associated in one's mind with the fierce tides of the Raz. But except in bad visibility or heavy weather, navigation in the area with a chart on a sufficiently large scale is not difficult because:
(i) The plateau is compact on the NE and E sides, and the fringes are indicated by the whistle buoy on the N, the above-water rock Ar Vas Du to the ENE, the Cornoc ar Vas Nevez tower to the E and Le Chat tower to the ESE. There are no dangers if a vessel is over ½ mile seaward of these visible marks.
(ii) The tidal streams on the Sein side of the Raz are not so strong as they are on the E side.
(iii) The entrance channels are clearly marked. However, when visiting the island for the first time, it is best to wait for settled weather with clear visibility and neap tides.

The Ile de Sein is sufficiently detached from the busy world to remain largely unspoilt. Its inhabitants live by catering for tourists, from fishing and by farming small plots of soil won from hard rock, which is always so near the surface that it is difficult even to find depth for burying the dead. The local fishing boats are mostly small, but the harbour is a base for larger vessels from Audierne and Douarnenez, which fish by day and anchor at Sein sufficiently early in the evening to patronise the numerous bars. When the fishing fleet is in, the harbour is crowded, but there is still room for a few yachts.

Though there is considerable tripper traffic with the mainland the island is a strange, out-of-the-way place which is worth visiting if only to see the curious rock formations, but it also has a practical use, as the harbour is convenient if you are late on the tide, especially when bound south. The facilities are quite good and the anchorage secure in southerly and westerly winds. It is exposed to the N and E; if there is a threat of winds from this quarter it is best to leave the Ile de Sein to visit another time, for if the winds are moderate there will be a swell in the harbour, and if they are strong it may be dangerous to remain.

Approach
Nerroth is the key to pilotage in the Ile de Sein. Situated in the approach to the harbour, it looks like a small island: in fact it is composed of three very large rocks; only at low water does it form a continuous island, with a finger of rocks extending from its southern end to the

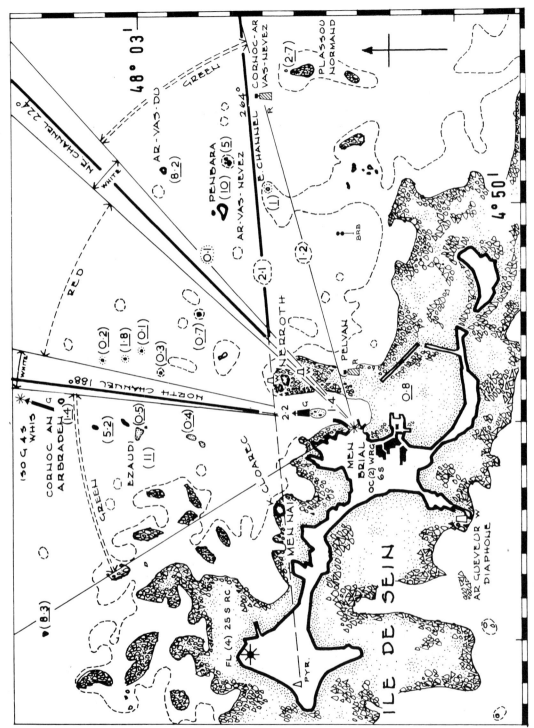

ILE DE SEIN   MLWS 1.2m; MLWN 2.6m; −0010 Brest, Index 3, MTL 3.8m
Based on French Chart No. 5252 with corrections   Depths in metres; right hand margin in cables

The north breakwater, Men Brial lighthouse and the lifeboat jetties. The rear leading mark for the north channel is the black-striped house over the left hand life boat jetty.

eastern breakwater. There are two white masonry beacons, at its northern and southern ends, which are important leading marks.

North channel. This is the principal channel and the easiest for a stranger. The channel is deep until abreast of Nerroth, after which the depth is 1.4m (5 ft) to the jetties.

   Having given a wide berth to all beacons and visible rocks (not less than ½ mile if approaching from the Raz), approach the Cornoc an Arbraden pillar whistle buoy (stbd) from the northward. Bring Men Brial lighthouse into transit, at 188°, with the third house from the left by the quay; this house is painted white with a black vertical stripe which should be kept just open to the left of the lighthouse if the latter tends to hide it. This transit leaves both the buoy and the rock which it marks very close to starboard. It is advised, therefore, to borrow say 50m to port until the rock is passed as the tides set very strongly across the channel. Thence follow the alignment; there are drying rocks on either side, but no dangers for 50m on either side of the line. When Nerroth is abeam Pelvan concrete beacon (port, R) will come into transit with the E end of the eastern breakwater, bearing 155°. Follow this transit leaving Guernic concrete beacon (stbd) to starboard. When the tower is well abaft the beam borrow a little to starboard of the transit, and when Men Brial lighthouse bears 220° the shoal is passed and course can be altered to SW for the anchorage.

By night: There must be enough light to make out Nerroth and the concrete beacon on Guernic on near approach. As it may not be easy to find the best water, it is desirable also that the tide should be high enough to allow some margin, preferably above half tide.

   Enter in the white sector of Men Brial light, leaving Cornoc an Arbraden buoy to starboard. When Nerroth is abeam alter course to 160°, and enter the red sector of Men Brial, leaving Guernic concrete beacon 60m to starboard. When the other white sector of Men Brial is entered it is safe to steer for the anchorage. The lights are:
Ile de Sein, main light; Fl (4) W 25s, 49m, **31**, *18*M.
   Radiobeacon, call SN, 303.4 kHz, 1/6 min, begins H + 2 min.
Men Brial; Oc (2) WRG 6s, 16m, 10M.
Cornoc an Arbraden by; Iso G 4s, 7m, 3M, Whistle.

Looking north across the anchorage. Guernic concrete beacon is in line with the end of the north breakwater.

North east channel. This channel carries 3.6m (12 ft) until it joins the north channel by Nerroth; thence depths are as for the north channel.

Make a position 1.5 cables NW of Ar Vas Du, a rock 8.2m (27 ft) high. Here the white masonry beacon south of Nerroth will be in transit with Men Brial lighthouse bearing 224°; follow this transit. When the white masonry beacon at the north end of Nerroth bears 265° turn to starboard, and leaving the white beacon ½ cable to port, join the north channel.

By night: There is a white sector of Men Brial light covering this channel, but sufficient light is needed for the deviation round Nerroth and into harbour. For the lights see above *North channel.*

East channel. This channel carries 2.3m (7 ft) until it joins the north channel by Nerroth; thence depths are as for the north channel.

The channel is entered ¾ cable N of Cornoc ar Vas Nevez tower (R). When coming up through the Raz be careful to avoid the shoals E and N of Le Chat and Plassou Normand to the SE of the Cornoc ar Vas Nevez tower. These shoals will all be avoided if the tower is kept bearing less than 290°. The leading marks for this channel are the white masonry beacon on the north end of Nerroth in transit, at 264°, with a pyramid with fluorescent orange top situated ¼ mile south of Ile de Sein main lighthouse. Also on the transit is Karek Cloarec, a rock which never covers, and behind it and just south of the transit is Men Nai, a promontory rising to 18m (60 ft) above datum. If the pyramid cannot be identified either of the above could be used instead, and they will in any case serve to confirm the identification. The marks must be held very closely, as Ar Vas Nevez drying 5m is close to the north of the transit, while shortly after there is a rock drying 1m close to the south.

68

The anchorage looking north-east, showing the inner lifeboat jetty and the white pyramid on the S end of Nerroth. *Provident* of the Island Cruising Club is scrubbing on the beach; she needs her legs, and previous reconnaissance for rocks.

On close approach to Nerroth, bear to starboard and round it to join the north channel, leaving the white masonry beacon ½ cable to port.

Near high water it is possible to make a short cut east of Nerroth by steering to leave Pelvan concrete beacon (port) close to port, then steering for 1 cable towards the southern quay to avoid rocks to starboard before rounding into the anchorage. This passage, which dries 2.5m (9 ft), is a SEVERE one which cannot be recommended to strangers.

Anchorage

The anchorage is immediately off the lifeboat slip, near Men Brial lighthouse and SE of it. Off the slip there is about 1.8m (6 ft), and 1m (3 ft) further to the SE. Near and south of the quays the whole harbour dries out. The fishing fleet enters the harbour in the evening, and is often there by day. Its position indicates the best water. The round red buoys appear to belong to the fishermen and do not leave much room to anchor between them and the slip; it may be necessary to anchor to the east of them. Permission can sometimes be got to use one.

The anchorage is sheltered from S to NW, and from E below half tide. Swell enters if the wind goes into the N and the anchorage would be dangerous in strong winds from any northerly direction. It is also exposed to the E when the rocks are covered. Yachts should not remain in the anchorage if fresh northerly or easterly winds are expected. The bottom is a layer of mud over rock. The stream in the anchorage is weak.

Facilities

Several small shops, restaurants, ship and engine repairs can be arranged, chandlery at the fishermen's co-operative shop. Water is scarce and yachts should bring enough with them.

The village has a considerable population; the houses are clustered together in a small area, with narrow alleyways. Bread comes on first vedette from the mainland.

Tidal streams: Southgoing, ebb stream

Position	begins Brest	direction	spring rate, knots
Off Pte du Van	−0130	SW	$1\frac{1}{2}$
Between Sein and Tévennec	−0045	SE	$2\frac{3}{4}$
Off La Vieille	−0045	SSE	$5\frac{1}{2}$
In centre of Raz	−0030	SW	$5\frac{1}{2}$
In southern part of Raz	−0045	SE	$5\frac{1}{2}$

There is a northgoing eddy between La Vieille and a position near La Plate.

Northgoing, flood stream

Position	begins Brest	direction	spring rate, knots
In southern part of Raz	+0535	NW	$6\frac{1}{2}$
In centre of Raz	+0550	NE	$6\frac{1}{2}$
Off La Vieille	+0535	NNW	$6\frac{1}{2}$
Between Sein and Tévennec	+0535	NW	$2\frac{3}{4}$
Off Pte du Van	+0605	NE	$2\frac{3}{4}$

There is a southgoing eddy for $\frac{1}{2}$ mile north of La Vieille. In the inshore Passe du Trouziard the streams are much stronger and in the approaches to the pass they do not run true with the channel. They turn earlier, the S stream beginning about −0120 Brest; the time the N stream begins is not known, probably about +0445 Brest.

The Raz de Sein is the area of sea between the Pointe du Raz on the mainland and the Ile de Sein. The scene viewed from the Pointe du Raz during gales, with the wind against a spring tide, is so impressive that it forms an inspiration to artists and photographers. Taken under reasonable conditions, however, the passage through the Raz presents no great difficulties and is a smoother passage than out at sea. It is largely a matter of timing. A yacht leaving the Four channel on the last of the fair tide can usually cross the Iroise, where the tides are less rapid and set nearly across the course, during the foul tide, so as to arrive at the Raz at the correct time, when the tide is just starting to turn fair.

The channel between La Plate tower and the rocks on the Ile de Sein is 2 miles wide. In the northern approach lies the island of Tévennec, surrounded by rocks; to the SW of Tévennec a rock, Basse Plate, narrows the western passage to $1\frac{1}{2}$ miles.

Approach and passage
The Raz de Sein is rough, especially in the overfalls off La Vieille, even in moderate winds if they are contrary to the stream, as may occur with a fair tide if sailing south against a SW wind. When wind and tide are together the passage is smoother than outside. In light weather at neap tides and in the absence of swell the passage may be taken at any time by vessels having auxiliary power. The seas caused by the irregular bottom knock the way off a boat

70

Tévennec, the small island and lighthouse in the northern approach to the Raz de Sein, bearing about SW.

La Plate tower (left) and La Vieille lighthouse, bearing about 060°. Behind them is the Pointe du Van, and to the right Pointe du Raz with Gorlégreiz off it. The Baie des Trépassés lies behind the Pointe du Raz.

very quickly. Except when wind and tide are together slack water for the passage is always to be preferred. There is a period of about half an hour of slack or weak stream each side of the turn of the tide. The Raz is temperamental and the seas met there vary considerably, but in strong winds contrary to the tide the overfalls are dangerous.

From the north. Steer for La Vieille lighthouse, bearing 180°, about midway between Pointe du Van and Tévennec. When ½ mile off La Vieille, bear to starboard to pass west of La Plate tower (card W), allowing for any tidal set. There are overfalls west of La Vieille and La Plate.

After passing La Plate the sea soon begins to moderate, but in rough weather the Masclougreiz, 9m (30 ft) and Cornoc Bras, 3.6m (12 ft) must be avoided as the seas break heavily over them. If proceeding seawards the Pointe du Van in transit, at 041°, with Gorlégreiz, the large rock between the Pointe du Raz and La Vieille, leads between the shoals. If bound for Penmarc'h, steer with Tévennec bearing 324° astern open to the left of La Plate.

By night : Steer for La Vieille light at 180° in the white sector. When Le Chat turns from green to white steer in that white sector until the directional isophase light on Tévennec opens; thence steer in that sector. Bound seaward steer out in the first white sector of La Vieille (017° to 035°); bound for Penmarc'h steer out in the second white sector of La Vieille

71

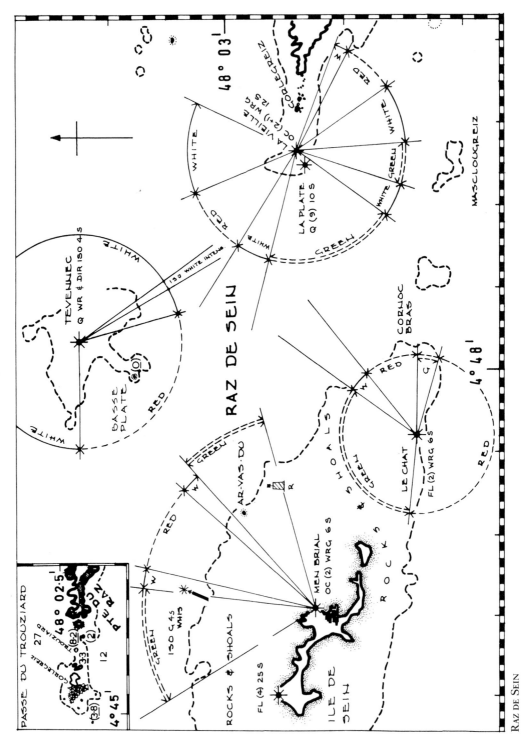

RAZ DE SEIN

PASSE DU TROUZIARD

TEVENNEC
Q WR & DIR ISO 4 S

BASSE
PLATE

WHITE

RED

WHITE

RED

RED

WHITE

ISO WHITE INTENS

WHITE

WHITE

LA VIEILLE
OC (2+1) WRG 12 S

CORLEC'REIZ

48° 03'

WHITE

GREEN

WHITE

GREEN

WHITE

RED

GREEN

RED

LA PLATE
Q (9) 10 S

MASCLOUC'REIZ

RAZ DE SEIN

CORNOC
BRAS

RED

W

G

RED

W

GREEN

GREEN

LE CHAT
FL (2) WRG 6 S

4° 48'

AR-VAS-DU

GREEN

RED

W

W

SHOALS

R

MEN BRIAL
OC (2) WRG 6 S

ROCKS

GREEN

ISO G 4 S
WHD

ROCKS & SHOALS

FL (4) 25 S

ILE DE
SEIN

PASSE DU TROUZIARD
48° 02·5'

CORLEC'REIZ
27
33
(8·2)
(2)
12
(3·8)

TROUZIARD

PTE DU RAOU

4° 45'

72

RAZ DE SEIN
Based on French Chart No. 5252 with corrections   Depths in metres; right hand margin in cables

(325° to 355°). When Le Chat light turns from green to red the vessel is clear of the southern dangers.

The lights are:

Tévennec; Q WR, 28m, 9M.
    also Dir Iso W 4s, 24m, 12M.
La Vieille; Oc (−−·) WRG 12s, 33m, 15M.
La Plate; VQ (9) W 10s, 19m, 12M.
Le Chat; Fl (2) WRG 6s, 24m, 8M.
Men Brial; Oc (2) WRG 6s, 16m, 10M.
Ile de Sein main light; Fl (4) W 25s, 49m, 31, *18*M.
    Radiobeacon, Call SN, 303.4 kHz, 1/6 min, begins H + 2 min.

From the north west. The approach is between Tévennec and Ile de Sein. There is the Basse Plate $\frac{1}{2}$ mile SW of Tévennec to be avoided; keep Coumoudoc islet open to the right of Gorlégreiz, bearing 118°. The dangers off Ile de Sein are fairly well defined by the whistle buoy, Ar Vas Du rock, which never covers, and a R tower. Follow these dangers on the Ile de Sein side, leaving them $\frac{1}{2}$ mile to starboard, and Le Chat tower (card S) $\frac{3}{4}$ mile to starboard. Or steer for La Vieille in transit with the southern limit of the cliffs SE of the Pointe du Raz, bearing 112°. When $\frac{1}{2}$ mile off La Vieille alter course to round La Plate as before.

The ebb stream SW of Tévennec is weaker than in the Raz, and the race itself appears weaker on the Ile de Sein side, though there is no official confirmation of this. In W or SW winds most of the passage is under the lee of the Ile de Sein plateau, and not so rough as east of Tévennec; care must be taken not to get set on to Cornoc Bras.

By night : Steer for Men Brial light on Ile de Sein, in the white sector (186° to 192°). When La Vieille turns from red to white steer in this white sector until the directional isophase light on Tévennec opens; thence proceed as described for the northern channel.

From the south. Follow the sailing directions given above in reverse. Watch for the set of the flood stream towards the Tévennec dangers. If going out east of Tévennec steer handsomely to starboard after passing La Vieille to put this lighthouse on a stern bearing of 180°. If going west of Tévennec steer handsomely to port until the NE-going stream is entered.

Passe du Trouziard. This passage is SEVERE, see page 25. It can only be taken by those with experience of these waters, in calm weather, at slack water, with good visibility and reliable auxiliary power.

Identify Gorlégreiz, which is the largest rock off the Pointe du Raz. At high water Gorlégreiz appears as two large slightly separated rocks, and Trouziard is the small rock midway between them and the shore. The passage lies between Gorlégreiz and Trouziard and is deep and clean, except for a 0.5m (1 ft) outlier to the north of the eastern end of Gorlégreiz. Approach on a N or SSW course, allowing for any cross set of the tide in the approach, and go through the centre of the channel. Soon after slack water, even at neaps, the

Passe du Trouziard from the N at high water, mean tides (Index 7), bearing about SSW. Trouziard looks very small at high water; the Pointe du Raz is just out of the picture on the left.

tide runs so hard that the yacht goes out of control and any sea makes the passage highly dangerous. Note that the tide turns early in the pass; see page 70.

Anchorage

There is a good fair-weather anchorage in the Baie des Trépassés, sheltered between NE and SE, in which to wait for the tide. The bay is sandy and shelving, so anchor in the most suitable depth; the best position is in the centre, facing the valley.

Passe du Trouziard, bearing 040° at low water. The yacht has been swept too far to the W; on this approach there is an outlier showing off Gorlégreiz.

74

13 Audierne

Charts: 2351, 2645
High water: −0030 Brest, Index 1, MTL 3.1m.
MHWS 5.3m; MLWS 0.9m; MHWN 4.1m; MLWN 2.1m.
Tidal streams: In the approach the NW stream begins at −0515 Brest, the SE at +0025 Brest. Streams in the approach are weak, but strong in the harbour itself.
Depths: The approach is deep until ESE of Ste Evette mole, where there is a depth of 2.2m (7 ft). The anchorage at Ste Evette has depths of from 2.7 to 1.0m (8 to 3 ft). The entrance and harbour dry by up to 2.0m (7 ft).

The port of Audierne, like all French fishing centres, is interesting, and the harbour is picturesque, although the outside anchorage is rather bleak. The harbour dries out, and yachts which cannot take the ground should only make a short visit at tide time; the shops are conveniently close to the quays. The entrance to the harbour can be dangerous in strong onshore winds and swell. There is a good anchorage outside at Ste Evette, protected by the land and a breakwater, except from the E and SE.

Approach and entrance
Audierne is situated in the NE corner of the bay of the same name, and the white slate-roofed houses will be seen from a distance clustered on the hillsides, with another group above the village of Portz ar Poulhan, 4 miles to the SE.

Approach from the west and south. There are no dangers until the vessel approaches within 1 mile of Pointe Raoulic, on which stands the harbour jetty. The channel, $\frac{1}{2}$ mile wide, lies between Le Sillon and adjacent rocks on the west side, and a group of rocks named La Gamelle, which only dry at spring tides, on the east side. If there is a swell the seas break on La Gamelle. There is a whistle buoy (card W) $\frac{1}{4}$ mile SW of La Gamelle, and a bell buoy (card S) $\frac{1}{4}$ mile SE of La Gamelle.

The approach may be made with the two lighthouses, one disused, to the west of Pointe Raoulic in transit, bearing 006°. The rear lighthouse, Kergadec, is on the hill, but the old front

The Raoulic jetty and entrance to the harbour. The church at Poulgoazec is indicated but is not easy to identify, either on the photograph or from the water.

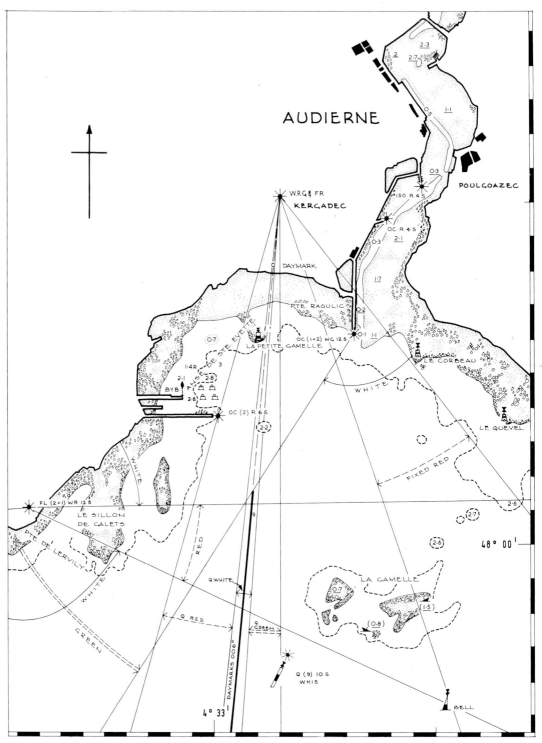

AUDIERNE   MLWS 0.9m; MLWN 2.1m; −0030 Brest, Index 1, MTL 3.1m
Based on French Chart No. 5937 with corrections   Depths in metres; right hand margin in cables

lighthouse, Trescadec, is in a gap between some houses and is not so easy to locate. This line leaves the whistle buoy (card W) about 1 cable to starboard. When the mole head bears NW alter course to round it, but not very closely. About 1 to 2 cables E of the end of the mole there is a patch with a depth of 2.2m (7 ft). If making for the inner harbour, leave the transit of the lighthouses and steer for the end of Raoulic jetty when it bears 034° and is in transit with Poulgoazec church on the eastern side of the river. The church is not very easy to see; it is small with a small steeple, and is situated on a grassy knoll, see photograph on page 75.

By night: Enter in the narrow white sector of Kergadec quick flashing light. When the light on the mole head bears NW alter course for the anchorage. If proceeding to the inner harbour alter course for the head of Raoulic jetty when the light on it turns from white to green, bearing 034°.

Eastern approach. There is no difficulty in the eastern approach as the channel between La Gamelle on the west and the land on the east is wide and carries a least depth of 2.5m (8 ft) on the leading line. The leading line is Raoulic jetty head in transit with Kergadec light bearing 332°. This leaves the bell buoy (card S) SE of La Gamelle about 3 cables to port, and two towers (card W) 3 cables and 1 cable to starboard. When a pyramid on the shore bears 070°, La Gamelle is passed and it is safe to steer for the Ste Evette anchorage.

By night: Enter with Raoulic and Kergadec FR lights in line. Pointe de Lervily light has a red sector covering La Gamelle. When this light turns from red to white the way is open to steer for the anchorage at Ste Evette. The lights are:
Pointe de Lervily; Fl (2 + 1) WR 12s, 20m, **14**, *13*M.
Kergadec; FR, 43m, and Dir Q WRG, 43m, 11M.
Jetée de Ste Evette; Oc (2) R 6s, 2m, 6M.
Jetée de Raoulic; Oc (––·) WG 12s, 11m, **14**, *11*M.
Coz Fornic; Oc R 4s.
Vieux Môle; Iso R 4s.

The outer anchorage
The Ste Evette anchorage ½ mile SW of the harbour entrance is good. It is sheltered from W and N by the land and from S by the mole, though some swell enters if there is S in the wind and this may be considerable if the wind is strong. The depths are 2.5 to 3.1m (8 to 10 ft) north of the end of the mole, decreasing steadily towards the shore. There are tightly packed mooring buoys in the anchorage, with a charge collected for their use. There may

Anse de Ste Evette, bearing about 260°, near high water. The ferry slip to the right of the lifeboat house is almost covered.

be room to anchor east of them, with less shelter from the south. The holding ground is not very good and there are a few rocky patches. It is best to tuck in behind the mole as far as depths allow, so as to get out of the swell. The northern of the two slips, used by the ferries, extends a long way; the end is marked by an inconspicuous (card E) beacon. A small tower (card S) marks a rock, called La Petite Gamelle, in the northern part of the anchorage; west and north of this the bay is shallow.

Land at the ferry slip, or above half tide, at the little pier in the NW corner of the bay. There is a restaurant facing the bay at Trescadec and a small store at Kergadec, but most of the shops are in the town over a mile away. It is also possible to land at Raoulic jetty and leave the dinghy in a pond near its root, but this pond dries out towards low water.

The harbour
Most of the harbour dries out at low water, and there is a bank, which dries, outside the harbour nearly 1 cable to the SE of the Raoulic jetty head. The best water lies near to the jetty as far as the bend in the wall some 2 cables from the entrance. Thence the channel passes near the end of the two spurs which project from the west side, with lights on their ends. The channel then crosses over to run along the quay at Poulgoazec, and then swings back to run alongside the quays at Audierne. The position of the channel shifts a little from time to time, and a stranger may not find the deepest water. The channel should be treated as drying 1m (4 ft), though on the best line there is more water as far as the main quays. Farther up the harbour dries 2m (7 ft) and more.

There is nowhere for a yacht which cannot take the ground to stay when the tide is out as the quays are occupied by fishing vessels. Those which can do so may dry out on either side of the harbour below the bridge.

There are lights on the spurs at Coz Fornic and Vieux Môle, to be left to port in the first reach. After passing these one must rely on the street lights. Strangers are not advised to attempt this channel on a dark night.

Facilities
Audierne is a substantial town with a population of 4000. There is a wide selection of shops, hotels and restaurants. There is a shipyard and engine repairs can be undertaken. It is on the tourist route, both in its own right as a picturesque place, and as a stopping place on the way to the Pointe du Raz. For nearest shop to Ste Evette, land at slip and turn left, $\frac{1}{2}$M. Water tap on roadside near slipway. Diesel from a garage in town.

Audierne harbour, looking NW, with the fish quays on the left.

Charts: 2351, 2645; French 6645
High water: −0020 Brest, Index 0, MTL 2.8m
MHWS 5.0m; MLWS 0.6m; MHWN 3.8m; MLWN 1.8m
Tidal streams: For streams in the offing see under Penmarc'h, page 83. In the harbour the streams are weak, except in the final approach channel.
Depths: In the approach channel and in the anchorage 2m.

In the entrance to St Guénolé. On the right the two leading marks for Groumilli are indicated, bearing about 125°; they are too distant to reproduce clearly. To the left of Scoëdic tower the church of Notre Dame de la Joie is indicated. Scoëdic tower is now green.

The small town of St Guénolé, situated about 1 mile north of Pointe de Penmarc'h, cannot be mistaken. It has a long and interesting history. Before the war the harbour, open to the westward, was untenable in bad weather sweeping in from the Atlantic. Then a sea wall was built, closing this entry, and a channel blasted through the rocks to the south, the quays extended and the harbour dredged. Although the entrance is exposed and dangerous in bad weather, the harbour now offers good shelter in all winds. A considerable fishing fleet is based here, but there is no local yachting activity, and yachts are not popular.

No attempt should be made to enter the harbour except in settled weather, with no swell. A first entry should be made with the tide more than half up, in daylight; a night entry should not be attempted unless the channel is well known. There is very little room for error in following the channel.

Approach
From the north. Bring Eckmühl lighthouse on a bearing of 145° and make good this bearing until Menhir tower (card W), lying about 1 mile W of Penmarc'h, bears 175°. Alter course to make good this bearing, 175°, which leads clear of all the inshore dangers and about 7 cables westward of St Guénolé sea wall. When Basse Gouac'h whistle buoy (stbd) is $1\frac{3}{4}$ cables ahead the leading marks for the Passe de Groumilli will come in transit, bearing 123°. They are masonry towers with BW horizontal bands; they will be seen to the left of Eckmühl lighthouse, see photograph.

79

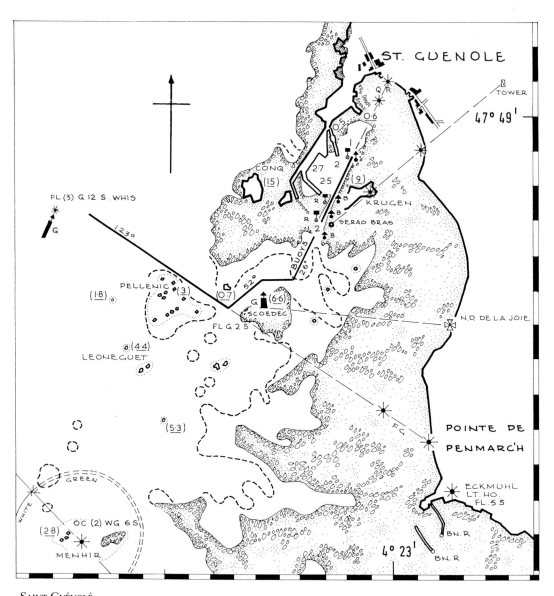

SAINT GUÉNOLÉ
MLWS 0.6m; MLWN 1.8m; −0020 Brest, Index 0, MTL 2.8m
Based on French Chart No. 5284 with corrections (No. 6645 supersedes)
Depths in metres; right hand margin in cables

The leading marks for the second line, bearing 052°, are indicated; the rock is conspicuous, the church only just shows through the houses. No. 1 concrete beacon on the right.

From the south. Give the Menhir tower (card W) a berth of 4 cables to starboard. When it bears 090° steer 020° for the whistle buoy (stbd). Pass the buoy on either hand and hold the same course for 1½ cables, when the marks for the Passe de Groumilli will come in transit, bearing 123°.

Entrance

Enter with the BW towers of the Passe de Groumilli leading lights in transit, bearing 123°. This transit leaves the Pellenic rocks, which dry, close to starboard; Scoëdec tower (stbd G) will be seen on the port bow. After 6 cables, before Scoëdec tower is reached, the church of Notre Dame de la Joie, on the coast ½ mile north of Penmarc'h, comes in transit with Scoëdec tower, bearing 096°. At about the same time a rock 9.6m (31 ft) high, seen between the outer two of three concrete beacons (stbd), comes in transit with a church tower on the east side of St Guénolé, bearing 052°. This rock, named Serao Bras, rises like a leaning tooth out of the sea at high water, and out of a flat expanse of rock at mid tide. The tower is square with a very squat steeple; it does not come into view until shortly before the alignment is reached. This transit is also marked by lights on GW metal columns.

Steer 052° on this transit; when Scoëdec bears 180°, borrow to starboard, steering about E magnetic, until the channel through the rocks opens bearing 026°. The channel, said to be dredged to 2m, is defined by 2 pairs of small R and G buoys and by Nos 3 and 5 green concrete beacons to starboard and Nos 2 and 4 red concrete beacons to port. The alignment is marked by two concrete poles near the town, carrying the leading lights, but these are not easy to pick up by day; they are a little way to the right of a large square white building, see photograph.

Steer on this alignment, 026°, until No. 4 port hand beacon is well abaft the beam, when steer round the end of the mole into the pool.

The final leading line: the poles carrying the lights are indicated, but they are not easily seen. The tide runs strongly through this channel, especially when the rocks at the side are uncovered. The anchorage is to the left inside.

By night: Only those who already know the harbour should attempt a night entry. Some, but not all, of the transits are lit. The lights are:
Eckmühl; Fl W 5s, 60m, **24**, *20*M, Siren 1 min.
      Radiobeacon, call üH (·· —— ····), 289.6 kHz, 1/6 min, begins H + 0 min.
Menhir; Oc (2) WG 6s, 19m, 8M.
Basse Gouac'h by; Fl (3) G 12s, 7m, **12**, *9*M, Horn.
Groumilli, front; FG, 9m, 6M.
Groumilli, rear; FG, 13m, 7M.
Intermediate: front Q (3) G 6s 5m; rear F Vi 12m.
Inner lead, front; Q R, 8m.
Inner lead, rear: Sync Q R, 12M.
Scoëdec tower; Fl G, 2s, with reflectors.
Channel buoys; Fl (2) R, 5s, and Fl G 2s.
Notre Dame de la Joie church is sometimes floodlit.

Anchorage and facilities
The pool is dredged to 2.5m (8 ft). Anchor out of the way of the fishing boats, probably near the lifeboat house, but the bottom is foul and a tripping line should be used. The bottom is rock covered with muddy sand.

    All shops. Shipyard. Several hotels. Buses to Quimper. Museum of prehistoric megalithic culture distant about 1 mile. Water could probably be obtained from the fish market on the quay. No petrol within reasonable distance.

Black Jack anchored outside the fishing fleet, looking N. Although they all have legs fitted, there is enough water here for most yachts.

The Pointe de Penmarc'h is a low headland, in contrast with the very high octagonal light-house of Eckmühl on it, which is 60m (200 ft) high. There are reefs of rocks extending in all directions from the headland, with numerous towers on them. In bad weather the whole scene is grim, but the point need not be closely approached except when on passage north of the Iles de Glénan. When rounding Penmarc'h progress often seems slow with Eckmühl lighthouse in sight for a long time, as the course follows an arc over 1 mile offshore.

Navigationally the principal consideration is the tidal stream. This does not compare in strength with that in the Four channel or the Raz de Sein, as the spring rates are only 1½ to 2 knots, except perhaps in the vicinity of the Menhir tower.

Some four miles south of Penmarc'h the streams are rotatory clockwise: N at −0325 Brest, E at −0020 Brest, S at +0240 Brest, WSW at +0600 Brest.

The tidal stream divides at the Pointe de Penmarc'h, the flood setting northerly towards Audierne and easterly towards the Iles de Glénan; the ebb sets in the opposite direction, the streams meeting off the Menhir tower, where there are overfalls in rough weather. North of Penmarc'h the NNW stream begins at about −0540 Brest, the SSE at about +0025 Brest, spring rates 2 knots. South of Les Etocs the E and NE stream begins about −0600 Brest, the W and WSW at about HW Brest, spring rates 1½ knots. The streams on the coast east-ward of Penmarc'h are much affected by wind.

There is a radiobeacon at Eckmühl lighthouse, for details see the previous chapter.

Pointe de Penmarc'h, bearing about E. On the left Eckmühl lighthouse, with the former one to the right of it; on the right Menhir tower (card W, but retains non-IALA colouring).

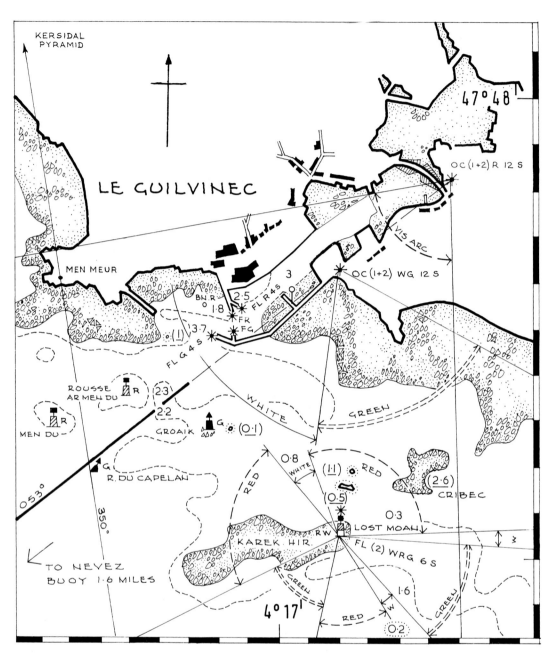

LE GUILVINEC
MLWS 0.6m; MLWN 1.8m; −0020 Brest, Index 0, MTL 2.8m
Based on French Chart No. 5284 with corrections (No. 6646 supersedes)
Depths in metres; right hand margin in cables

84

16 Le Guilvinec

Charts: 2351, 2645; French 6646
High water: −0020 Brest, Index 0, MTL 2.8m
MHWS 5.0m; MLWS 0.6m; MHWN 3.8m; MLWN 1.8m
Tidal streams: Outside, the E stream begins about −0610 Brest, the W at HW Brest, spring rates $1\frac{1}{2}$ knots, but much affected by winds. There is negligible stream in the harbour.
Depths: On the main leading line the least depth is 2.8m (9 ft), but more water can be found. In the SE approach the least depth is 0.2m (1 ft). The harbour is dredged to 2.5m (8 ft) in the outer part and dries in the inner part.

Situated some 4 miles east of Penmarc'h, Le Guilvinec (officially Guilvinec, but always called Le Guilvinec) is an important centre for fishing vessels of all kinds, and has processing factories. The town is not a tourist centre and derives its living entirely from the fishing industry. It has the attractions of a busy working town and there are a number of shops. Provided that care is taken to avoid the outlying rocks the approach is straightforward, and the harbour is sheltered. There is only limited room for yachts, which are tolerated rather than encouraged. There is no local yachting activity.

Approach

The landscape east of Penmarc'h is dotted with houses having slate roofs so that Le Guilvinec tends to be inconspicuous among them. It may be located by a somewhat thicker cluster of houses and the fishmarket, which is a long white building with a higher part at the west end; in appearance it is similar to a ship with the bridge aft. Also to be seen are the lighthouse, with a red top, on the north mole and the rear leading light structure, a rectangular building with a gable, the upper half painted black and the lower half white with a large red sphere topmark. Note that these two lights do NOT form the leading line.

Main western approach. From westward give Les Etocs, a prominent group of above-water and drying rocks, a good berth. Thence make a position $\frac{1}{2}$ cable to the NW of Nevez pillar buoy (card N). This buoy lies 3 cables SE of Raguen tower (card S) which is itself on the SE side of Les Etocs. From eastward make for the Basse Spinec whistle buoy (card S), and either leave it about $\frac{1}{4}$ mile to port and make for the Nevez buoy or when the north mole lighthouse is identified, make for it, bearing no less than 020°, the lighthouse seen just to the right of the fishmarket.

From the position $\frac{1}{2}$ cable NW of Nevez buoy the leading marks should be in transit, bearing 053°. They are: two enormous red spheres, the front on a beacon on the spur of the south breakwater and the rear on a rectangular building with a gable, the upper half painted black and the lower half white. It is safe to steer in with the conspicuous lighthouse, with a red top, on the north mole, bearing between 020° and 050°, until the buoys and beacons near the entrance are approached. On these bearings the north mole lighthouse will be approximately in transit with the eastern edge of the fishmarket.

The leading line crosses Basse aux Herbes with a depth of 1.8m (6 ft). Near low water, especially in rough weather, it may therefore be desirable to borrow ¾ cable to starboard while the *old* Penmarc'h light tower is in line with Locarec tower, bearing 292°; at night, in the red sector of Locarec light. After Basse aux Herbes is passed, return to the leading line, leaving

Men Du concrete beacon (port), 1 cable to port,
Capelan conical buoy (stbd), close to starboard,
Rousse ar Men Du concrete beacon (port), ¾ cable to port,
Groaïk tower (stbd), 1 cable to starboard.

South eastern approach. At sufficient rise of tide a shorter approach from the east may be followed; this can most easily be treated as drying 1.1m (4 ft), but with care a depth of 0.2m (1 ft) can be carried through.

First make a point 1 cable E of Les Putains tower (card S). Here Lost Moan tower (card E) should be in transit with the low building with a green top, on the outer, southern mole head, bearing 327°. Steer on this transit, nothing to westward, until Lost Moan is approached; then alter course to leave Lost Moan 1 cable to port. Thence steer for the mole head, leaving Groaïk tower (stbd) 1 cable to port. If the tide is so low as to make it necessary to avoid the rocks north of Lost Moan, steer sharply to port as soon as Lost Moan is abeam, passing ½ cable N of it. Note that the *striking* mark for the first rock is Rousse ar Men Du concrete beacon (port) in transit with Groaïk tower (stbd), bearing 292°, so that Groaïk tower must be kept on a bearing of 300°, well open to the right of Rousse ar Men Du concrete beacon, until Lost Moan tower is in transit with Les Putains tower, bearing 150°. Then steer 330° on this stern transit until Groaïk tower is abaft the beam, when alter course to enter harbour.

Southern Approach. This is the easiest daylight route with ample water provided the leading marks can be identified. Make a position midway between the Putains tower and Spineg buoy, 3 cables to the SW of Les Fourches rocks which never cover; then identify the Men Meur white painted rock at the W end of the Guilvinec waterfront buildings and a slender pyramid with large diamond topmark a mile to rear. Follow this line for 1¾ miles on 350° to the Capelan buoy, which is left to starboard to continue as on the western approach.

The entrance to Le Guilvinec, looking ENE. The lighthouse is on the end of the inner north spur; the outer south spur conceals the inner. The arrows show the leading marks.

By Night. Entry by the main channel is straightforward. Entry may also be made by the south eastern channel, at sufficient rise of tide, if there is enough light to judge distance off Lost Moan tower at 1 cable. Enter in the white sector of Lost Moan tower between 317° and 327°, round the tower at about 1 cable to port and continue in the white sector between 140° and 160°, until it is necessary to alter course to round the southern mole head. The lights are:

Basse Spineg by; Q (6) + L Fl W 15s, 7m, 5M. Whistle.
Basse Nevez by; Q W 7m, 8M.
Le Guilvinec front; Oc (––·) WG 12s, 9m, 10M.
Le Guilvinec rear; Oc (––·) R 12s, 19m, 11M.
Locarec; Iso WRG 4s, 11m, 8M.
North mole head; Fl R 4s, 11m, 9M.
South mole head; Fl G 4s, 5m, 6M.
Spurs; Fl (2) R 6s, and Fl (2) G 6s.
Lost Moan; Fl (3) WRG 12s, 7m, 8M.

Entrance and Anchorage
Steer to leave the head of the outer southern mole to starboard, and then the northern mole head and spur to port. The ends of the spurs are marked by flashing red and green lights. The entire lower part of the harbour is allocated to fishing boats and may not be used by yachts. The fish quays have recently been extended NE and a further area in this direction dredged to 3m, with a narrow strip on its SE side designated for yacht mooring: but there are discouraging restrictions for yachts; they may not enter or leave between 1600 and 1830 hrs, and only secure alongside a quay or fishing boat in emergency. Their stay may not exceed one night, and VHF watch on channel 12 is required. In order to keep clear of any possible port operation, bow and stern anchors are probably necessary, and landing may be a problem. The port is best left to the fishermen.

Facilities
The main part of town is on N side of harbour. Market day is Tuesday; excellent supermarkets. Showers at municipal baths near western pontoon on Thursdays, Fridays, Saturdays, and Sunday mornings.

The inner end of the S mole with the trawler lift. Front and rear leading marks are arrowed.

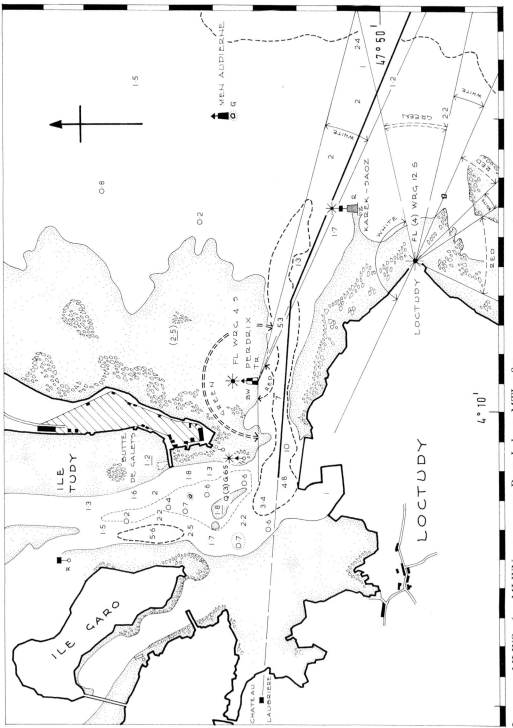

LOCTUDY   MLWS 0.6m; MLWN 1.9m; —0020 Brest, Index 0, MTL 2.8m
Based on French Chart No. 5301 with corrections (No. 6649 supersedes).   Depths in metres; right hand margin in cables

Charts: 2352, 2645, 3640, French 6649
High water: −0020 Brest, Index 0, MTL 2.8m
MHWS 5.0m; MLWS 0.6m; MHWN 3.7m; MLWN 1.9m
Tidal streams: In the offing the NE stream begins about −0610 Brest and the SW at HW Brest, spring rates 1½ knots. In the harbour the spring rates are: flood 3 knots, ebb 3½ knots.
Depths: The least water in the approach is 1.0m (3 ft). In the anchorage: off Loctudy there is 3m (10 ft); off Ile Tudy there is 1.3m to 2m (4 to 6 ft); on the opposite side of the channel to Ile Tudy there is a deep pool, but there are heavy moorings in it, there is 2m (6 ft) outside the pool.

Geographically Loctudy and Ile Tudy, on the peninsula facing Loctudy across the river entrance, lie between Le Guilvinec and Bénodet. Likewise, in character they stand midway between the wholly fishing port of Le Guilvinec and the holiday and yachting resort of Bénodet. At Loctudy and Ile Tudy fishing and sailing flourish together. The approach is sheltered in westerly winds and the anchorage is a good one.

Approach
From the west the outside approach is the same as for Bénodet (see page 92), turning to port shortly after passing the Basse du Chenal buoy. Many will prefer to coast along the shore, which is considerably shorter. Except near low water it is sufficient, after clearing Les Etocs near Pointe de Penmarc'h, to leave not less than ¼ mile to port Les Fourches (never cover), Les Putains tower (card S), Reissant (a small round rock which never covers), Les Bleds tower (card S), Men Du tower (card E), Karek Hir tower (card E), Men Bret tower (card E) and Karek Saoz tower (R). This course has a least depth of drying 0·1m (1 ft). Near low water it will be necessary to stand farther offshore, using the chart and the outer buoys.

From the E and SE the distant approach is the same as for Bénodet (see page 93) as far as Ile aux Moutons. Thence steer more to the NW, leaving to port Les Poulains tower (card N) and Men Diou tower (card E). Half a mile NW of Men Diou is a rock with 2m (6 ft) over it. If necessary this can be left to the SW by keeping Ile aux Moutons lighthouse midway between Les Poulains beacon and Men Diou tower. Thence leave ½ mile to port the buoys on Roche Malvic (card W), Basse du Chenal (card E) and Basse Bilien (card E).

By night: Follow the direction for Bénodet (see pages 92 and 93) until the white sector of Les Perdrix light is entered. Then alter course to keep in this sector until within 2 cables of the lighthouse. There are no navigation lights in the river, and it will be necessary to rely on the shore lights. A first entry should be made in adequate daylight. The lights are:
Basse Bilien by; VQ (3) W 5s, 4m, 5M, Whistle.
Loctudy; Fl (4) WRG 12s, 12m, 15, 11M.
Les Perdrix; Fl WRG 4s, 11m, 8M.
Le Blas; Q (3) G 6s, 7m, 2M.

Entering Loctudy, Les Perdrix tower should be midway between the houses indicated, bearing 294°.

Entrance

Bring the Perdrix tower (BW cheq) to bear 294°. On this bearing it will be just open to the left of the promontory of Ile Tudy and midway between two large houses on the shore (see photograph). This lead crosses the bar in a depth of 1m (3 ft); the sea breaks here when there is a heavy swell or rough conditions, especially on the ebb. Karek Saoz beacon should be given a good berth; there are said to be isolated rocks near it as a result of blowing up a wreck.

When Les Perdrix tower is about 2 cables distant alter course to port and steer 274° on the Château Laubrière, a conspicuous three-story house with symmetrical lower wings on each side, and a level roof-line between chimneys each end.

If proceeding northward to the Ile Tudy anchorage, turn to starboard after passing the Banc Blas beacon (stbd), leaving the middle ground, which dries 1.8m (6 ft), to port. Steer towards a position some 30m off the end of the jetty at Ile Tudy. One cable north of the jetty head is the Butte des Galets, a shingle patch on which it is easy to ground when it is covered near high water. Between 1800 and 1900 hours, entry is only permitted under power, sailing being prohibited.

Anchorage

The areas out of the fairway north west of the fish quay and off Ile Tudy jetty are now fully

The Château Laubrière, on the right, bearing 274°, leads into the anchorage.

Loctudy: the inner fishing harbour.

occupied with white mooring buoys, some likely to be available, but there is room to anchor further north, though this may entail a long dinghy journey across a fast tide.

After half tide, there is water for a draught of 1.3m to go 3 miles up river to Pont L'Abbé, but the river is not fully marked and there is limited room to dry out against the quays.

Facilities
At Loctudy there are all shops, restaurants and hotels, shipyard and marine engineer. Water by hose at the quay. The harbour is very animated when the fishing fleet is in, especially if dinghy racing is taking place too.

At Ile Tudy there are also all shops and hotels, but it is rather less sophisticated. There is a water tap at the root of the jetty. From both side of the river there are buses to Quimper.

Ile Tudy, from the recently enlarged fishing quay, near low water. Le Blas beacon on the left.

Charts: 2352, 2645, 3640
High water: −0020 Brest, Index 0, MTL 2.9m
MHWS 5.0m; MLWS 0.7m; MHWN 3.9m; MLWN 1.8m
Tidal streams: In the centre of the bay the streams are rotatory clockwise running N at +0600 Brest, NE at −0330 Brest, SE at −0015 Brest and WNW at +0245 Brest, spring rate about 1 knot. In the river the flood begins about −0540 Brest, the ebb at HW Brest, spring rates 2¾ knots.
Depths: The approach, entrance and river for several miles upstream are deep. The upper reaches of the river dry.

The port of Bénodet at the mouth of the river Odet, situated some 16 miles to the eastward of Penmarc'h, is one of the principal yachting centres in the north of the Bay of Biscay. It has good moorings and good facilities, and is a natural port of call for British yachts. The little town itself is a yachting and holiday resort, where a yachtsman can get most of the things he needs. The only trouble is that it is terribly crowded.

The Anse de Bénodet is a fine wide bay, some 5 miles across with sandy shores, sheltered from the N and W. The port of Loctudy lies on the west side, and to the east lie the Baie de la Forêt and Concarneau, which are partially sheltered from the W; to the south there are the Glénan islands only 12 miles away. The Odet river, which is completely sheltered, is navigable near HW nearly up to the cathedral city of Quimper; unless the yachtsman is in a hurry to sail south, he has plenty of local sailing to interest him. The whole bay is a centre of intense local sailing activity, with less popular waters to the west and to the south east. Communications with England are good for crew members leaving or joining.

Approach

From the west. After rounding Menhir tower off Penmarc'h make good 135° for 4½ miles, when the Basse Spinec buoy (card S) will bear 020°, ¾ mile. Thence, alter to 081° towards the Ile aux Moutons lighthouse. After sailing 8¼ miles on this course Bénodet main lighthouse will come in transit with Pointe de Combrit lighthouse, bearing 000°. Alter course and steer on this transit, which leaves Rostolou (card E) and Basse du Chenal (card E) buoys to port, and Roche Malvic buoy (card W) to starboard. When these buoys are well astern alter course to starboard for the entrance. In good weather a shorter course can be followed closer to the shore as suggested for Loctudy, see page 89; an intermediate course with more water lies outside the Basse Spinec, Les Putains, Karek Greiz, Basse Boulanger and Basse du Chenal buoys.

By night: The course of 135° from the Menhir tower lies on the edge of the white and green sectors of Menhir light. Follow this edge until Ile aux Moutons light turns from red to white, bearing 081°, and then follow this edge until Bénodet main light comes in transit with Pointe de Combrit light bearing 000°. Follow this transit, watching the Loctudy light; it will change from red to white to red to white to green to white. When it finally changes from green to white bearing 257°, the way is clear to steer to starboard to bring the Bénodet leading lights in line. Many lights will be seen but only the relevant ones are given in the following list:

Menhir; Oc (2) WG 6s, 19m, 8M.
Ile aux Moutons; Oc (2) WRG 6s, 18m, 15, 13M.
Pointe de Combrit; Oc (––··) WR 12s, 19m, 12M.
    Radiobeacon, call CT, 289.6 kHz, 1/6 min begins H + 3 min.
Bénodet main light; Oc (––·) W 12s, 48m, 15M.
Loctudy; Fl (4) WRG 12s, 12m, 15, 11M.

From the south east. Leave Basse Jaune whistle buoy (card E) to port, and make good a course of NW, leaving Les Pourceaux about 1½ miles to port. This rocky area is marked by a tower (card E) on its SE side and a buoy (card N) on its NW side. Continuing the same course leave Ile aux Moutons 1½ miles to port, Les Poulains tower (card N) to port, La Voleuse buoy (card S) to starboard and Men Diou tower (card E) to port. The leading lighthouses of Bénodet will then be seen and course should be altered to bring them in transit, bearing 346°, leaving Le Taro tower (card W) to starboard.

By night: Before the Basse Jaune buoy is abeam, get into the white sector of Ile aux Moutons light, and in, or south of, the narrow sector of the Ile aux Moutons directional light. Stay in this sector (and in, or south of, the directional sector) until *either* the directional sector of Concarneau rear leading light is entered, *or* Loctudy light is seen (it will be red) and Trévignon light has turned from white to green bearing more than 051°. When one or other of these occur steer to starboard and enter the white sector of Loctudy light, bearing 295°. Steer in the white sector of Loctudy light until Pointe de Combrit light opens, bearing 325°. Then steer for this light, crossing the green sector of Loctudy light, and bring the Bénodet leading lights in transit. Many lights will be seen, but only the relevant ones are given in the following list:

Basse Jaune by; Q (3) W 10s, 7m, 8M, Whistle.
Trévignon; Oc (––··) WRG 12s, 11m, 12M.
Concarneau rear; Dir Q W, 87m, 23M.
Ile aux Moutons; Oc (2) WRG 6s, 18m, 15, 13M.
    also Sync Dir Oc (2) W 6s, 17m, 24, 12M.
Loctudy; Fl (4) WRG 12s, 12m, 15, 11M.
Pointe de Combrit; Oc (––··) W 12s, 19m, 12M.
La Voleuse by; Fl (4) R 12s, Whistle.

Entrance
Bring the leading lighthouses in transit, bearing 346°. The tower of the main light is very conspicuous, but the front light, Le Coq, has been painted in green and white vertical stripes which tend to conceal it. It will be seen some way to the left of the conspicuous letters YCO on the grassy bank in front of the Yacht Club. This alignment leaves 2 buoys and one beacon (all port) to port and 2 towers (stbd) to starboard. When within 2 cables of Le Coq lighthouse

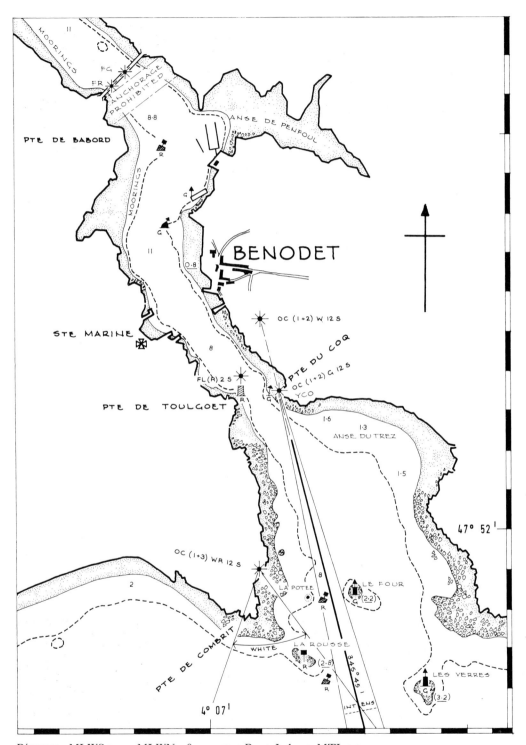

BÉNODET   MLWS 0.7m; MLWN 1.8m; −0020 Brest, Index 0, MTL 2.9m
Based on French Chart No. 5301 with corrections (No. 6649 supersedes)   Depths in metres; right hand margin in cables

The leading lighthouses at Bénodet. The conspicuous letters YCO on the right show the position of the yacht club.

bear to port and steer up the middle of the river, leaving a beacon (stbd) to starboard and a tower to port.

By night: Entrance is straightforward. The only navigation lights inside the entrance are the fixed red and green lights on the bridge. However, the shore lights give some guidance; they are on all night on the quays. In the season finding somewhere to moor may be a problem in the dark. The lights are:
Le Coq, front; Dir Oc (—–·) G 12s, 11m, **14**, *11*M.
Bénodet, rear; Sync Oc (—–·) W 12s, 48m, 15M.
Pointe de Toulgoët; Fl R 2 s.
Pont de Cornouaille; FR and FG mark the centre of the arch.

Anchorage and Mooring
There is good anchorage during offshore winds in the Anse du Trez on the starboard side of the entrance, especially if arriving in the dark. There is some hazard here from sail-board and Optimist schools, but it becomes peaceful at night.

The church, large hotel and town quay at Bénodet, with fishing boat buoys.

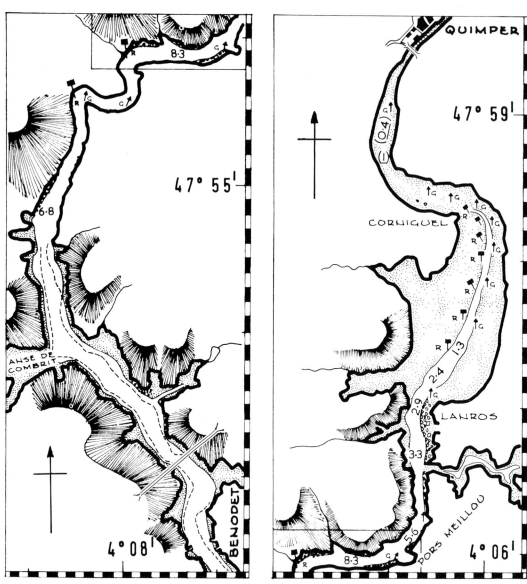

RIVER ODET
MLWS 0.7m; MLWN 1.8m; −0020 Brest, Index 0, MTL 2.9m
Based on French Chart No. 5368 (No. 6679 supersedes)
Depths in metres; right hand margin in cables

Bénodet, looking downstream from the Bridge.

Anchorage is prohibited in the channel. All the available space outside the channel between Pte du Coq and a mile above the bridge is occupied by permanent moorings. Visitors moorings, for which a charge is made, are provided (i) in a line of about 5 on the port hand side SE of Pte de Babord, (ii) off the Anse de Penfoul, (iii) on the port hand side beyond Pte de Babord. The harbour master dealing with yachts has his office on the quay at the Port de Plaisance in the Anse de Penfoul, where there are two long pontoons connected to the quay, and one unconnected but with a launch service. For W bank moorings, apply to Combrit at Ste Marine.

Yachtsmen intending to stay more than a couple of days should write in advance to the Port de Plaisance, giving details of the yacht and intended stay, and ask for a marina berth or mooring to be reserved for them.

Another possiblity is to secure to the quay, at tide time, to do any necessary business in the town and then go up the river where there is plenty of room.

Facilities

All the facilities of a sophisticated yachting centre, with shops, hotels, restaurants, engine repairs, yacht builder. Water tap on the quay at Penfoul; one can lie alongside the quay at tide time. Fuel from a barge at Penfoul.

Hot showers can be had at Penfoul or at the Yacht Club, which is less formal than its appearance from seaward would indicate.

Communications are good; bus or ferry to Quimper, whence there are good train services and occasional air services.

River Odet

The river Odet is a famous beauty spot and ferries ply regularly from Bénodet to Quimper on the tide. There is no difficulty in sailing up the first 5 miles in depths of more than 2m

(6 ft). The deep water is in the middle, the only obstruction is a rock on the sharp turn to starboard, which is marked by a beacon (stbd). Above Lanros the river is shallow, but well marked by beacons as far as the port of Corniguel; above that the river dries and the beacons are farther apart. A bridge prevents masted yachts reaching Quimper, but motor yachts can carry a depth of drying 1.5m (5 ft) up to the first quays on the port hand at Quimper. These quays form the best berth, even though one is liable to be among the sand heaps there; the bottom is very hard for drying out. The river, though still pleasant, is notably less attractive above Lanros, and the author's recommendation is to stop at that point.

In using the river, and especially in anchoring, it is important to remember that occasional large ships go up to Corniguel and need all the room there is. They must be given absolute right of way.

In looking for a place to anchor one wants to find a bight into which the worst of the tide does not get, and in which the mud will have settled; in the river much of the bottom is rock. Among several such places the Anse de Combrit and the bay opposite Lanros may be mentioned. There is a beautiful anchorage just below Lanros in the inlet on the eastern side, but care must be taken to avoid a rock on the south side of the entrance where it opens out. Keep close to the N side of the channel. A large area has 1m depth, and 2m can be found.

There are no facilities on the way up the river, but everything can be got at Quimper, which is a large city with an attractive cathedral with nave and chancel out of line. Quimper is famous for its pottery.

Bénodet road bridge, looking up River Odet.

Charts: 2352, 2645; French 6648
High water: −0020 Brest, Index 0, MTL 2.9m
MHWS 5.0m; MLWS 0.8m; MHWN 3.9m; MLWN 1.8m
Tidal streams: Near the islands the streams are rotatory clockwise setting N, 1 knot at +0600 Brest; ENE, 2 knots at −0230 Brest; S, 1 knot at HW Brest and WNW, 1 knot at +0330 Brest, spring rates in each case. Amongst the islands the streams run in the direction of the channels, the flood setting N and E and the ebb S and W, spring rates up to 2 knots.
Depths: There is enough water in the anchorages for most yachts at all tides. Above half tide there is enough water to sail freely in the channels and in the large pool between Penfret and St Nicholas, but near low water the pilotage becomes intricate and a number of the channels cannot be used.

Situated about 12 miles south of Bénodet, and 10 miles from Concarneau, this archipelago is an intricate mixture of islands, rocks and shoals. It is the home of the Centre Nautique des Glénans (CNG), which is almost certainly the largest sailing school, in Europe at least. Founded by Monsieur Philippe Viannay, it gives systematic training to young people at all levels from absolute beginners to ocean racing. The main base of the CNG is on Ile de Penfret, but there are also camps on a number of the other islands, and indeed in other parts of France and Europe. The fleets of CNG boats are in evidence everywhere among the islands. The CNG is very hospitable to visitors, but the latter should be careful not to impose on this hospitality, as the *moniteurs* have a very full programme.

The Ile de St Nicholas, where some of the more popular anchorages are, has a small café, some holiday cottages and the shell fish tanks of a famous restaurant.

The islands should be visited only in good weather as all the anchorages are somewhat exposed, at least at high water. They form a fascinating area to explore and practice one's pilotage, and a week or more could be spent happily knob-dodging. It is hoped that the plans in this book will suffice for a quick visit, using the main channels, but for any exploration the large scale French chart 6648 is essential. Although called Iles de Glénan, partie Sud, it covers all the islands. Chart No. 6647, Iles de Glénan, partie Nord, covers Ile aux Moutons and Les Pourceaux. A vessel should be fully provisioned before going to Iles de Glénan as no provisions of any kind can be bought.

Approach
The main islands are easily distinguished by the conspicuous lighthouse on Ile de Penfret, the largest and most easterly of the group; a stone fort having a tall concrete tower, the top of which is painted black on the SE side, on Ile Cigogne; a disused factory chimney on Ile du Loc'h; some houses on the SE side of Ile de Drenec; and the shell fish tanks with adjacent house and summer cottages on Ile de St Nicholas. A number of islets stretch out to the west of Ile de St Nicholas and the western edge of the archipelago is marked by Les Bluiniers tower (card W). The southern and south eastern sides are guarded by buoys (see chart 2352).

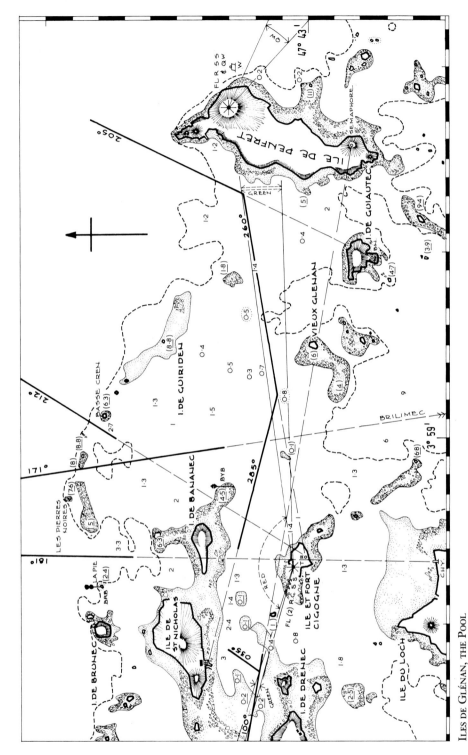

ILES DE GLÉNAN, THE POOL
MLWS 0.8m; MLWN 1.8m; −0020 Brest, Index 0, MTL 2.9m
Based on French Chart No. 5285 with corrections (No. 6648 supersedes)
Depths in metres; right hand margin in cables

Entrance

The entrances are described on the basis that one is aiming for the pool east of Ile de Bananec; from there the various anchorages are easily reached, if they have not been passed on the way in. The descriptions are already sufficiently complex, so the metric heights of rocks have not been translated into feet. The heights, above chart datum, are simply underlined, thus 'the 7.2m rock' means 'the rock, of which the top is 7.2m above datum'.

North eastern entrance. This channel carries a least depth of 1m (3 ft), but passes close to shoals of 0.7m (2 ft) and should be treated as carrying that depth. This is one of the easiest entries for a stranger. Leave the northern end of Ile de Penfret to port and steer 205° on the stone beacon on Ile de Guiautec. When Ile Cigogne concrete tower bears 260° alter course to make good the bearing, which also holds Ile de Penfret lighthouse dead astern. When the southern wall on the shell fish tank on Ile de St Nicholas bears 285° alter course on to this bearing.

Northern entrance. All three northern entrances should be regarded as carrying 1m (3 ft), although with careful pilotage through the pool, using the large scale chart, a little more water can be found. In the approach care must be taken to avoid Les Pourceaux rocks, marked on their SE side by a tower (card E).

   There are three entrances, here taken in order from east to west; the easiest for a stranger is La Pie, the third. The vital clues to the first two entrances are four rocks which never cover: Basse Cren (6.3m) in the E, then two adjacent rocks of Les Pierres Noires (8.8m and 8m), and finally in the W a single Pierre Noire (7.6m) which has others to the SW which dry not long after HW. All these rocks stand on compact rocky bases and must be distinguished from Ile de Guiriden to the SE; this has a considerable sandy expanse, which covers near high water, leaving only the rocky head (8.8m).

   The first entrance leaves Basse Cren (6.3m) 50m to 100m to port steering on Fort Cigogne tower, bearing 212°. Once Basse Cren is fairly passed the vessel can bear to port as convenient.

   The second entrance leaves the two adjacent heads of Les Pierres Noires (8.8 and 8m) 20m to 60m to port. Steer on Ile de Brilimec, bearing 171°, which leads fairly into the pool. As a check Ile Cigogne tower bears 200° in the entrance.

Les Pierres Noires, near low water, bearing 155°. The yacht is going through the second northern entrance. *A* is Ile de Guiautec with its beacon, *B* is Vieux Glénan and the rocks to the S of it, *C* is Ile de Brilimec.

Photo: Centre Nautique des Glénans.

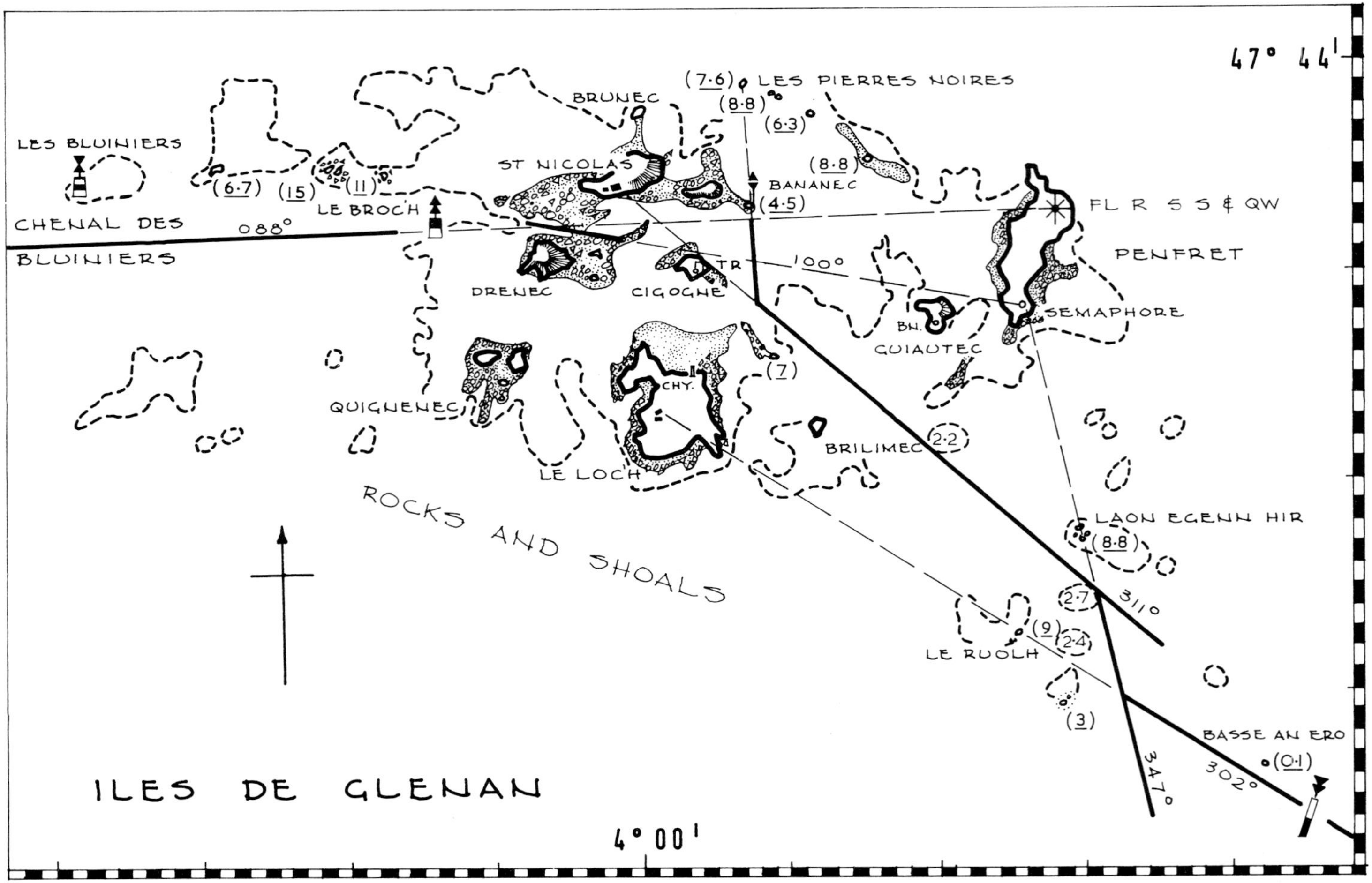
47° 44'
LES BLUINIERS
CHENAL DES BLUINIERS
088°
(6·7)
(15)
(11)
LE BROCH
BRUNEC
ST NICOLAS
DRENEC
CIGOGNE
TR
(7·6) LES PIERRES NOIRES
(8·8)
(6·3)
(8·8)
BANANEC
(4·5)
100°
FL R 5 S & QW
PENFRET
SEMAPHORE
BN.
GUIAUTEC
(7)
CHY.
QUIGNENEC
LE LOCH
BRILIMEC
(2·2)
ROCKS AND SHOALS
LAON EGENN HIR
(8·8)
(2·7)
311°
(9)
(2·4)
LE RUOLH
(3)
BASSE AN ERO
(0·1)
302°
347°
ILES DE GLENAN
4° 00'

ILES DE GLÉNAN
MLWS 0.8m; MLWN 1.8m; −0020 Brest, Index 0, MTL 2.9m
Based on French Chart No. 5368 with corrections (No. 6648 supersedes)
Depths in metres; right hand margin in cables

For the third entrance, La Pie, bring the chimney on Ile du Loc'h just open of the right hand side of the Ile Cigogne tower, bearing 181°. Steer so until inside Les Pierres Noires. Near low water the chimney dips behind the fort and it will be necessary to chose an alternative mark on the foreshore before it does so. Except near high water there is no problem about knowing when Les Pierres Noires are passed because the 5m rock marks the SW extremity of Les Pierres Noires. But the actual height of this rock is probably less than 5m, and it covers near HW springs. When La Pie beacon is in transit with the N side of Ile de Brunec, bearing about 280°, steer to port into the pool, unless one is going into the anchorage north of Ile de Bananec, in which case steer straight in.

La Pie and the pool N of Ile de Bananec. Arrows indicate the leading marks for the third northern entrance.

Western entrance. The Chenal des Bluiniers carries a least depth of 0.2m drying, but it is safer to regard it as drying 0.5m. If this gives insufficient margin, it is better not to use this entrance, but to skirt the north edge of the rocks and enter by the third northern route, described above. Visibility of 3 miles is needed except towards high water.

Make a position 1 cable S of Les Bluiniers tower (card W); if coming from the NW round this tower at not less than 1 cable distance. From this point steer E for Le Broc'h tower (card N). The dangers to the north of the channel will be avoided by keeping not less than ½ cable S of the line joining all the dangers that show. Do not go south of the transit of Ile de Penfret lighthouse and Le Broc'h tower, bearing 088°.

When Le Broc'h tower is approached steer to port to leave it about 1 cable to starboard. Bring the Semaphore, near the south end of Ile de Penfret, open to the left of Fort Cigogne by the width of the fort (not the tower), bearing 100°. Steer so until opposite the eastern part of Ile de Drenec; this island is in two clearly defined parts separated by a sandy strip which covers at HW. Thence steer 035° on the summer cottages to the east of the shell fish tank into La Chambre and thence out into the pool (see page 105). Near HW the detailed directions above can be disregarded; having passed Le Broc'h tower it is only necessary to sail ½ cable N of Ile de Drenec and then make straight for La Chambre or the pool as required.

The right edge of Fort Cigogne and the white gable on Ile de St Nicholas are indicated. These in transit, bearing 311°, form one of the lines for the SE entrance. It was reported in 1984 that increased building had made it difficult to identify the 'white' gable, now discoloured. A safer identification is the pair of dormer windows.

South eastern entrance. The channel shown on the French charts calls for local knowledge in the identification of rocks. The following directions should be safe for the stranger, provided that the visibility is sufficient. The channel carries a depth of 1.3m (4 ft).

First make a position close to the Basse an Ero buoy (pillar, card S). Do not confuse it with the spar buoy about 1 mile to the SE; if in doubt read the name painted on it. When approaching the buoy identify the white-painted gable of the large house on Ile de Nicholas; close to the buoy this is masked by Fort Cigogne. From a position close to the buoy identify the following: (i) Le Ruolh (9m), a rock with a vertical left hand side, and a smaller outlier on that side, bearing 302°. It will be seen in transit with Ile du Loc'h, the farmhouse on that island being just open to the left of it; see sketch. (ii) Laon Egenn Hir (8.8m), a shapeless bunch of rocks seen in transit with, or just to the left of Ile de Guiautec, on which there is a stone beacon with a ball topmark, bearing 323°. (iii) The Semaphore on the south end of Ile de Penfret, not to be confused with the lighthouse at the northern end which is to the right of the Semaphore. If all these identifications are satisfactory it is safe to proceed; if not, go away.

First steer 302° on Le Ruolh, keeping Loc'h farmhouse open to the south of it. This line leads 1 cable SW of Basse an Ero (0.1m). When the Penfret Semaphore comes in transit with Laon Egenn Hir bearing 347°, steer on that transit until the white gable of the house on Ile de St Nicholas opens to the right of Fort Cigogne. Then steer 311° on that transit until Ile Cigogne is approached. When the 7.6m western rock of Les Pierres Noires comes in transit with the 4.5m rock SE of Ile de Bananec, bearing 358°, steer on that transit. If the 4.5m is covered you have nothing else to worry about and the transit does not matter. When Cigogne tower bears 230°, alter course for the pool, or for La Chambre.

Sketch of Le Ruolh, bearing 302°, with Ferme du Loc'h behind. This was made near low water, and the high-water line on Le Ruolh is indicated.

104

Sketch of the Penfret Semaphore in transit with Laon Egenn Hir, bearing 347°. The gap in the rocks, seen here below the Semaphore, does not appear when looking from Basse an Ero buoy.

By night : A sectored light, Fl (2) RG, is shown, in summer only, from Fort Cigogne. The green sectors cover the final section (only) of the Bluiniers channel and the NE route through the pool.

Anchorages

East of Ile de Penfret. This anchorage is in the sandy bay south of the hill on which the lighthouse stands. Approach with the middle of the bay bearing 270°. This leaves a rock having 0.2m (1 ft) over it 1 cable to starboard and another rock, at the same depth, ½ cable to port. The latter rock is at the end of a ridge which extends less than 1 cable NE of an islet 11m high. The anchorage is well protected from the W, but completely exposed to the E.

South west of Ile de Penfret. There is good anchorage towards the southern end of the island outside the CNG moorings. The tide runs fairly hard here, but the islands give a good deal of shelter, even from the W, and it is well sheltered from the E. This anchorage should normally be approached from the north; from the south the pilotage is intricate and requires the large scale chart. At high water take care to avoid the 5m rock ¾ cable off the shore.

East of Ile Cigogne. Anchor in 1m to 1.4m (3 to 5 ft).

La Chambre. This anchorage, south of Ile de St Nicholas, is the most popular one for visitors. The depths are up to 3m (10 ft); although the best spots are occupied by moorings there is normally no difficulty in finding room to anchor. Do not anchor in the channel used by the vedettes, which is marked by 3 pairs of small port and starboard buoys.

It is important to avoid the rocky shoals extending SE from Ile de Bananec; they extend about 1 cable beyond the 4.5m head, the extremity now marked by a beacon (card E).

Coming from the pool keep the shell fish tank bearing 285° until the vessel is S of Ile Bananec. Then steer for the anchorage, which is usually clearly defined by the boats already there. Near low water it is necessary to avoid a shoal drying 0.1m (1 ft) just south of the eastern part of the anchorage; the nearer and more southerly of two 5m heads SW of Ile de St Nicholas in transit with Les Bluiniers tower, 272°, just leaves this shoal to the south.

The bottom in this anchorage is patches of weed on sand, but the water is clear and it is easy to ensure that the anchor is dropped on a sandy patch.

North of Ile de Bananec. There is a good anchorage in the bay NW of Ile de Bananec and E of Ile de St Nicholas. The depth shoals from 2m (6 ft); choose a spot according to tide and draft. There is a clean sandy bottom. The anchorage is exposed to the N and E at high water.

La Chambre. The shellfish tank is the low rectangular structure seen just over the head of the fisherman in the foreground.

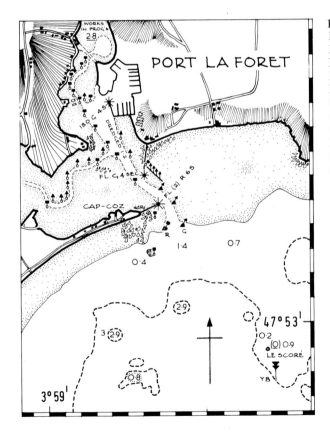

PORT LA FORÊT
MLWS 0.6m;
MLWN 1.8m; −0015
Brest, Index 0,
MTL 2.8m
Based on French
Chart No. 5359 with
corrections (No.
6650 supersedes).
Depths in metres;
right hand margin in
cables

20 Port La Forêt

Charts: 2352, 2645, 3641; French 6650
High water: —0015 Brest, Index, 0, MTL 2.8m
MHWS 4.9m; MLWS 0.6m; MHWN 3.8m; MLWN 1.8m
Tidal streams: Are weak in the bay.
Depths: Rivière de la Forêt is dredged to 2m (6 ft).

Baie de la Forêt lies just to the NW of Concarneau. It is rectangular in shape, with shoals on each side of the entrance. It thus affords anchorage in most weather, even in SW winds. The shelter is sufficient for many local boats to lie on permanent moorings in the summer off Beg Meil. The only harbour is Port La Forêt at the head of the bay. The E and NE sides of the bay are foul.

Approach
The entrance to the river lies to starboard of the wooded promontory of Cape Coz. Pass between the breakwaters of Cape Coz, to port, and Kerleven, to starboard. The inner channel is well marked by buoys and beacons on the lateral system. The moorings near the top of the river are reserved for fishermen.

By night: A night entry is possible if there is enough light to see the buoys and beacons marking the channel. The lights are:

Cape Coz breakwater head; Fl (2) R 6s. }
Kerleven breakwater head; Fl G 4s. } Lights in line on 134° clears Le Scoré.
Marina breakwater head; Iso G 4s. }

Mooring
There is room for several hundred yachts on pontoons. The harbour master will allot a berth. Anchoring is not permitted. Visitors' pontoon to starboard at entrance.

Facilities
It is intended to develop a holiday village complex, but progress is slow. The marina has food shop, café, chandlery, fuel etc.

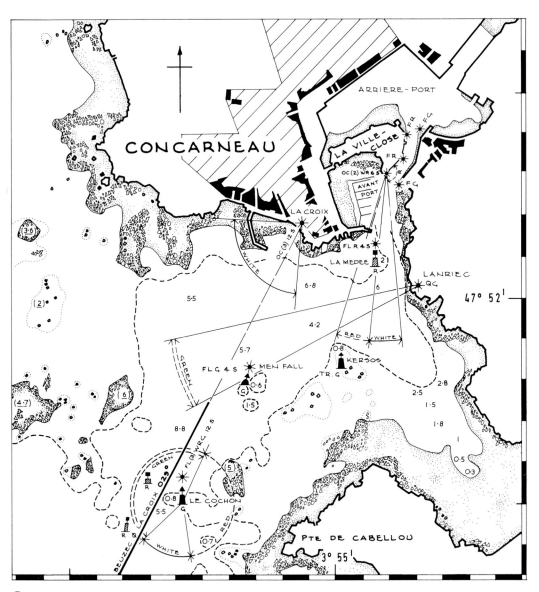

CONCARNEAU

MLWS 0.6m; MLWN 1.8m; −0015 Brest, Index 0, MTL 2.8m
Based on French Chart No. 5359 with corrections (No. 6650 supersedes)
Depths in metres; right hand margin in cables

Charts: 2352, 2645; French 6650
High water: −0015 Brest, Index 0, MTL 2.8m
MHWS 4.9m; MLWS 0.6m; MHWN 3.8m; MLWN 1.8m
Tidal streams: The streams in the harbour run about 2 knots springs.
Depths: The entrance is deep as far as La Médée tower, where there is a 2m (6 ft) shoal. The Avant Port has 1m to 2m (3 to 6 ft). The Anse de Kersos shoals steadily from 3m (10ft).

Concarneau is an important fishing port and it has some commercial traffic; the inner harbour is wholly devoted to these activities. The Avant Port, on the other hand, is wholly devoted to yachting, of which the port is also a busy centre. The approach is encumbered with rocks, but the fairway between them is deep and is so well marked that there is no difficulty at all, by day or by night.

The town is large and contains all resources; the Ville Close is picturesque, but so got up for the tourist that one is put off. Though rather off the route to the south it is a port of character, worth a visit; it is a good place for re-victualling.

Approach and entrance
Whatever the direction of approach the buildings on the hill rising up at the back of the town are unmistakable. Steer for a position about ¾ mile W of the tree-covered promontory of Pointe de Cabellou.

The official leading line is Beuzec belfry, about 1 mile inland, in transit with La Croix lighthouse, on the sea front, bearing 029°, but these marks are not particularly conspicuous. Le Cochon tower (G) is rather more easily identified and it is sufficient to steer to leave it 1 cable to starboard and a red buoy and a red tower to port. After ½ mile on this course Men Fall buoy (stbd) will be left to starboard. Course should ideally then be altered to steer for Lanriec lighthouse, bearing 070°. The lighthouse is not at all obvious, being just one cottage among many; it is distinctive in that it has only one small window and it has its name painted on it, see photograph. But it is sufficient to steer in the correct general direction, leaving Kersos concrete beacon (stbd) at least ½ cable to starboard and La Médée tower (port) at least ¼ cable to port.

Concarneau. The leading line, bearing 029°, is indicated; the former lighthouse is still visible on this line. Le Cochon tower (right) is now green and less conspicuous.

Lanriec lighthouse, bearing ENE, is indicated.

Round La Médée tower and steer for the Ville Close ahead until the breakwater is passed, when round up into the Avant Port past the floating breakwater.

By night: Approach in the white sector of Le Cochon and bring Beuzec and La Croix lights in transit, bearing 029°. Hold this course past Le Cochon and Men Fall buoy. As Men Fall is passed Lanriec light will open. Steer about 070° in the visible sector of this light until the Passage de Lanriec light on the Ville Close opens red and then turns white. When it turns from red to white steer about 000° in the white sector, leaving La Médée light to port. When the breakwater is passed steer into the Avant Port. The channel to the inner harbour is marked by four lights, two fixed green to starboard, two fixed red to port. The other lights are:
Beuzec; Dir Q W, 87m, 23M.
La Croix; Oc (3) W 12s, 14m, 13, *12*M.
Le Cochon; Fl (3) WRG 12s, 9m, 10M.
Basse du Chenal beacon tower (1 cable NW of Le Cochon); Q R.
Men Fall by; Fl G 4s, 3m, 4M.
Lanriec; Q G 13m, 7M.
La Médée; Fl R 4s, 6m, 4M.
Passage de Lanriec; Oc (2) WR 6s, 4m, 8M.

Mooring
Anchoring is not permitted in the harbour. The Avant Port is developed as a marina. Visitor's berths are available in the marina on the clearly marked centre pontoon, or less convenient but cheaper, on the floating wave-breaker.

The Avant-Port marina with floating wave-breaker, and narrow channel into the inner harbour.

The trouble is that there is only a limited number of places and great demand in the busy season. The alternatives appear to be to go into the inner harbour or the Anse de Kersos. All the quays in the inner harbour are reserved for fishing or commercial use. But there are double ended moorings on the northern side of the Ville Close. These are usually pretty full with tiers of boats of various kinds, but it is often possible to find a place. The inner harbour is fairly noisy and dirty and is not very attractive.

Although there are moorings in the Anse de Kersos there is room to anchor, going as far in for shelter as tide and draft permit. It is sheltered from N through E to SW, but exposed to the W and NW. There are no facilities and it is a long and exposed journey in the dinghy back to Concarneau.

If all else fails, and the wind is in the exposed quarter, it is not far to the anchorage off Beg Meil or to the marina at Port La Forêt, see page 107.

Facilities
All the facilities of a large town. Shops of all kinds, hotels and restaurants of every category. Bonded stores can be obtained from Echo Peche, which is to be found in a street behind the eastern quay of the inner harbour; it is most easily reached by dinghy. They are however only able to supply yachts proceeding directly to a foreign port. There are ship chandlers near the Avant Port and all kinds of repairs can be undertaken. Water, petrol and diesel by hose from the fuel point on the breakwater of the Avant Port. Launderette in the Rue Malakoff.

The early part of the flood stream divides at this headland, one branch turning NW towards Concarneau and the Baie de la Forêt, the other turning E, flowing past Ile Verte and along the land. The later part of the flood flows S and E round the point. This pattern is reversed on the ebb. Between the Pointe de Trévignon and Ile de Groix the stream is weak.

There is a wide passage between Ile Verte and Ile de Raguenès, although rocks extend $\frac{1}{4}$ mile off each island. The charts show a tower under construction on Men an Tréas about 3 cables E of Corn Vas buoy. The tower is not yet visible at HW, its site being protected by a card S spar buoy, 3 cables ESE of Corn Vas buoy.

Pointe de Trévignon, bearing very roughly NE.

The drying harbour at Trévignon, near high water.

23 Aven and Bélon Rivers, Port Manec'h

Charts: 2352, 2645
High water: —0020 Brest, Index 0, MTL 2.8m
MHWS 4.9m; MLWS 0.6m; MHWN 3.8m; MLWN 1.8m
Tidal streams: The available information about the tides outside is contradictory. The flood runs to the E, the ebb to the W at rates which are uncertain but not very great. The streams in the river are stronger.
Depths: The approach from the SSW or S is deep, but coming from the E inside Les Verrès there is a shoal having 2.6m (8 ft) over it. The bars into both rivers vary a little and should be treated as drying 1m (3 ft).

Beg ar Vechen lighthouse and the jetty at Port Manec'h, from the S.

Both rivers are very pretty and offer good anchorage. Both offer good restaurants, but not much else in the way of shops except at Port Manec'h and Pont Aven; the Bélon is famous for its oysters. Both have shallow bars, but whereas that of the Bélon is impassable in bad weather, the Aven bar is sheltered and rarely breaks. It is perhaps for this reason that the Aven is much more visited than the Bélon; given reasonable weather, I find the Bélon more attractive than the Aven.

Approach and entrance
The entrance is easy to locate by the Beg ar Vechen lighthouse at Port Manec'h, on the west side of the entrance. On the east side of the entrance there is a large white masonry beacon on Pointe Kerhermain, and a beacon (stbd) off the tip of the point.

Approach may be made from any direction having regard to the following dangers. To the W Les Cochons de Rousbicout lie within 4 cables of the coast and dry 0.3m (1 ft). To the SE Les Verrés dry 2.6m (9 ft), and are marked by a BRB tower; an outlier, called Le Cochon, lies $\frac{1}{2}$ mile NW of the tower and dries 0.6m (2 ft). There is a clear passage between Les Verrés and the land, carrying a depth of 2.6m (8 ft). Enter as convenient between Port Manec'h and the beacon (stbd) off Pte de Kerhermain, giving them a berth of $\frac{1}{2}$ cable.

By night: The white sectors of Port Manec'h (Beg ar Vechen) light lead in. The red sector

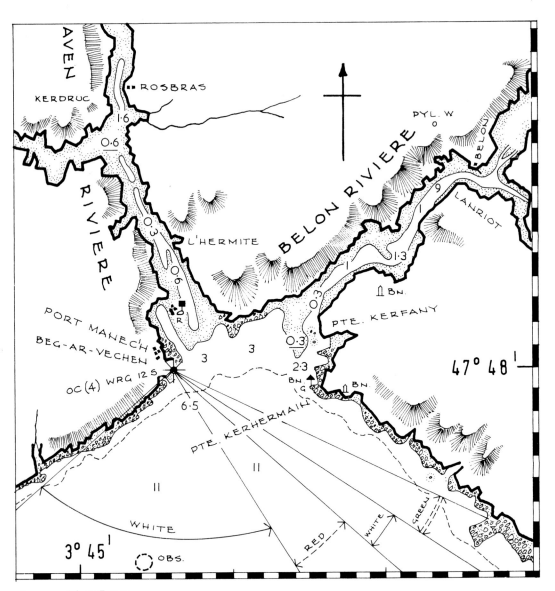

AVEN AND BÉLON RIVERS
MLWS 0.6m; MLWN 1.8m; −0020 Brest, Index 0, MTL 2.8m
Based on French Chart No. 5479 with corrections
Depths in metres; right hand margin in cables

114

The quay and village at Port Manec'h.

covers Les Verrés, and the green sector the rocks along the coast. Having made the entrance a stranger should anchor off Port Manec'h and wait for daylight. The only light is:
Beg ar Vechen; Oc (4) WRG 12s, 38m, 10M.

Port Manec'h

There is a shallow inlet between the bar and the western shore off the quay and village of Port Manec'h. There is 2.3m (7 ft) off the quay shoaling progressively as one goes north. Go as far in, for shelter, as draft, tide and permanent moorings will allow.

Land at the quay; there are shops and restaurants in the village, and water on the quay.

Aven River

As the bar dries 1m (3 ft) it may be necessary to wait for sufficient rise of tide. Although the depths change from time to time there is usually 1.8m (6 ft) when the rocks and the base of the beacon are covered. Leave the beacon (port) comfortably to port and proceed up the centre of the river. Half a mile up there is an inlet called Port l'Hermite on the eastern side. Here the river deepens for a little and up to 2m (6 ft) can be found. Moorings indicate the best places.

Farther up the river shoals and dries 0.6m (2 ft) before the deep pool is reached. This pool is just seaward of the narrows between Kerdruc, to port, and Rosbras, to starboard. There is a large number of permanent moorings which occupy the deepest part of this pool. There is still room to anchor, but it is necessary to moor to two anchors as there is little swinging room. There are a café and restaurant here, but no shops. Water by hose at the quay.

Above this point the river dries at low water, and few yachts go farther up, though it is navigable near high water for a further 2 miles to Pont Aven. The channel is not well marked with perches and there is much seaweed. It is really better for a dinghy excursion, but there is a quay drying 2 to 3m (7 to 10 ft) against which a yacht can berth. The town has shops and restaurants and is a famous haunt of artists.

Belon River

Make a position about $\frac{1}{2}$ cable W of the beacon (stbd) off Pte de Kerhermain; that is, about

Pointe Kerfany. Keep close to this point and then alter course, aiming well W of the hut across the river.

1 cable W of the point itself. Thence steer about 010° for the next headland (here called Pointe Kerfany, for want of a better name) on the east side of the river. This course leaves the bar, drying about 0.3m (1 ft), to port and a bay with a popular bathing beach to starboard. This course passes over three small rocks, awash at datum.

Aim well W of this hut; thence the river bends back towards the next headland on the SE side.

On arrival off Pointe Kerfany keep close to it, as the shore is clean except for rocks immediately edging it. Thence steer towards the NW side of the river, leaving a quay to starboard, and heading well W of the hut on the shore shown in the photograph. This leads up a channel with 0.3m (1 ft), but it is narrow, so that it is not easy to find the best water. As the tide rises there is much more latitude.

Having reached the NW side of the river steer back towards the headland forming the SW side of a large bay. Steer to leave the headland fairly close to starboard and follow round well into the bay, leaving to port the inner bar, which projects from the NW side of the river. There are stakes marking oyster beds on the bar, but there are also similar stakes planted in the bay, and it is not easy to distinguish the channel between them. Once past the bar the channel leads straight up, keeping rather to the E side. It is best to enter after half tide, when there is no need to keep to the channel.

After rounding the corner anchor as convenient below the local boats on moorings. There are landing slips on each side of the river, but the better facilities are at Lanriot on the SE side, where there is a restaurant but no shops. There is some local yachting activity in addition to the oyster culture; fishing boats occupy most of the moorings near the village. Yacht moorings extend a long way upstream. Fresh winds from S or W quickly bring swell making the bar impassable.

This cottage well open of the headland on the SE side leads up the river.

The village of Lanriot, taken from the anchorage below the moorings.

Charts: 2352, 2645
High water: −0020 Brest, Index 0, MTL 2.8m
MHWS 4.9m (16 ft); MLWS 0.6m (2 ft); MHWN 3.8m (12.5 ft); MLWN 1.8m (6.0 ft)
Tidal streams: Outside the flood sets to the E, the ebb to the W, rates uncertain, but probably not exceeding 1½ knots springs. There is little stream in the harbour.
Depths: The harbour dries; about 1.3m (4 ft) at the quay.

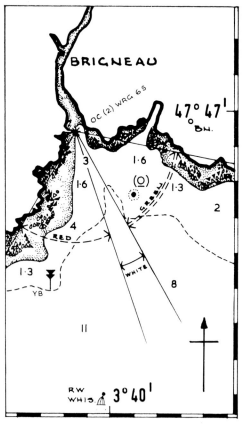

BRIGNEAU
MLWS 0.6m; MLWN 1.8m; −0020 Brest,
Index 0, MTL 2.8m
Based on French Chart No. 5479, much enlarged with corrections
Depths in metres; right hand margin in cables

The quay at Brigneau, looking seaward.

The entrance to Brigneau, bearing about 335°. The lighthouse on the head of the jetty does not show clearly in the photograph; it is just to the right of the daymark behind it. The quay is visible below the trees inside the harbour.

The port of Brigneau lies in a small inlet about 3 miles SE of Port Manec'h. In onshore weather the swell gets right in and it is untenable, but in fine weather it is an interesting and pretty place for a visit. The quay dries out; in very fine weather one could stay afloat anchored at the entrance. Activity is divided between a sailing school and a small fishing fleet.

Approach and entrance
The port can be identified by the factory on the west side, and a conspicuous squat white masonry beacon ½ mile to the east.

There is a RW landfall whistle buoy about 1 mile S of the entrance. From this one should steer to starboard of the entrance until the lighthouse on the head of the breakwater bears about 335°, when it will come in transit with a white board in front of the house just inside the entrance, see photograph.

From the west one need not go as far south as the buoy, provided that one leaves the beacon (card S), marking the rocks off the entrance, 1 cable to port. After passing the beacon, continue on a NE course for 3 cables; it is not safe to round up at once for the entrance.

Enter, leaving the breakwater end fairly close to port and secure to the quay to port. Part of the quay is allotted to the sailing school and part to the fishermen. No doubt the school would be willing to make a berth available to a yacht wishing to stay. The bottom dries about 1.3m (4 ft) alongside the quay.

Facilities
Village shop, cafés. Water tap on the quay. Two-stroke mixture at the café up the hill 100m from the quay.

Charts: 2352, 2645
High water: −0020 Brest, Index 0, MTL 2.8m
MHWS 4.9m; MLWS 0.6m; MHWN 3.8m; MLWN 1.8m
Tidal streams: Outside, the flood sets to the E, the ebb to the W, rates uncertain, but probably not exceeding 1 knot springs. There is little stream in the harbour.
Depths: There is 3m (10 ft) just inside the breakwater where the fishing boats lie. Inside this the harbour shoals rapidly, and the quays dry 0.7 to 1.5m (3 to 5 ft).

The port of Doëlan, though larger than the other small ports on this coast, is still very small. It supports a small but active fishing fleet, and there is a number of yachts which take the ground at the back of the harbour. The harbour is exposed to the S and entry should not be attempted except in settled offshore weather. It is a pretty little place and quite a resort of artists.

Approach and entrance
The port is easily recognised by the conspicuous buildings and the two lighthouses. In line with them is a masonry beacon inland, which is one of the marks for the measured distance

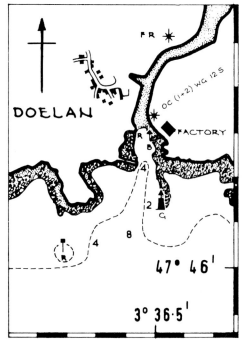

The quay on the west side of Doelan, looking SW. The café on stilts is a great resort of artists.

Doëlan
MLWS 0.6m; MLWN 1.8m; −0020 Brest, Index 0,
MTL 2.8m
Based on French Chart No. 5479, much enlarged with correction
Depths in metres; right hand margin in cables

Doëlan rear lighthouse is just open to the right of the front one, bearing 014°.

offshore. Enter with the lighthouses and beacon in transit, bearing 014°. The transit leaves to port a beacon (red) and to starboard a tower (green).

By night : Approach and enter with the leading lights in line. Coming from the direction of Lorient, a vessel can avoid the rocks off the shore west of Lorient by keeping out of the green sector of the front light, which covers them. The lights are:
Front; Oc (– – ·) WG 12s, 20m, 12M, Green sector 305° to 314°, 7M. W Tower, G band.
Rear; Q R, 27m, 8M. W Tower, R band.

Mooring
There is no room to anchor and lie afloat, as the entrance is taken up with moorings for the fishing vessels. Although partly sheltered by the breakwater, these moorings are very heavy to enable the vessels to ride out rough weather. The local people are friendly to visitors and the best course is to try and obtain permission to use one of these moorings.

There is a very heavy chain, which should be taken to the bows; made fast to the end of the chain is a stout rope leading to a stern mooring farther inshore. Leaving the end of the rope made fast to the chain, lead the rope alongside the vessel and after hauling in the slack, make it fast astern. In this way the vessel is moored bow and stern, facing seaward.

Alternatively one can dry out at one of the quays. Near the entrance to the harbour there is a landing slip on each side; these are marked by starboard and port beacons, of which the port hand one is a few metres inside the end of its slip. The quays lie inshore of these slips. There is one on the port hand, but this is not suitable for drying out, as the bottom slopes outwards. The first two quays on the starboard hand are, however, suitable. The bottom at both of these dries about 1.5m (5 ft).

Facilities
There are a baker and a grocer at some distance on the west side; there is a restaurant close to the quay on this side. There are no shops on the east side. There is a scrubbing grid up the inlet on the west side which could only be used by a yacht with a long straight keel as the blocks are about 1.5m (5ft) apart. It should be sighted before it is used.

121

26 Le Pouldu

Charts: 2352, 2645, 2646
High water: −0020 Brest, Index 0, MTL 2.8m
MHWS 4.9m; MLWS 0.6m; MHWN 3.8m; MLWN 1.8m
Tidal streams: Outside the flood sets to the E, the ebb to the W; the streams are weak. The streams in the river are fierce, up to 6 knots springs.
Depths: The bottom is sandy and both the position and depth of the channel are liable to change. Without prior exploration it should be regarded as drying 2m (7 ft), but there is often more water in the channel, if it can be found.

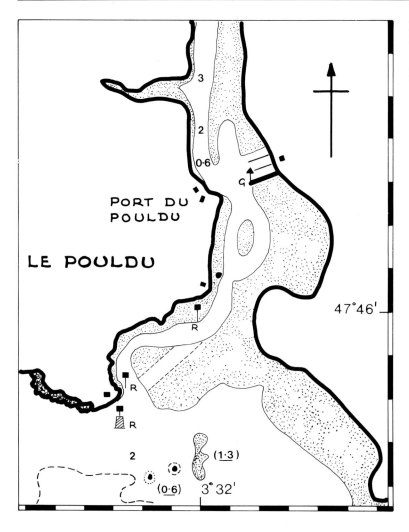

LE POULDU
MLWS 0.6m; MLWN
1.8m; −0020 Brest, Index 0,
MTL 2.8m
Based on French Chart
No. 5479, much enlarged
with corrections
Depths in metres; right
hand margin in cables

The entrance to Le Pouldu. At the left is indicated the white house on the cliff (the former Fenoux pilot station), with the tower marking the entrance below it and to the right. The house indicated on the right is not now visible.

Le Pouldu, at the mouth of the Laita or Rivière de Quimperlé, has a character quite different from its neighbouring ports. If we can liken Aven to a miniature Salcombe and Doëlan to a miniature Dartmouth, here we have a miniature Teignmouth. It has a much more open valley, shifting sands and searing tides, and because of these it is much less frequented by cruising men. A visit is only practicable in fine settled weather as the bar breaks heavily when the wind is onshore, and should be made at mean tides, as there is scarcely enough water at neaps and the tides are uncomfortably strong at springs. At low water the water in the anchorage outside is a deep peaty colour, justifying the name Le Pouldu (The Black Anchorage).

Approach
The entrance is not difficult to make out from a reasonable distance. Half a mile to the west is the town of Le Pouldu. The western side of the actual entrance is a cliffy headland, on the top of which is a white house with a round tower, the former Fenoux pilot's station. The eastern side of the entrance is low and sandy. Approach with the western headland bearing about 010°.

Entrance
The channel shifts frequently and unpredictably, and it is only possible to give alternatives as to where it may lie. The chart opposite shows a sandy spit extending from the east side of the entrance to confine the channel to a curve close below the low cliff between two port hand beacons. This channel seems to be permanent, but the strong tides tend to cut through the sandy spit, the main channel then following the more direct route between the port hand beacons indicated by the dashed lines. This leaves a steep-sided sandy island between the direct channel and the under-cliff one, its position varying considerably. It may even come close to blocking the latter route.

Without previous reconnaissance near LW or local advice, entry should only be attempted under calm conditions shortly before HW, though under these conditions there may be no indication where the channel lies. It can only be misleading to give precise directions and it is safer to try to follow the under-cliff route unless there is evidence against it. The tower outside the entrance and the first port hand beacon should be left about 50m to port; then swing steadily to port to follow the shelving bank below the cliff, to leave the second beacon about 20m to port. Beyond this is a headland with a single house near the point, and here the channel tends to be narrow with steep unstable sand on the east side; the chart shows a patch of rocks, covering near HW on the west side, which is the greater danger.

The next reach, from the rock patch to the marina breakwater, is more uniformly shallow, usually with an unmarked middle ground of sand. The best water is more likely to be found by following the west bank until the next point is reached, with two hotels and a small jetty. Thence one can enter the small marina behind the east bank breakwater, or find deep water for anchoring in the pool beyond the moorings under the west bank.

The river is navigable at HW up to Quimperlé, but is crossed by a low bridge 2 miles up, giving no access to masted vessels. The channel is said to be poorly marked and difficult.

Facilities

There are two hotels on the west bank, and further hotels and shops at Le Pouldu Plage, 1 mile. Near the east bank marina there are shops, a restaurant and sailing school at Guidel Plage with much development in hand.

Looking NE from the outer headland near LW; the alternative channel is shown, with a sand island separating it from the under-cliff route. The arrow marks the second port hand beacon.

The E bank breakwater and small marina, near LW.

Charts: 2352, 2645, 2646
High water: — 0020 Brest, Index 0, MTL 2.8m
MHWS 5.0m (16.5 ft); MLWS 0.6m (2 ft); MHWN 3.9m (13 ft); MLWN 1.7m (5.5 ft)
Tidal streams: Off the harbour the flood runs to the E, and the ebb to the W, spring rates 1¾ knots. There is no stream in the harbour.
Depths: Shoal steadily towards the shore.

The port of Lomener, with the adjacent Anse de Stole, is a small harbour on the north side of the channel between Ile de Groix and the mainland. It is exposed to the S, and would be uncomfortable in fresh winds, and dangerous in gales, from the S. But a considerable fleet of fishing vessels and yachts lie on moorings, both in the harbour and in the Anse de Stole, so the shelter must be sufficient for normal summer conditions.

It is sheltered from the N, and in settled fine weather, when the Vent Solaire is in evidence, it provides good shelter for a night's stop when on passage; better indeed than Port Tudy opposite, where the excitement begins in the early hours of the morning when the wind freshens from the NE.

Approach and entrance
The harbour is not difficult to identify. It lies about half way along the coast forming the northern side of the channel north of the Ile de Groix, with a very prominent block of flats (see photo) near the root of the breakwater.

The approach between the rocks round the Grasu tower and the shoal of Les Trois Pierres (if the tide makes this relevant) is with the block of flats bearing about 335°. Avoid the drying 0.4m

Lomener, from the end of the mole. The prominent building helps identification.

shoal off the breakwater end, making the final approach with the right hand end of the breakwater in line with the flats.

Anchorage
The harbour is crowded with moorings, but one can anchor outside them. There is a landing slip on the spur inside the harbour. Avoid the breakwater wall as there are vicious rocks at its foot.

Alternatively anchor south of the moorings in Anse de Stole. Note that there are rocky spurs on each side of the anchorage which dry at low water. Care must be taken to anchor clear of these; the position of the moorings will help in this.

Facilities
All the ordinary shops of a small seaside resort, hotels. Water from a tap on the quay. Shellfish can be bought from fishermen on the quay.

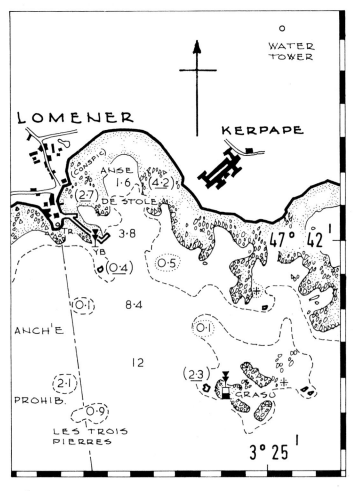

LOMENER
MLWS 0.6m; MLWN 1.7m; −0020
Brest, Index 0, MTL 2.8m
Based on French Chart No. 5912
with corrections
Depths in metres; right hand margin
in cables

126

28 Lorient and Port Louis

Charts: 2352, 2646, 304
High water: −0020 Brest, Index 0, MTL 2.8m
MHWS 5.0m (16.5 ft); MLWS 0.6m (2 ft); MHWN 3.9m (13 ft); MLWN 1.7m (5.5 ft)
Tidal streams: Outside, between Ile de Groix and the shore, the flood sets E and SE, the ebb W and NW, spring rates $1\frac{3}{4}$ knots. The main flood and ebb into and out of the harbour run through the Passe du Sud, spring rate $1\frac{1}{2}$ knots. In the Passe de l'Ouest there is a slack for 2 hr, starting at HW, the spring rates of the flood and ebb are 1 knot.

The strongest streams occur in the narrows off the citadel of Port Louis, where the spring rate is $3\frac{1}{2}$ knots; on extreme tides the ebb can reach $4\frac{1}{2}$ knots if the rivers are in flood. During the last of the flood and the whole of the ebb stream here sets to the W on to La Jument and Le Pot.

Once through the narrows the streams are weaker, spring rates everywhere less than 2 knots. Generally the streams flow in the direction of the channels, but just to the north of the narrows the stream is rotatory anti-clockwise, the main strength being NE $1\frac{1}{2}$ knots 4 to 3 hr before HW and SSW 1 knot 4 to 5 hr after HW.

Depths: The main channels are deep. Enough water can be found in all the usual anchorages, except Locmalo, for any ordinary yachts. The Baie de Locmalo has 3m (10 ft) just inside the entrance, but as little as 0.6m (2 ft) off the pier at Locmalo.

The city of Lorient is a combination of naval base, fishing harbour, commercial port and yachting centre. The main naval base is in the north of the harbour, but to the south of the city the submarine pens remain as a reminder of World War II. Bombing devastated the city during the war, but it is now rebuilt and is a thriving active place. It is the principal fishing port of Brittany; the fishing vessels, ranging in size up to the largest deep-sea stern trawlers, have the exclusive use of the Port de Pêche at the south end of the city, to the east of the submarine pens. Farther to the north, at Kergroise, are the quays used by commercial vessels.

Port Louis, situated near the harbour entrance on the east side, also has a fishing fleet. It is named after Louis XIII, and the fortifications were created by Richelieu.

The principal yachting centres are Kernével, near the entrance on the west side, Port Louis opposite, and, somewhat less popular, Pen Mané to the north of Port Louis. The 'Port de Commerce' in the centre of the city was the operational base of the French East India Company, and it is from this that the city takes its name. There is still a very limited commercial activity here—the ferries for Port Louis and the Ile de Groix start here, and sand dredgers unload at the quays—but much of it is now devoted to yachting. Near the entrance there are pontoons and moorings for a considerable number of locally based boats, and the wet dock has been restored as a yacht harbour. It is reserved primarily for visiting yachts, for which it offers a convenient berth in the heart of the city. Lorient is a good place for changing crew as communications are good, and there is plenty to explore if one has a day in hand.

It is possible to go up the River Blavet to Hennebont, whence with a draft not exceeding 0.8m (2 ft 9 in.) one can enter the Brittany canal system. After going up the Blavet to Pontivy one climbs over the hills and down to Redon, whence one can reach St Malo, Nantes or the sea via the Vilaine.

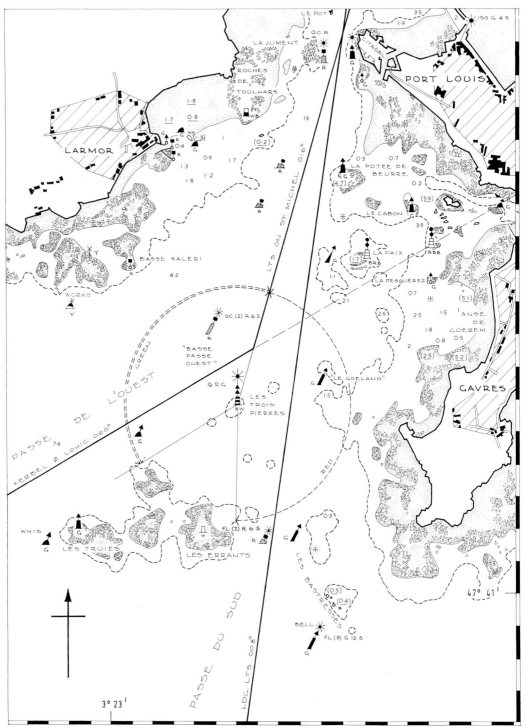

LORIENT APPROACHES   MLWS 0.6m; MLWN 1.7m; −0020 Brest, Index 0, MTL 2.8m
Based on French Chart No. 6470 with corrections   Depths in metres; right hand margin in cables

Approach

The approaches to Lorient are partly sheltered by the Ile de Groix, some 4 miles to the SW. They are well marked and the huge white grain silo in the commercial port is conspicuous. There are two channels: the Passe du Sud and the Passe de l'Ouest. Not all the leading marks are easy to identify, but the numerous buoys and beacons make navigation easy without them.

The larger ships using the port have little room to manoeuvre in the channels and all yachts should get out of their way in good time. Ships above a certain size carry a sphere by day (a red light by night) at the yard arm or masthead and these have absolute right of way over all other vessels. Sailing vessels must not hinder powered vessels of over 20m (65 ft) overall length.

Passe du Sud. The approach to this channel lies NE of the E end of Ile de Groix and ½ mile W of Pointe de Gâvres on the mainland. Steer with the citadel of Port Louis bearing 010° until the leading marks are made out, or the yacht's position is located by the channel marks.

The daymarks for the leading line are situated at the south end of Lorient; the front mark is a rectangular white board with a red vertical stripe and the rear mark a red board with a white vertical stripe. In transit they bear 008°. This transit passes the following channel marks:

Bastresse Sud	G pillar bell by	2 ca to stbd
Les Errants	R can by	½ ca to port
Bastresse Nord	G pillar by	¾ ca to stbd
Les Errants	W tower & statue	2 ca to port
Les Trois Pierres	BW card N tower	1½ ca to port
Le Goëland	G pillar by	¾ ca to stbd
Basse Passe Ouest	R pillar by	3 ca to port
	G pillar by	½ ca to stbd
La Paix	BRB beacon tower	1½ ca to stbd
	R by	2 ca to port
	R by	1½ ca to port
La Potée de Beurre	G beacon tower	¾ ca to stbd
Le Pain de Sucre	G beacon	1 ca to stbd
La Jument	R tower	½ ca to port
La Citadelle	G beacon tower	½ ca to stbd
Le Pot	R can by	close to port
No. 1	G conical by	¾ ca to stbd
Le Cochon	R beacon tower	½ ca to port

Traffic signals, on the simplified system, are made for large ships only, from the signal station on the citadel of Port Louis. No yacht should enter the narrows when one of these signals is shown.

Passe de l'Ouest. This channel is entered ¾ mile S of the conspicuous Grasu tower (card S). The leading marks are: front; Lohic, a black square in a black frame on a white wall, rear; Kerbel lighthouse, a circular white tower. In transit these bear 060°. Hold this transit until two

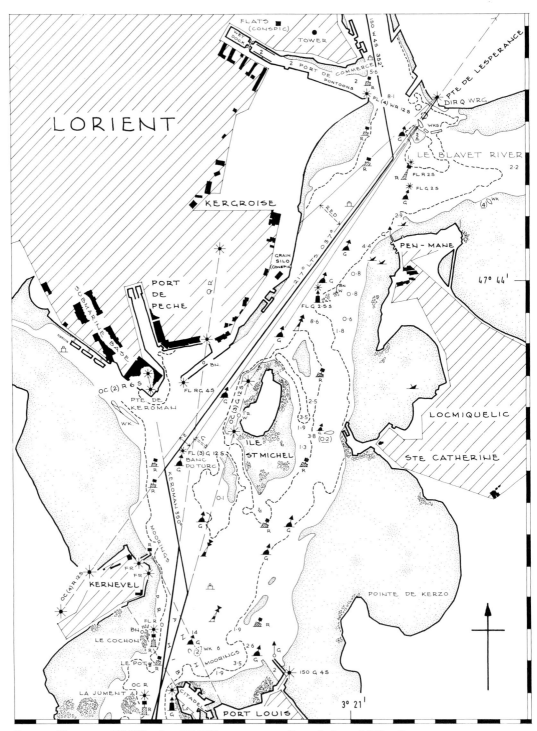

LORIENT HARBOUR   MLWS 0.6m; MLWN 1.7m; −0020 Brest, Index 0, MTL 2.8m
Based on French Chart No. 6470 with corrections   Depths in metres; right hand margin in cables

The citadel at Port Louis, from inside the harbour, looking S.

white towers with green tops on the west side of Ile St Michel come in transit, bearing 016°, or carry on and enter by the 008° transit of the Passe du Sud. This transit passes the following channel marks:

Loqueltas	R spar by	2 ca to port
Banc des Truies	YBY (card W) by	$1\frac{1}{2}$ ca to stbd
Les Truies Ouest	G conical whistle by	2 ca to stbd
Les Truies	G tower	2 ca to stbd
	G conical by	$\frac{3}{4}$ ca to stbd
Les Trois Pierres	BW (card N) tower	1 ca to stbd
Basse Passe Ouest	R pillar by	1 ca to port

thereafter as for Passe du Sud.

By night: Both entries are well lit making a night approach simple. Several of the leading lights have narrow intensified sectors on each side of the leading line. It should not be assumed that anywhere in the intensified sector is clear of danger. Les Trois Pierres light open, green, clears all the natural dangers to the south of the Passe de l'Ouest, but not the unlit G stbd buoy. The second leading line, bearing 016°, of this entrance is indicated, not only by the leading lights at its northern end, but by the boundary of the red and green sectors of Les Trois Pierres light. The lights are:

Passe du Sud, front; Dir Q R, 16m, **15**, *12*M.
Passe du Sud, rear; Dir Q R, 28m, **16**, *15*M.
Bastresse Sud by; Fl (3) W, 12s, 4m, 8M, Bell.
Les Errants by; Fl (2) R 6s.
Passe de l'Ouest, front; Dir Q W, 7m, **18**, *9*M.
Passe de l'Ouest, rear; Dir Q W, 30m, **17**, *15*M.
Banc des Truies by; Fl W 4s, 6m, 8M.
Les Trois Pierres; Q RG, 11m, 6M.
Basse Passe Ouest by; Oc (2) R 6s, 3m, 4M.
Ile St Michel, front; Dir Oc (3) G 12s, 8m, 10M.
Ile St Michel, rear; Sync Dir Oc (3) G 12s, 14m, **14**, *11*M.
La Citadelle; Oc G 4s, 6m, 5M.
La Jument; Oc R 4s, 5m, 6M.
Le Cochon; Fl R 4s, 5m, 6M.

Harbour

There are two principal channels up the harbour. The main channel goes to the west of Ile St Michel, passing Kernével and the fishing and commercial harbours before rejoining the other channel off Pen Mané. It then leaves to starboard the River Blavet before the entrance to the Port de Commerce is reached on the port side. Thence it becomes purely naval. The minor channel goes to the east of Ile St Michel, passing Port Louis, Ste Catherine, and Pen Mané before rejoining the main channel.

Both channels are well buoyed and need not be described in detail. Note that there is a wreck, marked by one buoy, in the centre of the minor channel off Ste Catherine. There is plenty of water to pass to the west of the buoy.

By night : Only the main channel is lit. After passing through the narrows on either of the alignments given under *Approach*, there are three further alignments. The first, bearing 350°, is marked by the Kéroman lights. The second, bearing 037°, is marked at both ends; at the south by the Kernével lights and at the north by the Pointe de l'Espérance directional light. The third, bearing 352°, is marked by the white sector of a light at the Arsenal. The lights are:

Kéroman, front; Dir Oc (2) R 6s, 25m, 12M.
Kéroman, rear; Sync Dir Oc (2) R 6s, 31m, 12M.
Banc du Turc by; Fl (3) G 12s, 4m, 5M.
Port de Pêche; Fl RG 4s, 7m, 6M.
Kernével, front; Dir Oc (4) R 12s, 10m, 14, *10*M.
Kernével, rear; Sync Dir Oc (4) R 12s, 18m, 14, *12*M.
Pengarne Fl G 2.5s.
Pte de l'Espérance, front; Dir Q WRG, 8m, 9M.
Arsenal; FG, 23m.
Arsenal; Dir Iso WRG, 6m, 9M.
Porte de Commerce; Fl (4) WR 2s, 7m, 9M.

Anchorage, mooring and facilities

Port Louis. Anchor NE of the citadel between the yacht moorings and the G buoy marking the end of the ruins of the former jetty. Depths of 3m (10 ft) or more, shoaling towards the shore.

Land at the jetty. There are shops and restaurants and a good ferry service to the old Port de Commerce in the centre of Lorient. This is the best anchorage though disturbed by wash.

Kernével. This is a fashionable yachting centre with good shops and restaurants, chandlers, shipyard etc. All of the available space out of the ship channel is occupied by moorings. The only hope is that the club boatman will be able to provide a vacant mooring.

Pen Mané and Ste Catherine. There is room to anchor out of the channel and clear of the moorings off these two villages, which have landing slips.

The hard at Kernével.

Port de Commerce. The wet dock is a fully pontooned yacht harbour in pleasant surroundings, as the roads are well set back. As entry past bridge and sill is only possible from about 2 hr before to 1 hr after HW, it may be more convenient for a short stay to use the pontoons provided by the same authority for yachts awaiting entry; these lie on both sides of the harbour just outside the dock, and access to them is independent of tide height. The pontoons near the entrance to the Port de Commerce are for local boats, and more disturbed by ferry wash, but it may be possible to find a berth there temporarily unoccupied.

Everything is at hand for the wet dock; shops, banks, main post office, chandlery; water by hose. Shipyards and sailmakers in Lorient. Washing accommodation and showers in the office building. Charges are reasonable, but rise to discourage a long stay. But there is another charge for each opening of the bridge (it is cheaper if several boats go through together) and this makes a one night stay fairly expensive. Bonded stores are only available from one of the ship-chandlers, all of whose premises are in the Port de Pêche at the southern end of the town.

Locmalo. Entry can only be made at sufficient rise of tide. There are two approaches, for both of which the large scale chart, No. 304, is essential. The first is to approach north of La Potée

Port de Commerce, looking NW towards the bridge and inner dock. There is now a pontoon each side of the channel to the bridge. Port Tudy ferries use the quay in the foreground.

The slip at Larmor, with the conical-topped water tower in the background, bearing about 335°.

de Beurre, with the north side of Ile aux Souris bearing 112°, in transit with the end of the ferry slip on the south side of the entrance to the Baie de Locmalo. This transit leads in between the rocks. On approaching Ile aux Souris and the detached above-water rock on its western side alter course to leave Ile aux Souris to starboard and steer on the north side of the channel. Then pass between the red and the green towers, and anchor as the depths allow.

The better approach is from the SW, on the transit of the Passe de l'Ouest, until Le Cabon tower (green) bears N. Then steer midway between Le Cabon tower and the detached rock to the west of Ile aux Souris, to join the channel already described.

Anse de Goérem. This sandy bay is situated south of Port Louis, on the west side of a sandy peninsula. Rocky shoals extend seaward north and south of the anchorage. Enter the bay on an easterly course midway between Le Goëland green buoy and La Paix tower (BRB). The northern dangers are marked by La Pesquerez beacon (stbd) which must be left well to port as there are rocks, awash at datum, up to $\frac{1}{2}$ cable south of it. The dangers to the south are not so well marked. Sound the way in and anchor at a suitable distance off the sands. The anchorage is sheltered from the E and to some extent from the S, but is exposed to the W. Land on the beach, where the village of Gâvres has shops and restaurants.

Larmor. The approach to this anchorage on the west side of the entrance is straightforward. It is sheltered from W and N; although it is exposed to other directions a large number of small boats lie on moorings in the summer, so it must be tenable in ordinary summer weather. If the wind does come onshore, shelter inside the harbour is not far off. Anchor outside the moorings. It is an attractive anchorage off a very popular summer resort with all shops, hotels and restaurants. Outboard motor specialist. Bus service to Lorient.

River Blavet. There are a number of rural anchorages up the river. The lower part has a narrow channel between wide mud flats; lines of large mooring buoys help in locating it, but it is best taken on a rising tide.

Charts: 2352, 2646
High water: −0020 Brest, Index 0, MTL 2.8m
MHWS 5.0m (16.5 ft); MLWS 0.6m (2 ft); MHWN 3.9m (13 ft); MLWN 1.7m (5.5 ft)
Tidal streams: Between the Ile de Groix and the mainland the flood runs to the E, the ebb to the W, spring rates $1\frac{3}{4}$ knots. Off Pointe de la Croix, at the eastern end, the flood runs to the S, the ebb to the N, spring rates 1 knot. To the SE of Les Chats, the southern point, the streams are rotatory clockwise, the greatest rates being ESE $1\frac{1}{4}$ knots at −0130 Brest and SW 2 knots at +0300 Brest.
Depths: At Port Tudy 3m (10 ft) on the moorings, the inner part of the harbour dries. At Loc Maria 1m (3 ft) in the anchorage, the jetty dries.

The Ile de Groix is a fairly high island, edged for the most part by cliffs; it is about 4 miles long by $1\frac{1}{2}$ miles wide. Although the coast is rocky it is reasonably clear of outlying dangers for about 3 miles eastward from Pen Men, the western extremity, on both north and south coasts. The eastern end of the island, on the other hand, is foul; E of Port Tudy rocks extend 3 cables offshore, off Pointe de la Croix the sandy shoals extend $1\frac{1}{2}$ cables seaward and there are several dangerous wrecks further out, and S of Pointe des Chats the rocks extend 1 mile.

The principal harbour, and the only secure one, is Port Tudy, half way along the northern shore. It was formerly a great tunny fishing port; some inshore fishing activity remains, and it is a very popular staging point for yachts. Half a mile west of it is Port Lay, a small harbour protected by a breakwater. In addition to fishing boats a sailing school operates here, but the harbour dries out beyond the pierheads and the swell gets in when the wind is in the north. Although a suitable objective for a day sail, it is not a harbour at which to spend the night and is not treated in detail here. Yachts should not anchor off it, as it is in a prohibited anchorage zone, but there are a number of moorings laid by the sailing school, which could be used for a short time by arrangement.

Port Lay, the harbour entrance.

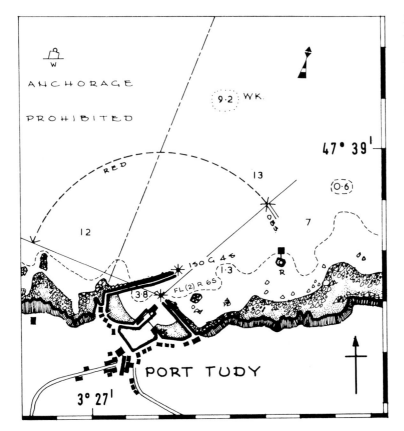

Port Tudy, Ile de Groix
MLWS 0.6m; MLWN
1.7m; —0020 Brest, Index 0,
MTL 2.8m
Based on French Chart No.
5912 with corrections
Depths in metres; right hand
margin in cables

On the south side of the island there is the pretty little harbour of Loc Maria, which is well worth a visit under the right conditions, but is dangerous if the wind comes in from the south.

Port Tudy

This is the only safe harbour in Ile de Groix. It is a good one except in northerly and especially in north easterly winds, when the swell penetrates the outer basin between the pierheads. When the Vent Solaire is in evidence this happens in the early hours of the morning, and as yachts lie in tiers on the moorings, and very few French yachts use springs when so doing, a noisy and enjoyable party is had by all.

Pen Men, at the NW end of Ile de Groix, bearing roughly NE.

Pointe de la Croix (the NE corner of Ile de Groix). The sands are conspicuous, and extend a long way seaward at low water. The lighthouse is indicated, bearing about 330°.

The port was formerly one of the principal tunny ports, since it was easy to make and leave under sail, but with the advent of the marine engine the tunnymen have gone to the more convenient mainland ports. There is still some local fishing activity and the port is a very popular staging post for French and English yachts on passage along the coast.

Approach and entrance
The harbour is easily identified and the approach is straightforward from the W and N. There are some buoys but no other dangers. From the E and SE care must be taken to avoid the dangers off the coast, which extend in places outside the line of buoys and beacons. A safe line is with the harbour lighthouses in transit, bearing 217°. This transit leaves close to starboard a buoy (card E) $\frac{1}{2}$ mile off the entrance; the buoy marks a wreck with 9m (30 ft) over it. The transit leaves just over 1 cable to port a rock with 0.6m (2 ft) over it, and it also clears a number of other dangers closer inshore.

When close to the harbour bear to port and enter midway between the breakwater heads, steering in parallel to the northern breakwater; there are rocks at the base of the head of the eastern breakwater. If the ferry to the mainland is manoeuvring to enter or leave, stand off as it needs all the room there is.

By night: The buoys in the approaches are unlit. The light on the eastern breakwater is obscured over the dangers to the east of the harbour, so it is safe to steer in with this light showing and open to the left of the light on the north breakwater. It cannot be seen in transit with the latter as it is obscured by it. The lights are:
Pen Men; Fl (4) 25s, 59m, **30**, *20*M, Siren (4), 1 min.
      Radiobeacon, call GX, 289.6 kHz, 1/6 min, begins H + 5 min.
East mole; Fl (2) R 6s, 11m, 6M.
North mole; Iso G 4s, 12m, 6M.

Port Tudy, with the wet basin in the foreground.

Anchorage and Mooring

A wet dock has been formed from the inner part of the inner harbour by the addition of a retaining wall and dock gates. Outside the dock the inner harbour is shallow, although moorings are available. Both sides of the quay are reserved for ferries, although it is possible to go alongside just outside the dock gates for short periods when there is sufficient rise of tide.

In the outer harbour, yachts moor between the large white mooring buoys, ensuring that ferries are left room to manoeuvre. Long warps are needed, and in the season, particularly weekends, these buoys become very crowded. There is no room to anchor, and in any case, the bottom is said to be foul.

In the inner harbour yachts moor bow and stern between rows of orange mooring buoys. The bottom at these buoys is at about chart datum, but at neap tides smaller yachts will stay afloat.

The wet dock is opened between 0600 and 2200 from approximately 2 hours before to approximately 2 hours after local HW. There are pontoons to which electricity and water are connected, and visitors are directed to a vacant berth. There is said to be 3m depth throughout the wet dock. A charge is made for all three parts of the harbour.

Facilities

There are cafes and restaurants and bread may be obtained by the harbour. All shops and a hotel in the town, $\frac{1}{2}$-mile up the hill. Marine engineer and slipway; water at pontoons; petrol at outer harbour and diesel from fuel depot at SE corner of inner harbour. Frequent ferry to Lorient (Port de Commerce), whence good communications to all parts.

Loc Maria

This charming unspoilt little harbour is situated on the south of Ile de Groix, $\frac{3}{4}$ mile west of Pointe des Chats. The approach is open to the Atlantic, but the harbour itself is well sheltered from the W through N to E. A jetty provides some protection from the S, though with moderate southerly winds some swell penetrates round the end, and the harbour would be dangerous in strong winds or swell from this quarter. The harbour is shallow; the bottom dries as far as the head of the jetty. There are depths of 1m (3 ft) off the end of the pier, where most yachts will be able to lie afloat except at spring tides.

Approach and entrance

The distant approach must be made from the chart. If coming from the east or south east it will be necessary to make a detour round Les Chats. The tidal streams are quite strong at springs, the ebb generally setting westerly and the flood easterly, but the directions vary from point to point.

Make a position 1 or 2 miles S of Loc Maria bay. On the eastern side will be seen the harbour and village, a tower (stbd) and a white masonry beacon on the shore. On the western side is another, smaller, village. Between the villages is a small group of houses on the NW side of the bay, with a small masonry beacon in front of them, see photograph.

Approach with the tower (stbd) bearing 005°, until the houses and beacon to the NW of the harbour have been identified. The lead for the channel, which carries about 0.2m (1 ft), is the masonry beacon in transit with the centre window of the white cottage, bearing about 350°. This cottage is the right hand one of three, and has a lean-to shed on its right hand side, see photograph; the windows now have blue shutters.

Loc Maria; the small beacon, here seen in front of the left edge of the house, should be in line with the centre window.

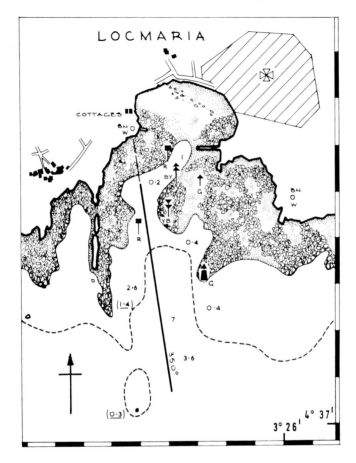

Loc Maria, Ile de Groix
MLWS 0.6m; MLWN 1.7m; −0020
Brest, Index 0, MTL 2.8m
Based on French Chart No. 5479,
much enlarged with corrections
Depths in metres; right hand margin
in cables

Follow this transit until the vessel is about halfway between the two cardinal beacons marking the middle ground; near low water, deeper water may be found by borrowing to the west when the outer port hand beacon comes abeam. Then bear to starboard for the pierhead keeping rather closer to the inner port hand beacon. There is a channel to the east of the middle ground, but it is shallower than the western channel, and directions for it are not given here. There are no lights and a night entry should not be attempted.

Anchorage
The harbour is now choked with small-boat moorings, and there is no room to anchor in it. Vessels able to take the ground will find space. Others should anchor outside the harbour. A suitable spot with good holding is just to the west of the leading line, with the outer middle ground beacon in transit with the beacon tower, and the head of the jetty bearing about 060°. Lying alongside the jetty is impossible owing to the lines of small boats on moorings, but it may be used for landing.

Facilities
Shops and a restaurant in the village. Good bathing beaches.

140

30 Etel

Charts: 2352, 2646
High water: −0020 Brest, Index 0, MTL 2.8m
MHWS 5.0m (16.5 ft); MLWS 0.6m (2 ft); MHWN 3.9m (13 ft); MLWN 1.7m (5.5 ft)
Tidal streams: The tidal streams offshore do not exceed 1 knot and are much affected by wind. Streams in the river attain 4 to 5 knots at springs, but are somewhat weaker for 1½ hours after high and low water. The streams continue to run the same way for about 1 hr after high and low water. That is to say, a vessel arriving on the bar at high water will find that the tide is still flowing strongly into the river. On spring tides there is hardly any slack.
Depths: The bar varies greatly; it usually has about 0.5m (1 ft) but has been known to dry 4.5m (15 ft). The river is deep except for the middle ground near the entrance and a patch having 2.6m (8 ft) west of the water tower. There is 1.5 to 2.5m (5 to 8 ft) beside the quay in the harbour.

The Etel River should not be approached by night, or in bad visibility, or on the ebb. First visits are not recommended in strong onshore winds, otherwise there is no more delightful place, with its clean blue water and extensive sands.

The entrance lies on the mainland halfway between Lorient and Quiberon, 8 miles due E of Groix. The aspect of the coast is low and sandy, but Etel can be easily recognised by its two water towers dominating the dunes. Three miles to the NW of the town the lonely church steeple of Plouhinec and two radio masts will be readily identified. To the S, the rounded hummock of Rohellan island will appear. A mile E of the actual entrance, the tower (card S) on Roheu rocks, which are covered at high water, will be left to port. One mile to starboard, in the direction of Rohellan, will be seen the Poul-haut rocks.

Etel entrance, looking SSE. Rohellan is to the left of the fisherman *Marie Yvonne*, and Poul haut just visible between her and the Chaudronnier tower, replaced by a beacon. You will not, alas, see a sailing fisherman there nowadays. *Photo: R. Twist*

141

The lighthouse and house with Fenoux signal mast.

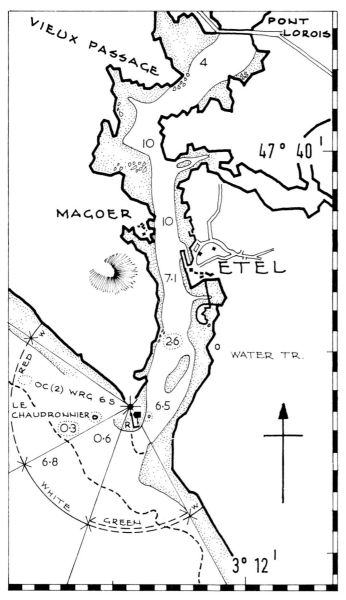

VIEUX PASSAGE

PONT LOROIS

4

47° 40'

10

MAGOER

10

ETEL

7.1

2.6

WATER TR.

0

RED W

OC (2) WRG 6 S

LE CHAUDRONNIER o

0.3

R

0.6

6.5

6.8

WHITE

GREEN

W

3° 12'

Fenoux signal mast, with arrow vertical.

ETEL
MLWS 0.6m; MLWN 1.7m; −0020
Brest, Index 0, MTL 2.8m
Based on French Chart No. 5560 with corrections
Depths in metres; right hand margin in cables

Etel quay. Anchor to the south of the lifeboat house, at the bottom of the picture.   *Photo: Combier, Mâcon*

Entrance

A convenient approach is with the water towers in transit, bearing 042°. Having left the Roheu tower to port, the yacht will begin to feel the indraft into the Etel River, which is very weak until the bar is crossed, when it becomes very strong indeed, and attains 6 knots near the lighthouse.

There is usually about 0.5m (1 ft) of water on the bar, but it has been known to dry as much as 4.5m (15 ft). The channel shifts, but its direction is known to the pilot operating the Fenoux Semaphore on the dunes, near the lighthouse. The lighthouse is a red lattice-work pylon; the Fenoux mast rises from a white house. The pilot is on duty from 2 hr before high water until high water. The correct signal is to hoist your ensign at the masthead. The Semaphore arm makes a complete turn or wags from side to side to indicate that the pilot has seen you and will guide you. If he hoists a red flag, a vessel should heave to and wait for the water to rise. If he hoists a black ball, or puts the arrow horizontal and leaves it there, a vessel must go away, for either she is too late and the ebb is too strong, or seas are breaking on the bar, which may not be realised from seaward.

Otherwise the course should be held, and a watch kept on the *upper* arm of the arrow. When this is vertical (after the salute) carry on. When it is moved to port, as seen from the yacht, alter course to port, and when it is moved to starboard alter to starboard. The upper arrow will point naturally the way to go.

A beacon (port) marks the western side of the entrance. About 150m from the beacon the Fenoux instructions are abandoned, and the middle of the entrance sought, care being taken to avoid the white sandy spit, which never shifts, on the starboard hand. Keep about 100m from the beacon, though there is plenty of water at high tide. Once across the bar, the water will be smoother, and the vessel should keep on the west side of the river, as the best water lies on this side nearly as far as Etel.

143

Local boats may be seen entering without apparently using the pilot; they have special walkie-talkies, but visitors are directed by the Semaphore.

By night : The entrance bar should not be attempted at night.

Anchorage and mooring

The best anchorage is just to the south of the conspicuous lifeboat house at the SW corner of the quays. By sounding it is possible to get far enough in to be out of the main tidal stream, except perhaps at springs. Beware of moorings which run under with the tide, and only show at slack water.

There is a small marina (150 boats) inside the jetty, with a least depth of 2m 50 (8 ft). Do not moor alongside the main jetty as this is regularly used by the fishing fleet; the local ferry works from the outer end of the first (southernmost) marina pontoon, and this should be left clear.

It is possible to anchor just above Etel on either side of the river. The tide is very strong, 6 knots springs, but the holding is good; even so, a long scope would be needed. There is also an anchorage just beyond Vieux Passage. Here there is good holding out of the worst of the tide, but do not go into the bay north of this, which is foul and shallow. One can anchor off Magöer, with a kedge to stop swinging into the shallows.

Facilities

All shops, several restaurants, and repairs to engine and hull; the capitainerie is on the quayside by the marina, with showers and toilets. Water on the pontoons. Buses to Auray etc. Swimming and sail-board hire in the landlocked pool a quarter of a mile to the south of the marina.

The Inland Sea

Above the bridge at Pont Lorois there is a wide expanse of water, the arms of which extend 5 miles inland. The bridge is said to have a clearance in the region of 10m (30 ft). There is water up to St Cado, about 1 mile, above which the channel dries. No reliable directions can be given, but it is an interesting place to explore in the dinghy, with adequate power to cope with the tides.

There is a strong eddy at the bridge. Thence steer to port, leaving to starboard a reef marked by a perch. Then the channel turns sharply to starboard, leaving an islet to port, and then back to port before swinging right round to starboard to St Cado. There is an ancient oratory at St Cado; this is a good place for a picnic, as are the islands studding the inland sea.

31 Belle Ile

Charts: 2353, 2646
High water : −0030 Brest springs, −0005 Brest neaps, Index 1, MTL 2.9m
MHWS 5.2m; MLWS 0.7m; MHWN 3.9m; MLWN 1.9m
Tidal streams: In the channel to the NE of Belle Ile the streams are rotatory clockwise, except close to the shore. They set NW at low water, SE at high water, spring rates up to $1\frac{1}{2}$ knots at the north end, up to 1 knot in the middle, and about $1\frac{1}{2}$ knots at the south end. The streams probably run harder close to the north and south points of the island. The streams in the harbours are weak.
Depths: The approaches to the harbours are deep. Le Palais has 3m (10 ft) in the usual anchorage, Sauzon dries, Port du Vieux Château has about 1.5m (5 ft).

Belle Ile is the largest island off the south coast of Brittany, being about 10 miles long and up to 5 miles wide. The NE coast is fairly free from outlying dangers, except at its ends off Pointe des Poulains and Pointe de Kerdonis. This side of the island is sheltered from the prevailing winds and has two harbours, Le Palais, which is one of the best in Brittany, and Sauzon, which is a drying harbour with an anchorage outside which is good in offshore winds.

The Atlantic side of the island is rugged, deeply indented and has a profusion of rocks. It is picturesque, and the island attracts many tourists. The only inlet on this side that provides some kind of harbour is the Port du Vieux Château, 1 mile south of Pointe des Poulains. This has no quay, roads or facilities, but has become a popular objective for yachts since attention was drawn to it in the first edition of this book. The danger is that here the Atlantic swell can rise and bar the entrance.

The island has a long and interesting history. It was taken by the English in 1572. After the English had withdrawn attempts were made to fortify it, but the main fortifications, including those which make such an impressive background to Le Palais harbour, were built by Vauban at the end of the 17th century. It was blockaded in 1761 and surrendered to the English after a long siege. It was held by the English for two years, but then exchanged for Minorca.

Les Poulains lighthouse, at the north end of Belle Ile, bearing about SW. It is near low water and Les Chambres rocks show clearly to the right of the island. These are now buoyed.

Le Palais harbour, out of season. This is a 1980 photo, and does not show the mooring buoys added in 1981.

Le Palais

Le Palais is a very good harbour, and there is good anchorage outside in offshore winds. The harbour itself has a narrow entrance facing SE, but some swell sometimes gets through into the harbour. Winds from the NE are the worst; strong NE winds cause seas to break over the breakwater. Even strong NW winds can cause some swell in the harbour. The harbour is, however, well sheltered from the S and W. If the outer harbour becomes too uncomfortable it is possible to dry out in the inner harbour or go into the wet dock, or through it to a new marina. Once a principal sardine fishing port it is now mainly a holiday resort, though some fishing continues. It is very popular not only with yachts on passage but as an objective for the large fleet of yachts in Quiberon Bay. It becomes very overcrowded in the season, especially at weekends. The town is the capital of Belle Ile, so there are shops of all kinds.

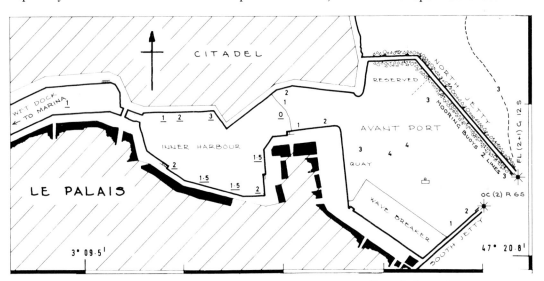

LE PALAIS, BELLE ILE   MLWS 0.7m; MLWN 1.9m; —0030 (sp), —0005 (np) Brest, Index 1, MTL, 2.9m
Based on French Chart No. 5911, with corrections
Depths in metres; right hand margin in cables

Approach and entrance

There are no difficulties of any kind in the approach. Steer for the lighthouse on the end of the northern jetty and enter between the pierheads, giving a fair berth to the northern one at low water springs. Keep a lookout for the frequent ferries to Quiberon, which enter and leave at a good speed and take up most of the channel.

By night: As by day, keeping a sharp lookout for unlit buoys which are sometimes moored near the entrance. The lights are:

Main light (Goulphar); Fl (2) W 10s, 87m, **28**, *23*M, Siren (2) 1 min sounded ½ M to SW of light.

    Radiobeacon, call BT, 303.4 kHz, 1/6 min, begins at H + 1 min.

Pte des Poulains; Fl W 5s, 34m, **24**, *17*M.

Pte de Kerdonis; Fl (3) R 15s, 35m, 12M.

North Jetty; Fl (2 + 1) G 12s, 11m, 9M.

South Jetty; Oc (2) R 6s, 11m, 8M.

Anchorage and mooring

Outside the harbour, anchor to the east of the north jetty in 3m (10 ft), keeping well clear of the fairway. This is a safe anchorage, with good holding ground, in offshore winds. Anchorage is prohibited between the citadel at Le Palais and the approaches to Sauzon, because of cables, but the anchorage recommended above is just clear of the prohibited area.

    Inside the harbour, yachts secure fore and aft between 3 rows of mooring buoys under the north jetty. Yachts also secure in a cluster round the large mooring buoy to port inside the entrance, taking a line to the buoy and breast ropes to their neighbours.

    There are also drying berths, mainly used by the fishermen, against the walls of the inner harbour, part of which has been recently dredged, and a wet dock which is principally used for laying up. The gates open about 1 hr each side of high water. Beyond the wet dock, through a lifting bridge which opens daily 0730 hrs, lies La Saline marina, completely secure with water and electricity on pontoons.

Facilities

There are all shops handy, restaurants and hotels. Banks open in the morning for cashing cheques. Water from a tap on the Syndicat d'Initiative by the dinghy landing or, in quantity, by hose on application to the harbour master, at 0900–1130 and 1300–1530. Petrol and diesel from the garage adjacent to the dinghy landing. Showers at the municipal baths, every day but Monday, at varying hours. It is possible to hire bicycles or self-drive cars to visit the island. Frequent ferries to Quiberon, whence trains and planes to Paris and elsewhere.

Sauzon

This peaceful little harbour is situated less than 2 miles SE of Pointe des Poulains. It dries out, but there is a good anchorage outside which has recently been improved by the building of an outer breakwater each side of the entrance; the harbour is less crowded than Le Palais and may therefore be preferred, but the anchorage, whether inside or outside the new breakwaters, is still completely sheltered only from the S and W. There is some local fishing and active sailing.

Approach and entrance

The harbour is not hard to identify, except when the sun is behind it. The Gareau tower (stbd) off the Pointe du Cardinal north of the entrance will be seen if approaching along the coast in either direction. The ends of the outer breakwaters are marked by low white lighthouses with red and green tops.

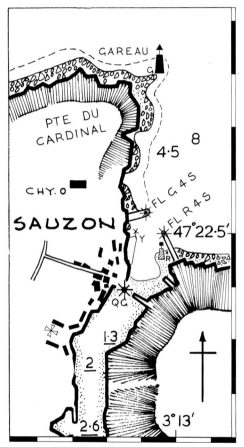

SAUZON, BELLE ILE
MLWS 0.7m; MLWN 1.9m;
− 0030 (sp), − 0005 (np) Brest,
Index 1, MTL 2.9m
Based on French Chart No. 5911
Depths in metres; right hand margin
in cables

The half-tide ledge, near LW.

The harbour, near HW.

Sauzon harbour entrance, with the new outer breakwaters.

By night : The main light, a white and green tower on the inner west breakwater is QG 9m 5M, the old sectored light being discontinued. Outer mole heads are Fl G 4s and Fl R 4s.

Anchorage and mooring
There are mooring buoys outside the outer north mole, and plenty of room to anchor outside them clear of the fairway. Between the outer and inner moles on the east side there are some buoys and also limited room to anchor in better shelter; the old port tower still stands here. Between the moles on the west side, the situation may not be immediately obvious: a yellow pole beacon, X topmark, marks the N end of a flat ledge about 5 yards wide, extending halfway towards the main lighthouse. Yachts lie E and W, with bow anchors in the fairway, sterns warped to iron loops on the ledge. The ledge however covers at half tide, and a yacht arriving nearer high water may have no evidence of its existence. She must take a stern warp over it to rocks on the bank behind.

The harbour dries out, but yachts can lie against the inner side of the east breakwater. Many boats take the ground in the harbour, with a bottom generally hard; the limited space near the entrance necessitates fore and aft mooring there, but there is plenty of room higher up for those prepared to dry out for longer each tide.

Facilities
All shops, hotels, water from a tap on the quay. Cycles for hire.

Port du Vieux Chateau (Ster Wenn)
This anchorage is in a fiord on the west coast of Belle Ile, a little over 1 mile south of Pointe des Poulains. It was described, in the first edition of this work, as one of the most beautiful in France; in consequence it has also become one of the most overcrowded by day visitors. It has also been likened to a lobster pot: easy to get into and hard to get out. The onset of bad weather, or heavy swell, which can be caused by bad weather elsewhere, would make the entrance a death trap.

149

The sailing directions and plan should be regarded with caution, as the largest scale chart published is on too small a scale to show much detail. The plan is much enlarged from the original chart. The names Pointe Dangereuse and Pointe Verticale are fictitious though appropriate; the name Pointe du Vieux Château is attached to what is believed to be the correct point—official charts differ.

Approach and entrance

In the approach from northward the dangers off the Pointe des Poulains must be avoided, and the tidal charts must be consulted as the streams are strong near the point and set across the rocks. A detour may be made round Poulains Basse Occidentale buoy (card W), and a yacht without auxiliary power should not risk being becalmed between this buoy and Port du Vieux Château with a northerly-running stream. Alternatively, if the rocks of Les Chambres and Le Cochon are showing, as they generally will be, the Pointe des Poulains may safely be rounded close inside them.

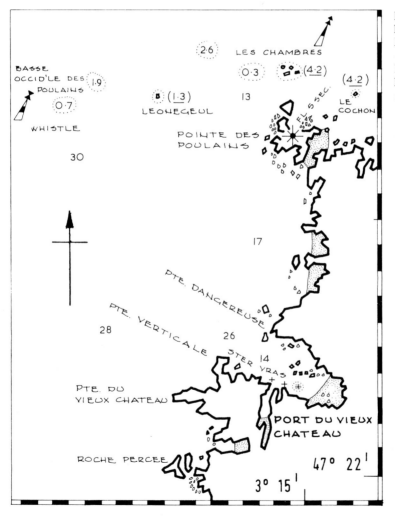

Port du Vieux Château, Belle Ile
MLW 0.7m; MLWN 1.9m; −0030 (sp), −0005 (np) Brest, Index 1, MTL 2.9m
Based on French Chart No. 135, much enlarged with corrections
Depths in metres; right hand margin in cables

The Port du Vieux Château is divided into two parts: the main inlet called Ster Vras which is seen from seaward, and a smaller inlet called Ster Wenn, which opens out on the south side of Ster Vras. Ster Vras is over 2 cables wide and $\frac{1}{2}$ mile long. Ster Wenn is under $\frac{1}{4}$ cable wide and $\frac{1}{4}$ mile long.

The entrance to Ster Vras is not so easy to locate as it appears on the chart, as there are several inlets looking similar from seaward, but on nearer approach it is easy to identify. The north side of Ster Vras is encumbered with rocks as much as 3 cables off Pointe Dangereuse, but the southern side is steep-to, there being 15m (50 ft) almost alongside. Pointe Verticale forms a vertical cliff on the south side of the entrance and it is this cliff which makes identi-fication easy. Half a mile to the south of Pointe Verticale is the peculiar pierced rock named Roche Percée (see photograph). The prominent Hôtel de l'Apothicairerie will also be seen on the skyline, just beyond Roche Percée.

Pointe Verticale, then, lies 1 mile SE by S from the Poulains Basse Occidentale buoy, but it is better not to approach the last half mile on this bearing for two reasons: one, because due allowance must be made for the stream which may be setting across the entrance to Ster

Roche Percée is a useful landmark, $\frac{1}{2}$ mile S of the entrance to Port du Vieux Château.

Ster Vras and the entrance to Ster Wenn (Bottom left)   *Photo: J R Blomfield.*

151

Ster Wenn, looking N.   *Photo: J R Blomfield.*

Vras; two, because approaching from a more westerly direction ensures that a good berth is given to the sunken rocks off Pointe Dangereuse and the northern arm of Ster Vras. The stream weakens as Ster Vras is entered, and so does the swell, especially in southerly winds.

The cliffs along the southern shore of Ster Vras may be skirted in safety. No sign or hint of the existence of Ster Wenn will be seen until, quite dramatically, the entrance opens up to starboard. Open Ster Wenn fully, when course may be altered sharply to starboard to enter. If Ster Wenn is overcrowded, there is a possible less sheltered anchorage up Ster Vras, which ends with a sandy beach. But proceed with great caution and only in settled weather, as the French chart shows rocks.

Anchorage

The inlet is deep near the entrance, and narrower than it looks in the photograph. Sail up the west side, meanwhile preparing to lower sail quickly and anchor, for there is little room for manoeuvring. About 3 cables up, the inlet divides into two. The main part continues up to a sandy end. The inlet on the starboard side is short. Beware of a rope spanning the main part, to which small boats are made fast. Anchor or use a mooring in the centre of the main inlet; it is wise to use a tripping line. The depth is about 1.5m (5 ft); there is just room for a 10m (35 ft) yacht to swing on her anchor, and if necessary a rope can be carried to a rock ashore to steady her.

The water is smooth in all winds except NW. It seems inconceivable that any sea can make the double turn to enter this snug retreat, even in a severe gale. It is stated, however, that surge enters when there is a heavy onshore wind, and therefore the anchorage is dangerous. Accordingly, the anchorage must be regarded only as a fair weather one.

Facilities

The only facilities are a ladder up the rocks to a fisherman's store on the east side, and a natural dinghy landing place in the inlet on the west side. There are no houses, but a road passes near the head of Ster Vras, and at the head of Ster Wenn a footpath leads to Grotte de l'Apothicairerie which is worth seeing; there is a large hotel there and the distance is only about ¾ mile.

The water is transparent, and every rock can be seen. There are lovely walks on the headland on the west side. The anchorage is indescribably beautiful, and when visited in 1958 it was completely deserted, except for two open fishing boats.

152

32 Presqu'île de Quiberon

Charts: 2353, 2646
Tidal information: See under the individual ports.

The name of Quiberon is familiar because it was the scene of the great sea-battle in 1759, when, in a November gale and gathering darkness, Hawke led his fleet into the bay to victory among the rocks and shoals and strong tides which will be described.

The peninsula itself is about 5 miles long, and is joined to the mainland by a sandy neck which is little over 100m wide. North of this a narrow arm of sand dunes continues for some 3 miles before widening to merge with the broader mainland. The total length of the projection seawards is therefore about 8 miles, and the geological formation continues for nearly 15 miles to the SE, in the shape of an archipelago of rocks, islets and shoals, between which there are navigable passages, which are described in the next chapter. Houat and Hoëdic are the only inhabited islands in this archipelago.

Presqu'île de Quiberon itself looks somewhat sinister from seaward; it is sandy in the north, but rocky towards the south and was formerly strongly fortified. Ashore, however, the whole peninsula is dotted with seaside resorts, for it has a long coastline and the sandy beaches are ideal for bathing. The town of Quiberon is the capital, and it has two harbours, Port Maria on the SW side and Port Haliguen on the NE, each a little over $\frac{1}{2}$ mile distant. Quiberon has a population of about 4000, a railway station, an airport and many shops, for it serves the whole district. Accommodation varies from the luxury hotel to the camping site.

Port Maria is not much used by yachts, nor is there much room for them, as the harbour is very crowded with fishing boats and the ferries to Belle Ile. Port Haliguen, the yacht harbour for Quiberon, is on the NE side of the peninsula; it has all the facilities of a marina. This side of Quiberon is sheltered from the prevailing winds and there are several anchorages available in winds from NW to S. At Port d'Orange, $2\frac{1}{2}$ miles farther north, there is merely a jetty and a somewhat indifferent anchorage. There are oyster beds in parts of the NW corner of Quiberon Bay, which are marked by orange buoys.

Yet farther north on the NE side of Quiberon peninsula is an almost landlocked bay, but it is very shallow, both in the bay and the approaches, except for a winding unmarked channel. Here is the Anse du Po, which is only one mile from Carnac, where the alignments of standing stones form one of the greatest sites of the megalithic culture.

The only other harbour on the Quiberon peninsula is Portivi, on the west side. This is exposed to the west, and when there is a heavy swell the sea is said to break nearly 1 mile to seaward. The anchorage is, however, a pleasant one in fine weather.

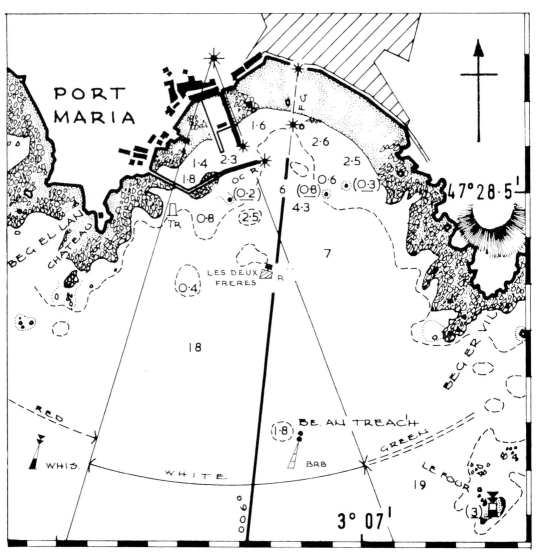

Port Maria (Quiberon)
Based on French Chart No. 5352 with corrections
Depths in metres; right hand margin in cables

Port Maria

High water: −0020 Brest, Index 1, MTL 2.9m
MHWS 5.1m (16.5 ft); MLWS 0.7m (2.5 ft); MHWN 3.9m (13 ft); MLWN 1.8m (6 ft)
Tidal streams: Some 4 miles SW of Port Maria the streams are rotatory clockwise, the main strength being NE, 1½ knots at −0330 Brest and W, 1½ knots at +0240 Brest. There is no stream in the harbour.
Depths: Maximum about 2m (6 ft), much of the harbour dries.

Port Maria, before the ferry terminal was enlarged.   *Photo: Jos Le Doare, Châteaulin*

This is an artificial harbour, situated just E of Beg el Lan on the SW extremity of the Quiberon peninsula. There is a conspicuous château with towers situated on this point. The harbour is used by many fishing vessels and is the terminal for the ferries to Belle Ile; it is sheltered from all winds.

Approach and entrance
The approach is well marked. Coming from the W or NW a whistle buoy (card S) is left to port over ½ mile from the entrance. Then steer 070° until the leading marks, two BW masonry beacons E of the breakwater, come in transit, bearing 006°. Leave Les Deux Frères can buoy (R) about ½ cable to port and follow the transit carefully, as a drying rock has been reported close to it, about a cable north of the buoy. When the harbour entrance opens up behind the breakwater steer in.

By night: Approach in the white sector of the main light. In good time bring the leading lights in transit, and steer so until the entrance between the south and east mole lights opens up. The lights are:
Main light; Q WRG, 28m, 15M.
Leading lights, front; Dir Q G, 5m, 10M.
Leading lights, rear; Dir Q G, 13m, 10M.
East mole; Iso G 4s, 9m, 6M.
South mole; Oc (2) R 6s, 9m, 8M.

Anchorage
The deep water, 1.4 to 2.2m (4 to 7 ft), lies on the SE side of the harbour parallel with the southern mole, and rocks and rocky bottom lie on the landward side. There are rocks at the base of the mole, which should not be approached too closely.

155

The berth at the east mole is used by the ferries to Belle Ile and the enlargement of the ferry terminal leaves no reasonable room to lie afloat, though it should still be possible to dry out. Alternatively, in settled northerly winds it would be possible to anchor clear of the fairway and W of the seaward leading light, keeping outside the yellow buoys marking the limit of pedal-boat activities.

Facilities
Several hotels, restaurants and shops of all kinds. Ferries to Belle Ile and Houat. Bus service to Carnac and Auray. Railway at Quiberon, $\frac{1}{2}$ mile away. Good chandlery.

Port Haliguen

High water: −0010 Brest, Index 1, MTL 3.0m
MHWS 5.3m (17.5 ft); MLWS 0.6m (2 ft); MHWN 4.0m (13 ft); MLWN 1.8m (6 ft)
Tidal streams: Off the harbour the N stream begins +0445 Brest, the S stream at −0220 Brest, spring rates 1$\frac{1}{2}$ knots.
Depths: The approach is deep. In the harbour there is up to 3m (10 ft).

Port Haliguen is a newly built yacht harbour with pontoon berths. A simple village encircles the old drying harbour. Every yachting facility is provided by the marina, there are excellent beaches handy and the resources of Quiberon are only $\frac{1}{2}$ mile away. It is a very pleasant harbour.

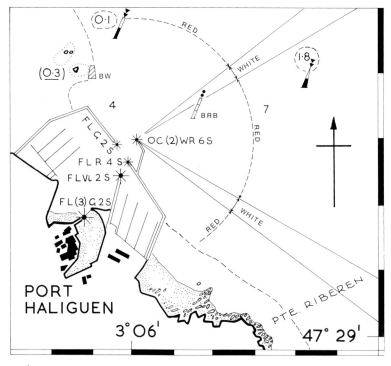

PORT HALIGUEN (QUIBERON)
MLWS 0.6m; MLWN 1.8m;
− 0010 Brest, Index 1,
MTL 3.0m
Based on French Chart No.
5352, enlarged with corrections
Depths in metres; right hand
margin in cables

Approach and entrance

The approach to Quiberon Bay through the Teignouse passages is described in the next chapter. Port Haliguen is situated less than 2 miles NW of the SE extremity of the Quiberon peninsula. The immediate approach is easy, keeping the lighthouse bearing about W, and leaving to starboard a YB buoy (card S). Another buoy BRB marks a wreck just outside the harbour entrance.

Enter between the breakwaters and leave the middle jetty to starboard. Very large yachts secure temporarily to a buoy just inside the eastern arm, near the middle jetty head. Secure to the short pontoon at right angles to the jetty; this is the reception berth, labelled *Ponton d'Acceuil*. Report to the harbour office which will allocate a permanent berth if they wish you to move.

By night: Approach in the white sector of Port Haliguen light (299°–306°), or on the white sector of Port Maria light (246°–252°). The protective spur off the east breakwater must be avoided. The lights are:

Port Maria, main light; Q WRG, 28m, 15M.
Port Haliguen, outer breakwater; Oc (2) WR 6s, 10m, 12M.
Port Haliguen, inner E breakwater; Fl R 4s, 10m, 5M.
Port Haliguen, west breakwater; Fl G 2s, 6m, 1M.
Port Haliguen, middle jetty; Fl Vi 2s.
Port Haliguen, old harbour; Fl (3) G 12s, 5M.

Port Haliguen, near LW out of season. Port office in the foreground.

Mooring

Visiting yachts must use the eastern basin. Leaving the central jetty to starboard, berth at the short pontoon at right angles to it near the tip and go to the harbour office, where a berth will be allotted if they wish you to move. Very large yachts moor temporarily to the first buoy to starboard on entering the eastern basin and seek a permanent berth from the harbour office. Alternatively, anchor outside between the fort and the breakwater (southern) off the Ecole de Voile.

Facilities

The facilities of a major marina; fuel, showers, repairs, a club. Water laid on to the pontoons. Baker and *alimentation* by the quay, where fish and shellfish can be bought. All shops, hotels and restaurants at Quiberon, 1 mile away, where there are connections by bus, train and plane to all parts. Supermarket half way along the road to Quiberon.

Port Haliguen, NW part. The dredging shown is now complete and pontoons are in place. Fishing harbour in the foreground dries.

Charts: 2353, 2646
Tidal streams: La Teignouse: NE begins −0610 Brest, SW begins −0005 Brest, spring rates 4 knots.
Le Beniguet: NE begins +0535 Brest, SW begins −0045 Brest, spring rates 3 knots.
Ile aux Chevaux and Les Soeurs: NNE begins +0535 Brest, SSW begins −0050 Brest, spring rates $2\frac{3}{4}$ knots.
Depths: All four channels are deep.

For a distance of some 15 miles SE of Quiberon there are reefs of rocks, shoals and the two islands of Houat and Hoëdic. Between the reefs and rocks there are several navigable passages, but only four which are suitable for the stranger. The Passage de la Teignouse is the big-ship route, well lit at night; it is about 3 miles from Quiberon. In addition to the main channel, some short cuts are described, formerly rated SEVERE, see page 25. The Passage du Beniguet, which lies close NW of Houat, is narrower but quite straightforward by day; there are no lights by night. The Passage des Soeurs lies between Houat and Hoëdic; it is wider than Le Beniguet, but also unlit. The Passage de l'Ile aux Chevaux is the short route between Le Palais and Hoëdic.

Passage de la Teignouse
This is a well marked principal channel, $\frac{1}{4}$ mile wide, and small vessels have plenty of margin, as there is deep water on either side of the marked channel. There are no difficulties other than those caused by bad visibility or bad weather. The strong tides cause a steep sea when wind and tide are opposed, so that with a contrary wind the passage should be taken as near slack water as possible.

From the south west. Bring the white lighthouse on La Teignouse to bear 036°. This line leads S of Goué Vas Sud buoy (card S), which must not be confused with Goué Vas NW buoy (card N), situated $\frac{1}{2}$ mile to the NW of it. Steer on this course, 036°, leaving
   Goué Vas Sud buoy (card S) 1 cable to port,
   Basse du Milieu Lanby stbd 1 cable to starboard,
   Goué Vas Est buoy (port), 1 cable to port.
When this last buoy is abeam alter course to 068°. The official lead for this is the church at St Gildas (10 miles away) bearing 068°, but all that is necessary is to steer out between Basse Nouvelle buoy to port and La Teignouse NE buoy to starboard.

From the east. Reverse the above directions.

By night: Enter the visible sector, 033° to 039°, of La Teignouse auxiliary fixed light before Port Maria main light turns from white to green. Steer in this sector between the buoys.

When the vessel is approximately between Basse du Milieu and Goué Vas Est buoys, alter course to 068° to pass between the two eastern buoys. When Port Haliguen light turns white bearing 305°, all the dangers are cleared and course can be altered as required.

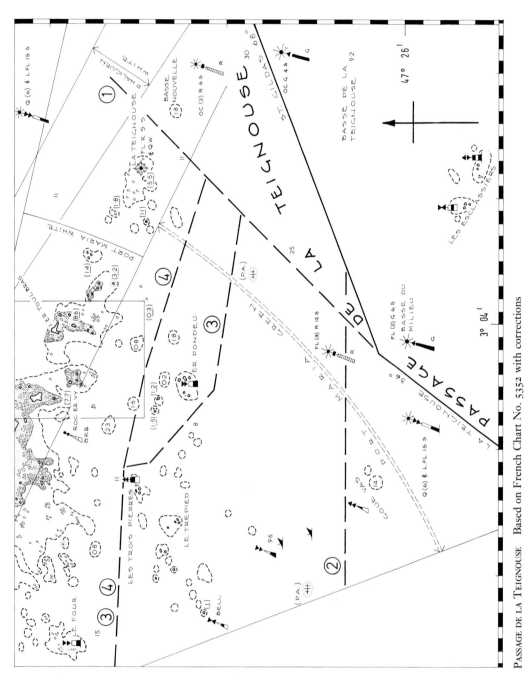

PASSAGE DE LA TEIGNOUSE   Based on French Chart No. 5352 with corrections
Depths in metres; right hand margin in cables

La Teignouse, bearing about NW, near low water. Note the outlying rock on the channel side.

From the east or north. Avoid the dangers off La Teignouse by keeping in the white sector of Port Haliguen light. Enter between the two eastern buoys and steer 248° to pass between Goué Vas Est and Basse du Milieu buoys. Steer out 216° between the buoys, in the fixed sector of La Teignouse light. When Port Maria main light turns from green to white all dangers are passed. The lights are:

Port Maria, main; Q WRG, 28m, 15M.
La Teignouse; Fl R 5s, 19m, 13M.
La Teignouse aux.; Dir QW, 14m, 9M.
Goué Vas Sud by; Q (6) + L Fl W 15s, 6m, 5M.
Basse du Milieu Lanby; Fl (2) G 6s, 9m, 8M.
Goué Vas Est by; Fl (3) R 12s, 6m, 5M.
Basse Nouvelle by; Oc (2) R 6s, 4m, 5M.
La Teignouse NE by; Oc G, 4s, 4m, 8M.
Port Haliguen; Oc (2) WR 6s, 10m, 12M.

Short cuts
These are only practicable by day. The strong tides set across all but the first two, and they are therefore best taken near slack water, and with reliable auxiliary power. In many cases they shorten the distance, and with contrary winds they may avoid some tacking.

   (1) South and E of La Teignouse the only danger is Basse Nouvelle, carrying 1.8m (6 ft), which can generally be disregarded. Thereafter there is nothing until the shoals round Les Esclassiers towers are reached. There is, therefore, no need to worry about passing between the two eastern buoys. Leave La Teignouse itself not less than 1½ cables to the N, and be careful to avoid the wreck nearly 1 mile SW of it.

   (2) Pass not more than 2 cables N of Goué Vas NW buoy (card N) and steer E to pass either side of Goué Vas Est buoy (port), where the main channel is joined or short cut No. (1) used, being careful to avoid the wreck mentioned there.

   (3) From Port Maria, or the NW, leave Le Four tower (card S) at least ½ cable to port and steer in the direction of La Teignouse lighthouse, bringing it to bear 093°, well open to the left of Les Trois Pierres tower (card N). When Les Trois Pierres tower is abeam, round it at a distance of at least ½ cable, and bring it in transit astern with Port Maria main light bearing 312°. Steer 132° on this stern transit until Er Pondeu tower (card S) is abeam, when alter course as requisite to leave La Teignouse to port. The wreck mentioned in short cut (1) must be avoided by keeping Er Pondeu tower open to the left of Le Four tower.

   (4) The dog leg to the S of Er Pondeu tower in short cut (3) is taken to avoid a number of shoals to the NW, N and NE of the tower. Near high water these will be well covered, see

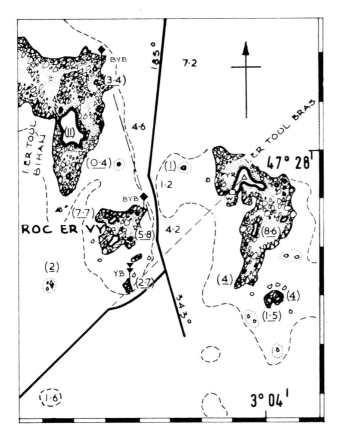

ROC ER VY PASSAGE
MLWS o.6m; MLWN 1.8m; − 0020 Brest, Index 1, MTL 3.0m
Based on French Chart No. 5352 with corrections
Depths in metres; right hand margin in cables

plan, and one can continue on after passing Les Trois Pierres tower, leaving Er Pondeu tower about ¼ mile to starboard. The principal dangers are the 1.5m and 1.2m rocks NW of Er Pondeu; to clear these keep Les Trois Pierres tower bearing less than 280° until the dangers are passed.

(5) Roc er Vy Passage. This short cut offers a substantial saving in going from the NW to Port Haliguen; it should only be attempted near slack water in good weather, with a wind which will lead through all the changes of course or reliable power. The channel is very narrow and the tides run hard through it. The location of a card S beacon on the 2.7 rock S of Roc er Vy has made it easier than it used to be, and under reasonable conditions it need not perhaps be still classified as SEVERE (see page 25).

Bound East and North. Follow short cut no. (4) to a position about 3 cables E of Les Trois Pierres tower. Before committing the yacht to the channel the following must be positively identified:

The white pyramid on Ile er Toul Bras,
The beacon (card S) on the 2.7 rock S of Roc er Vy,
The beacon (card E) on the E side of Roc er Vy,
The beacon (card E) on the NE outlier of Ile er Toul Bihan.

Follow the transit of the 2.7 rock beacon on the Ile er Toul Bras pyramid, bearing about 48°; when within 100m of the beacon, alter course to starboard to pass it at 30 or 40m; continue to make good a course on the white pyramid until the two card E beacons on Roc er Vy and Ile er Toul Bihan come in transit, bearing 343°. Steer with the farther beacon slightly open to the right of the nearer one. When within about 100m of the near one alter course to starboard and pass it at a distance of 30 to 40m, rounding it and bringing it in transit astern with Er Pondeu tower (card S), bearing 185°. Steer out 005° on this transit; all dangers are cleared when the Ile er Toul Bihan beacon is abeam.

Bound south and west. Make a point 1½ cables E of the beacon (card E) on Ile er Toul Bihan. Before committing the yacht to the channel identify positively
    The beacon (card E) on Roc er Vy,
    The beacon (card S) on the 2.7 rock south of Roc er Vy,
    Er Pondeu tower (card S).
    Steer 185° on the transit of Roc er Vy beacon with Er Pondeu tower until within 100m of the former. Round it at a distance of 30 or 40m and bring Ile er Toul Bihan beacon just open to the right of it, bearing 343° astern. Steer 163° on this transit until the 2.7 rock beacon is abeam. Steer 220° until it is passed and then shape a course to pass N of Les Trois Pierres tower (card N) and south of Le Four tower (card S).

Passage du Beniguet
For the plan for this passage see under Houat in the next chapter.

Although this passage is not so well known as La Teignouse, it is quite easy. It lies immediately to the NW of the island of Houat, and is often used by yachts going between Belle Ile and Houat.

Coming up from the south leave Le Rouleau tower (card W) to starboard. The passage itself goes between Le Grand Coin tower (card E) and Bonen Bras tower (card W). Keep closer to Le Grand Coin tower and well clear of both Bonen Bras and the shoals, with a least depth of 1.5m (5 ft), which extend 3 cables to the NNE of it. Le Grand Coin tower bearing 248° (and in transit with Pte de Taillefer, N of Le Palais, if the visibility is good) clears these shoals.

Passage de l'Ile aux Chevaux
No plan is given; chart 2353 is sufficient.

This is the direct fine-weather route from Le Palais to Hoëdic, and is an attractive alternative to Le Beniguet for reaching Houat.

Steer E from Le Palais for the Ile aux Chevaux. The Pot de Fer, 1 mile NNW of Ile aux Chevaux, must be passed on either side. It is marked by a BRB spar buoy, and can be safely cleared by keeping the northern tangent of Ile aux Chevaux clear to the N or clear to the S of Hoëdic. Keep 2 cables N of Ile aux Chevaux; the outling danger dries 5.7m (18 ft) and hardly ever covers.

Bound for Houat steer for Try Men, the steep-to isolated rock off the south end of Houat. Pass this closely; there is a rock with 1.3m (4 ft) over it about ½ mile off. Beg Pel and the rocks north of it are steep-to and can be passed at less than ½ cable. Thence leave the Men er Houteliguet BRB tower ½ cable to starboard. To port will be seen the magnificent sweep of Tréac'h er Gouret, one of the sights of Brittany. It is a magnificent beach for bathing, but unfortunately anchorage off it is prohibited owing to cables. Steer to leave the rock Er Yoc'h, 25m (80 ft) high, ½ cable to port, the beach on the point of En Tal well to port and the rock Er Geneteu, 16m (50 ft) high, ½ cable to port. Thence follow the directions in the next chapter.

Bound for Hoëdic, leave Men er Vag shoal to starboard; it is marked by a BRB spar buoy and the clearing mark is Le Palais breakwater open N of Ile aux Chevaux astern. Thence leave Les Soeurs tower (card W) to starboard and follow the direction for the Passage des Soeurs given below.

Passage des Soeurs

No plan is given for this passage, chart 2353 or 2646 is adequate.

Bound north east. Make a point 2 cables W of Er Palaire tower (card W), which is itself 1 mile W of Hoëdic. If the visibility is good this will bring the church of St Gildas in transit with Er Rouzès tower (card E), bearing 019°. If St Gildas church, which is 10 miles away, cannot be seen, bring Er Rouzès tower 3 or 4 times its own height to the left of Les Soeurs tower (card W). Leave Les Soeurs tower ½ cable to starboard. The channel is quite wide and it is not necessary to follow the alignments closely. Having passed Les Soeurs tower steer out as requisite.

Bound for Hoëdic do not bring Les Soeurs tower to bear more than 255° (270° if the tide is high enough to cover safely a shoal with 1m (3 ft) on it), until the west side of Hoëdic is shut in behind the Pointe du Vieux Château, bearing 175°; this point is the NW headland of Hoëdic.

Bound north leave Er Rouzès tower (card E) at least 1 cable to port.

34 Houat and Hoëdic

Charts: 2353, 2646
High water: −0020 Brest, Index 1, MTL 3.0m
MHWS 5.2m; MLWS 0.6m; MHWN 4.2m; MLWN 1.9m
Tidal streams: The tidal stream in Passages du Beniguet and des Soeurs are given on p. 159. North of Hoëdic the NE stream begins at +0600 Brest, the SW stream at −0020 Brest, spring rates 2 knots. Half a mile E of Les Grands Cardinaux the flood runs NNE, the ebb SW, spring rates 2½ knots.
Depths: In the harbour at Houat there is 2 to 2.5m (6 to 8 ft) near the breakwater; the southern side of the harbour dries. In the open roadsteads of Hoëdic depths shoal steadily towards the shore.

Houat

Pronounce as English 'what', but with the 'a' sound of 'hat'.

Houat, a strangely shaped island about 2 miles long, lies 7 miles east of Le Palais and 10 miles south of La Trinité. At its eastern end there are long promontories; En Tal on the NE is low, the southern one is higher, with off-lying rocks. Between these headlands lie the remarkable sands of Tréac'h er Gouret, and the disused harbour. The new harbour lies to the west of En Tal. This harbour is very snug and well protected from the swell, but it is small and the local fishing vessels nearly fill it. As it is a very popular objective for a weekend sail from the mainland, it becomes very overcrowded at weekends, and it should only be visited mid-week during the season.

Approach

The easiest approach is from the north and east. Coming from the north one will try to come down with the ebb stream, but it is better to avoid arriving near low water, so as to have more room to manoeuvre inside the harbour.

Coming from the north steer towards the eastern end of the island. Nearly 1 mile N of it is the conspicuous rock La Vieille, 19m (60 ft) high. Once this is identified it is easy to locate the harbour, which bears 200°, ¾ mile from it. Pass either side of La Vieille; it is clean to the N and E, less so to the SW, and shoals extend about 1 cable to the S. A convenient lead which goes W of La Vieille, is to keep the church in transit with the breakwater lighthouse.

From the east the outer NE rock Er Geneteu, 16m (50 ft) high, can be passed at a distance of ½ cable. There are rocks near the direct line from it to the harbour, and a yacht should stand well out into the bay before shaping up for the harbour.

By night: Green sectors of the breakwater light cover La Vieille and also the dangers to the east and west of the harbour. Approach in either white sector and anchor off the harbour, or enter if there is enough light to berth. The light is:
Houat; Oc (2) WG 6s, 8m, 8M.

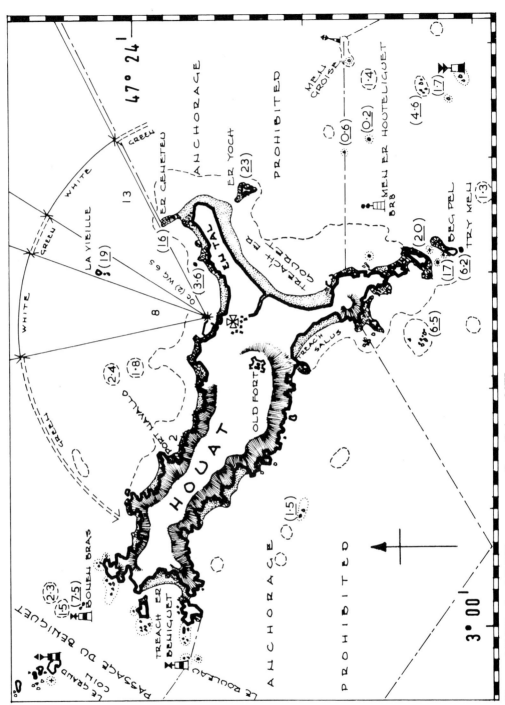

HOUAT   MLWS 0.6m; MLWN 1.9m; −0020 Brest, Index 1, MTL 3.0m
Based on French Chart No. 135 with corrections   Depths in metres; right hand margin in cables

Approaching Houat, the leading line is the lighthouse in transit with the church.   *Photo: B. M. Dépinay*

Entrance and anchorage

Turn sharply round the breakwater head, leaving it 20m to starboard, as there are shoals to port. Yachts and fishing vessels lie in a closely packed line parallel with the breakwater, but not too close to it as it has stones at its foot. Plenty of good fenders are essential. There is about 2 to 2.5m (6 to 8 ft) most of the way along, with a shallower patch probably about 1m, (3 ft) near the outer end. There will seldom be any room.

The fishing vessels have stern moorings, and lie with bow lines to the breakwater. Yachts usually anchor and take stern lines to the breakwater; if a tripping line is used, avoid buoyant line and bring the end on board or it is likely to be fouled when the fishermen leave in the dark. The fishing vessels usually go out in the early hours and return in mid-afternoon.

One can anchor outside the harbour, but the holding is not good. In fine weather it is exposed to the Vent Solaire at night. The anchorage at Port Navalo, 1 mile to the west, is better.

Many yachts anchor off Treac'h er Gouret and Treac'h Salus despite being prohibited because of high tension cables. The latter offers good protection from the Vent Solaire in fine weather. The anchorage in Treac'h er Beniguet is also attractive, sheltered from N to S by E.

Facilities

The shops can supply simple needs and tourist fodder, but they are very limited. Hotel.

Houat harbour near HW. There will be little water and some rocks later where the boats are now lying in mid-harbour.

167

Tréach Salus Beach near LW, looking SSE. A prohibited anchorage, but *Knuckleduster* has dried out with a clear conscience.

Water is available in the village, and from a tap between the beaches. The island is noted for its succession of wild flowers: roses in May, carnations in June, yellow *immortelles* in July and sand lilies in August. There are wonderful beaches on the north side of En Tal, at Tréac'h ar Gouret in the east, Tréac'h Salus in the SE and Tréac'h er Beniguet in the west.

Hoëdic

This island, rather over 1 mile long and ½ mile wide, lies about 4 miles SE of Houat. There are many detached rocks off its west, south and east coasts. There are two harbours. Argol

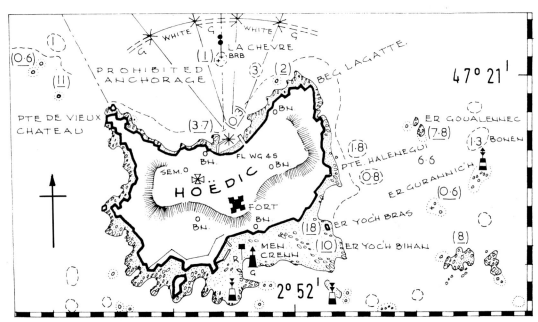

Hoëdic   MLWS 0.6m; MLWN 1.9m; —0020 Brest, Index 1, MTL 3.0m
Based on French Chart No. 5482 with corrections   Depths in metres; right hand margin in cables

Argol harbour, looking WSW. The semaphore building is on the extreme left edge of the photo.

harbour, on the N side, is very small; most yachts will prefer to lie outside. The southern harbour and its approaches are dangerous in strong winds from S and E, but in settled fine weather offer the best anchorage.

Approach

From the north make for the centre of the island, taking care to avoid La Chèvre in the close approach, see below. From Houat leave Men Groise beacon (card E) and Er Rouzès tower (card E) to starboard. Thence steer for the north side of the island, keeping Houat church open to the south of Er Rouzès tower; this line passes SW of La Chèvre. From the east, making for the north side of the island, leave Beg Lagatte, the NE point of the island, about 2 cables to port, and continue on a course of about W into the bay as there are drying rocks to the west of Beg Lagatte.

La Chèvre, a small group of rocks drying 1m (4 ft), marked by a BRB beacon, form the principal danger in this approach.

For the approaches from the south and west see chapter 33.

By night: Approach in one of the white sectors of the harbour light. A green sector covers La Chèvre. The light is:
L'Argol; Fl WG 4s, 10m, 10M.

Anchorages

L'Argol harbour has little room for a large yacht. To avoid sunken rocks in the approach and outside anchorage do not bring the head of the eastern jetty to bear more than 180°. The bottom shoals steadily; anchor in any convenient depth. A road leads to the village.

The southern harbour is best approached using one of the French charts Nos. 5482 or 135. The harbour itself dries 2.8m (9 ft) and is often crowded; most yachts will prefer to anchor outside, where there is good shelter from the Vent Solaire in fine weather. If the French chart is not on board approach with the SE tower (see chart on p. 168) in transit with the right edge of the fort, bearing 320°. On close approach leave the tower to starboard and make for a point to

Hoëdic Southern harbour entrance near LW, the neap tide anchorage outside, Men Crenn Tower and port hand beacon.

the S of Men Grenn tower (stbd), fetching a slight curve to avoid the rocks SE of Men Grenn. Anchor S of Men Grenn tower. Yachts which can take the ground, and others at neaps, can pass between Men Grenn tower and the port hand beacon and anchor beside other vessels. Thence the way to the harbour is open.

There is an anchorage, sheltered from N through W to S on the south east side of the island. Approach leaving Er Gurannic'h tower (card E) to port and Er Goualennec rock, 7.8m (25 ft) high, to starboard. Bonen, with 1.3m (4 ft) over it, lies N of the tower, out to about 3 cables. If the tide is low, avoid Bonen by entering on a southerly course, passing close to Er Goualennec, which is clean on its eastern side.

Steer SW for Er Yoc'h Bras, 18m (60 ft) high; this rises out of rocky flats, which cover. Keep Men Crenn tower (stbd) beyond Er Yoc'h Bras in transit with the right hand tangent of the latter. Steer so until the beach immediately south of Pointe Halénegui (see plan) bears about NW when steer into the bay and anchor off the beach as far in as draft and tide allow. The bottom is sand with patches of weed, but the water is clear and one can avoid anchoring in the weed. There is absolute seclusion here with a rough field path to the village.

Facilities
A yacht should be fully provisioned before visiting Hoëdic. There is a small village store at which a few necessities can be bought, and a café. The nuns bake the bread.

The Southern harbour and Roch Melen card S tower.   *Photo J R Blomfield*

Charts: 2353, 2358, 2646
High water: −0015 Brest, Index 1, MTL 3.0m
MHWS 5.4m; MLWS 0.7m; MHWN 4.2m; MLWN 2.0m
Tidal streams: The currents outside vary from point to point; 4 miles south of La Trinité the flood sets NNE, the ebb SW, spring rates 2 knots.
Depths: The river is deep in the channel until the last reach, approaching the quay, where there are patches with only 2m (6 ft).

La Trinité, situated 1½ miles up the river Crac'h on the west side, is one of the most popular yachting centres on the Bay of Biscay. It is not in itself exceptionally pretty, but it has good facilities and good communications and is the centre for a remarkably interesting cruising area, which also affords good courses for racing. It is, in consequence, more of a place to yacht from than to visit, though visitors are made welcome and all reasonable needs can be met.

In the marina the shelter is excellent from all except strong S and SE winds which send in a sea near high water when La Vaneresse, the sandbank protecting the harbour, is covered. In addition to its yachting activity it is a great centre for oyster culture. Anchoring is prohibited in the main channel between the entrance to the river and the town. Speed limit 5 knots. Power vessels over 20m (65 ft) overall, barges, and tows of oyster-culture vessels have priority over all other vessels.

Approach
The entrance to the river is not conspicuous. It is most easily identified by the rear leading lighthouse, although this is masked on some bearings.

By day, approaching from La Teignouse, the wooded hill about 30m (90 ft) high will be seen to the west of the entrance. La Trinité nestles behind it, but there are some villas on it. To the east the lighthouse will be seen. Some 2 miles from the entrance lies Le Souris buoy which is a spar buoy, BRB; this buoy must not be confused with Le Rat (same shape, same colours), situated about 1 mile to the NNW. From Le Souris buoy the Petit Trého buoy (port) will be easy to find; this buoy marks the outer dangers on the port side of the entrance to the river.

From the S or SE leave the conspicuous island of Méaban 1½ miles to starboard, leave the Basse de Buissons buoy (card S) to starboard and make for the leading line, the two lighthouses in transit, bearing 347°. Many of the dangers on the east side of the leading line are marked by beacons, but Roche Révision, with 0.4m (1 ft) over it, is unmarked.

Entrance
The river is entered between Mousker rock 7.3m (24 ft) high, painted white on top, to star-

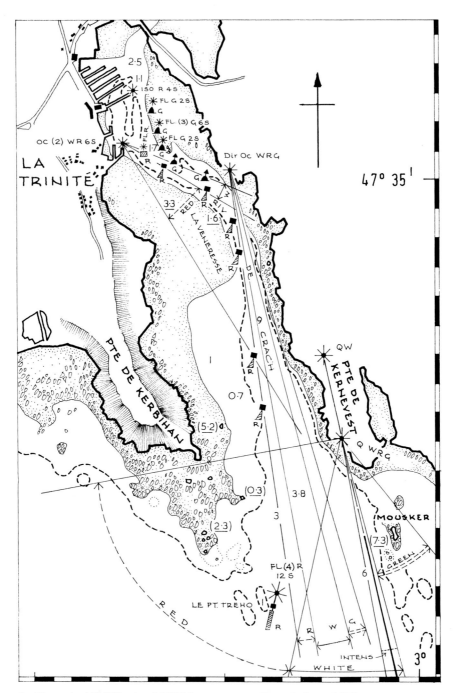

2.5

1.1

ISO R 4S

FL G 2S
▲ G

FL (3) G 6S
▲ G

OC (2) WR 6S

FL R

1.7

FL R

▲ G

FL G 2S
▲ G

Dir Oc WRG

LA
TRINITÉ

G ▲
R
R ▲ G
R ▲ G
R

3.3 RED

R ▲ G
R W
1.6

LA VENERESSE

R

R

47° 35'

R

R

DE

9 CRACH

QW

PTE DE KERBIHAN

1

0.7

(5.2)

R

R

PTE DE KERHEVEST

Q WRG

(0.3)

3.8

MOUSKER

3

(2.3)

(7.3)

GREEN

FL (4) R
12 S

6

LE PT. TREHO

R

R   W   G

RED

INTENS

3°

WHITE

LA TRINITÉ   MLWS 0.6m; MLWN 2.0m; −0015 Brest, Index 1, MTL 3.0m
Based on French Chart No. 5352 with corrections   Depths in metres; right hand margin in cables

La Trinité harbour and bridge; in the foreground, Eric Tabarly's hydrofoil trimaran, *Paul Ricard*.

board, and Le Petit Trého buoy to port. The river is so well marked by buoys, as shown on the plan, that no directions are needed. Near No. 3 buoy there is a shoal with about 2m (6 ft) over it; yachts of deep draft should consequently keep close to No. 10 buoy near low water.

By night: Approach with the leading lights in transit, bearing 347°, or in the white sector of the front light, with the rear light open to the left of it. When the entrance is reached proceed up the river in the narrow white sector of the directional light. When the harbour light turns from red to white continue in the white sector of that light.

The lights, amended in 1984, are:
Front leading light: Q WRG, 10m, 12M.
Rear leading light: Q W 20m, 17M.
Le Petit Trého by; Fl (4) R 12s.
Directional Oc WRG, 9m, 14M.
Harbour; Oc (2) WR 6s, 7m, 11M.
No. 12 by; Fl R 2s.
No. 5 by; Fl G 2s.
No. 7 by; Fl (3) G 4s.
No. 9 by; Fl G 2s.
Marina pierhead; Iso R 4s.

Mooring
Anchoring is forbidden below the bridge (clearance 10m at HWS). Visitors berth at the marina on the first or second pontoons above the breakwater.

Facilities
All shops, restaurants and hotels. All the facilities of a busy yachting centre; chandlers, shipyard, repairs of all kinds. Water by hose on the quay and pontoons; petrol and diesel by hose from a fuel barge in the harbour. Showers at the Yacht Club or to N of the marina. Good scrubbing berth, with a level concrete bottom, by the Yacht Club.

173

Charts: 2353, 2358, 2646, 2359
High water: (Port Navalo) as Brest, Index 0, MTL 2.8m
MHWS 5.0m; MLWS 0.6m; MHWN 3.8m; MLWN 1.7m
Tidal streams: Outside, in the middle of the bay, the streams are rotatory; SSW at +0300 Brest, they turn clock-
wise to NW at −0600 Brest and on to NNE at −0300 Brest, they then swing anticlockwise to N at HW Brest
and back to SSW at +0300 Brest, spring rates 1 to 2 knots. Nearer to the entrance the streams strengthen. Off
Pointe de Port Navalo the flood begins −0440 Brest, the ebb at +0055 Brest, spring rates 7 knots.
Depths: The approach and entrance is deep.
Note: Tidal information for the interior of the Morbihan is given below under the headings 'Auray River',
'Vannes Channel' and 'Southern and Eastern Morbihan'.

This inland sea, which receives the waters of three rivers, though it is fed mostly by the tide, has an area of about 50 square miles. The islands are said to be equal in number to the days of the year, but there are not more than 60, and this figure includes the isolated rocks. Many are wooded and all, with the exception of Ile aux Moines and Ile d'Arz, are privately owned. Most are uninhabited, and in these cases landing is not objected to. Ile Berder is a convalescent home, and if wishing to penetrate inland it is usual to ask permission. Ile aux Moines with its pine woods, restaurants, good shops and plage is the island most visited. Ile d'Arz has picturesque walled farms, such as Ker Noel. The Séné peninsula (known as L'Angle, and lying east of Boëdic) was the home of the Sinagots, a separate community of fishermen. On Gavrinis, visitors have the right of way to the celebrated carved tumulus (if locked, key at Larmor-Baden).

As a cruising ground the Morbihan is exceptionally interesting and offers innumerable anchorages in sheltered water. Only near the narrow entrance off Port Navalo is it open to the sea. Within the entrance, off Grand Mouton and south of Ile Longue, Gavrinis and Ile Berder the streams attain $8\frac{1}{2}$ knots at extreme spring tides. They are fierce in the narrows between the islands, but farther from the entrance they moderate and in the upper reaches are not strong.

Navigation in the Morbihan is not so difficult as it appears on the chart as the islands are easy to identify. There is deep water in the main channels and dangers are marked by beacons or buoys. Chart 2358 is recommended if it is intended to explore the more out-of-the-way channels. The best time for cruising in the Morbihan is at neap tides, but even then the navigator will have to be quick in his pilotage, as with a fair stream the speed across the bottom will be faster than he is accustomed to. It is a help to tick off in pencil each landmark as it is passed.

The tidal streams are often fast enough for their direction to be seen from their surface appearance. The streams tend to follow the directions of the channels, but sometimes they run on one side of a channel and there is a slack or reverse eddy on the other, with a clear

Baguen Hir Tower, near low water. The lighthouse at Port Navalo is marked, just showing above the trees and bearing 043°.

dividing line between them. Using the eddies those with local knowledge can make surprising progress against a foul tide. If you leave the main channel begin to turn in very good time, or you will be swept past your destination.

Approach and entrance

The outer approach to the Morbihan presents no difficulty. Peering above the trees is Port Navalo lighthouse, on the east side of the entrance, with a second tower like a lighthouse close to it; more conspicuous are the Petit Mont, a hill 42m (140ft) high, on the peninsula 1 mile to the SE of it, and the white lighthouse within Le Crouesty marina.

As soon as they can be recognised come on to the line of the leading marks. They are the white pyramid on Le Petit Veisit in transit with Badène church spire, 3 miles behind it, bearing 001°, see photograph. This transit leaves Basse de Méaban buoy (card S) ½ mile to port, Petit Mont ¾ mile to starboard, Baguen Hir tower (which is now card E, BYB) half a mile to port and Port Navalo lighthouse 1 cable to starboard. The transit leads close to the Pointe de

The leading marks for the entrance to the Morbihan. The pyramid (A) on Le Petit Veisit in transit with Badène church (B), bearing 001°. Also shown are Le Lieu port hand buoy (C) and Le Grégan card S tower (D).

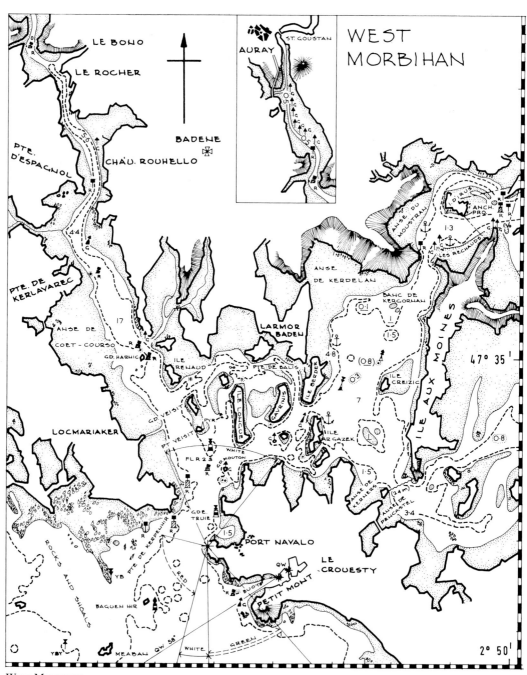

WEST MORBIHAN

WEST MORBIHAN
MLWS 0.6m MLWN 1.7m; 0000 Brest, Index 0, MTL 2.8m
Based on French Charts Nos. 5420 and 3165 with corrections
Depths in metres; right hand margin in cables

Port Navalo; if in doubt borrow to port, especially on the ebb, as the tide is weaker on the western side.

The flood sweeps past the Pointe de Port Navalo, then swings across towards the Pointe de Kerpenhir, then back again towards Le Grégan tower. The approach is rough on the ebb if there is an onshore wind. The entrance channel is marked on its western side by two towers Kerpenhir (port) and Goëmorent (port) and on its eastern side by the Grande Truie tower (card W, YBY), on the northern side of the bay on which Port Navalo stands.

For further directions for the Auray River see page 178, and for the Vannes Channel see page 181.

A gale warning light is shown by day from Port Navalo lighthouse. Int Qk Fl for forces 6 or 7; Qk Fl for force 8 and above, between 1 July and 15 September.

By night: There are no lights in the Morbihan. The lighthouse makes it possible, if there is a little light, to get into Port Navalo anchorage and there await daylight. Enter in the white sector of Port Navalo light, keeping on the west side of the sector, near the red sector, in the close approach. Petit Mont (42m, 140 ft) will be left to starboard, and when the next hill, 28m (90 ft) high, is abeam enter the red sector. Round the lighthouse at a distance of 1 cable and steer into the bay roughly midway between the lighthouse and Pointe du Mouton, 29m (90 ft) high, to the N. Pass through the white sector and anchor on the edge of it in a depth of about 1.5m (5 ft). The lights are:
Port Navalo; Oc (3) WRG 12s, 32m, 16M.
Le Lieu by; Fl R 2s.
Le Crouesty, front leading light; QW 10m, 15M. ⎱
⠀⠀⠀⠀⠀⠀⠀⠀rear leading light; QW 27m, 15M. ⎰ intensified 056.5°–059.5°

Anchorage
Le Crouesty marina has been built in the bay to the S of Port Navalo. It is useful if one arrives off the entrance at the wrong time of tide, but few would prefer it to one of the many anchorages in the Morbihan. The entrance channel carries 1.5m (5 ft) and is well marked. By night, leading lights on 058° take one straight in. Visitors moor to starboard until allotted a berth. All the usual facilities.

There is a tolerable anchorage in Navalo Bay, in depths of 1.5m (5 ft) off the end of the pier, but it is exposed to the S and W and troubled by the wash from ferries. At neaps it may be possible to get farther in, but there are many moorings.

Facilities
Land at all tides at the outer jetty, but dinghies must not be left blocking the way for passengers on the ferries. At tide time land at the eastern jetty by the village. Simple shops and restaurants. Ferries to Auray and Vannes.

Departure
When leaving on the flood, steer boldly out into the stream to avoid being set on to the Grand Mouton, see page 181.

Auray River

High water: (Auray) +0025 Brest, Index 1, MTL 3.0m
MHWS 5.2m; MLWS 0.7m; MHWN 4.0m; MLWN 1.9m
Tidal streams: Flood begins −0510 Brest, ebb begins +0025 Brest, spring rates 3 to 3½ knots.
Depths: The river is deep as far as Le Rocher, though the last mile of the deep channel is narrow, so that it may be better to regard it as carrying 1m (3 ft). Above Le Rocher it shoals rapidly and the channel bottom is only just below datum. The anchorage at Auray in midstream has been dredged to 3m (10 ft), and more in places, but the quays dry.

This fine river on the west side of the Morbihan provides eight miles of varying scenery. The town of Auray, at the head of the navigable river, stands on a steep hill on the west side of the river with the old port of St Goustan on the east side. Auray is quite a large town; much of it is fifteenth century, with the steeples of the church and chapel standing on the hill. The old port of St Goustan is now small, but at one time had a substantial trade. Benjamin Franklin landed here from America to negotiate a treaty with France during the War of Independence. The river runs southwards between wooded shores, through a narrow cleft at Le Rocher, then gradually widens out between mud banks and oyster beds, until near the entrance it merges into the Morbihan scene of islands and fast tidal streams.

The river is often visited by English yachts, but is relatively less popular with the local people, so that one can easily find quiet spots away from the crowds. Auray has good communications, so that it is quite a good place for changing crew.

The river

In passing the Morbihan entrance, see page 177, keep nothing E of the 001° transit of Le Petit Veisit pyramid and Badène church. When the tide is up a bit one can pass fairly close to Goëmorent tower (port), but there is only 1.4m (4 ft) some 1½ cables to the E of it, so near low water the leading line must be strictly held. Once the tower is passed steer a little to port, leaving Le Lieu buoy (port) to starboard. The essential thing is not to get set by the main stream of the tide into the Vannes channel to the NE. Beyond Le Lieu buoy Le Grégan tower (which is now card S, YB) is left about 2 cables to starboard. Thereafter the tides set fairly up and down the channel, except for local sets between the islands on the east side, especially north of Grand Veisit.

Steer for Grand Harnic, leaving the islands of Petit Veisit, Grand Veisit and Ile Renaud to starboard. Grand Harnic has two conspicuous clumps of trees and is easy to identify. On approaching it steer to leave a can buoy to port; after passing Grand Harnic steer between a buoy (port) to the N of it and a beacon (stbd) to the N of the buoy.

North of this the channel is wide, though there is a big shallow bay, the Anse de Coët Courso to port. A course of 325° will take the yacht to the port hand buoy off the Pointe de Kerlavarec and on to the Catis buoy (stbd). Here the channel is narrower and there are extensive mud flats on either hand. The yacht should be steered in a gradual sweep round the mud on the starboard hand until she heads for the middle of the narrows off Pointe d'Espagnol with the Château Rouhello (conspicuous with lawn in front and trees either side) well open.

The withies on the oyster beds help to identify the channel, but if more precise directions are required keep the red buoy a little open westward of the green buoy astern until the château bears 025°, when steer for it on that bearing, giving the red beacon off Pointe d'Espagnol a moderate berth.

Above Pointe d'Espagnol the deep water lies on the east side of the river off the château. Then, as the Anse de Kerdreau opens, the channel bears to port towards the narrows seen ahead. The shallow Anse is left to starboard, together with a green beacon marking the edge of the mud. The deep channel now crosses to the other side of the river; this is its narrowest part. The river is much prettier here, passing between steep rocky shores and thick woods to Le Rocher.

The deep part of the river ends above Le Rocher, and it can only be navigated up to Auray with sufficient rise of tide. The channel almost dries, but there is plenty of water in the pool at Auray. The channel is clearly marked; the trickiest bit is where it crosses the remains of a Roman bridge $\frac{1}{2}$ mile above Le Rocher. There is a drying shoal in midstream, marked by a red buoy which should be left well to port. The only visible remnant of the bridge is a flat square of turf over stones on the bank to port.

Anchorages
One of the beauties of the Morbihan is that it is possible to find an endless variety of anchorages according to weather and individual preference for solitude or company, steep banks or saltings. Some well known anchorages are given, but many others can be found.
Locmariaker. This village is on the west side of the river near the entrance opposite the Veisit islands. There is a channel to it, with about 0.6m (2 ft), marked by port hand beacons, but it is narrow and used by the ferries. The quay dries 1.5m (5 ft). Yachts can take the ground between the village quay and vedette jetty. It is possible to anchor off the entrance and go in by dinghy, but this anchorage is rather exposed, and subject to strong tides.
Larmor Baden. This village lies 1 mile to the east of the Auray River, between it and the Vannes Channel. It is approached from the Auray River by passing between Grand Veisit and Ile Renaud and leaving Ile Radenec to starboard. It can also be approached from the

Le Rocher.

St Goustan. The boat is anchored about at the end of the deep water; the foreground will now be fully occupied by buoys.

Vannes Channel, by passing close east of Ile Longue, or more simply between Gavrinis and Ile Berder.

It is possible to anchor near Pointe de Balis, or farther east; though moorings make the latter difficult, it is closer to the pier. The tides run hard through the channel (flood E, ebb W), and it is best to work into one of the bays as far as draft and depths allow.

Le Rocher. Once an excellent and popular anchorage, but now full of permanent moorings. If one is available, land at the small inlet downstream on the east side.

Port du Bono. An inlet to starboard just north of Le Rocher. There is 1m (3 ft) as far as the jetty and 0.5m (1 ft) at the quay but the holding is bad. The new bridge, but not the old, has ample clearance. A dinghy excursion can be made to the hamlet and chapel of St Avoye; land on the port side $\frac{1}{2}$ mile above the old bridge at Le Bono.

St Goustan. There are moorings in the middle of the river opposite the quays and visitors' fore and aft moorings further down. There is enough water at most tides over a considerable length. The water shoals rapidly on the turn to the bridge and, especially at springs, the ebb pours violently through the bridge and eddies make the upper end of the deep water an uneasy berth. The quay should only be used as a temporary berth at high water.

Facilities

All shops and restaurants at Locmariaker, Larmor Baden and Le Bono but nothing at Le Rocher. At St Goustan there are simple shops and restaurants on the quay and all the facilities of a substantial town up the hill at Auray, including a marine engineer. Good train service, though the station is some way from the town and further from St Goustan. Buses to all parts, including La Baule for the airport and Carnac for the megaliths.

Vannes Channel

High water: (Vannes) +0200 Brest, Index see below, MTL 3.0m
MHWS 4.7m (15.5 ft); MLWS 1.3m (4.5 ft); MHWN 4.0m (13 ft); MLWN 2.1m (7 ft)
The tide tables in this book will not give very good results for Vannes, as the tidal wave is distorted in passing up the channels. The Index varies from 0 at neaps to −3 at springs. Chart datum is the level of LAT at the *entrance*; coming up the channel even the lowest tides do not fall below 0.4m to 0.9m (1 to 3 ft) above this level.
Tidal streams: Inside the entrance the stream divides, a weaker portion running up the Auray River. Part of this sweeps past Larmor Baden and rejoins the main Vannes Channel at the south end of Ile Berder, where it causes turbulence and a back eddy close to the shore. The main torrent follows the main channel; the spring rate is about 8 knots. The irregularities of the channel produce whirlpools and the yacht's head is thrown from side to side, but not so as to make it difficult to keep in the channel. The way the water climbs up the Grand Mouton beacon is remarkable. Once through the narrows south of Ile Berder the rate decreases a little, but the stream continues in a narrow jet towards Ile Creizic, and thence near the Ile aux Moines to the narrows NW of that island. Here the stream is fierce, sweeping across from the Pointe des Réchauds in a wide curve along the mainland side and south of Ile d'Irus. This sets up an eddy, so that NW of Ile aux Moines the current runs SW almost continuously. After passing the narrows north of Ile aux Moines the stream fans out and becomes weaker, nowhere exceeding 4 knots. The ebb stream roughly reverses the flood, but it is important to keep towards the south side of the narrows between Ile Berder and Ile ar Gazek if one does not want to be swept up the channel west of Ile Berder, to Larmor Baden. It is important to realise that not only is local high water progressively later as one goes up the channel (2 hr between Port Navalo and Vannes), but the streams do not turn until about 1½ hr after local high water or low water.
Depths: The channel is deep to Ile aux Moines; thence deep water can be carried to Ile de Boëdic, but the deep channel is very narrow in places and it is easier to regard it as carrying 0.7m (2 ft). Thence to Conleau it carries 2.5m (8 ft), after which it shoals progressively, but see the note above on low water levels.

Tide rips in the narrows, looking S towards Er Lanic.

The channel

After passing the entrance (see page 177), immediate steps must be taken not to be swept by the tide onto the Grand Mouton rock, which lies to starboard and is marked by a green beacon with a green conical topmark. Steer to leave Le Lieu buoy (port) close to port and turn sharply to starboard only when the Grand Mouton beacon is safely passed. The channel is now clear before you. Leave Ile Longue to port, a beacon (stbd) and the island of Er Lanic to starboard, Gavrinis to port (there is a landing place here marked by beacons), a buoy (stbd) and Ile ar Gazek to starboard, and Ile Berder to port.

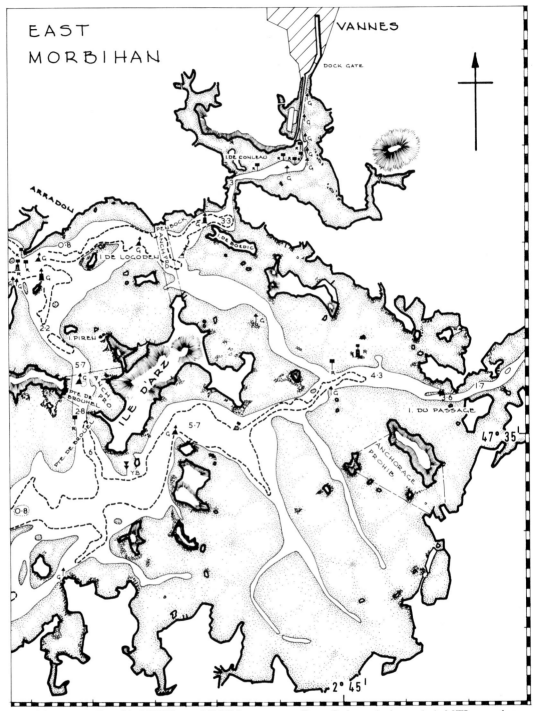

EAST MORBIHAN   Roughly MLWS 1m; MLWN 2m; +0100 Brest, Index, 0 (np), −1 (sp), MTL 2.9m but see
text   Based on French Charts Nos. 5420 and 3165   Depths in metres; right hand margin in cables

Pointe des Réchauds, Ile aux Moines, bearing NNE. This is the east side of the narrows between the island and the mainland.

A wide expanse of water, some of it shallow, now opens, but it is best to keep in the jet of tide setting towards the small Ile Creizic. Leave to port the two cardinal buoys marking middle grounds, steering midway between the second and the N end of Ile Creizic. After passing this turn towards the N, keeping fairly close to (but not less than 1 cable off) the Ile aux Moines shore. This avoids the Kergornan shoal which dries 1m (4 ft) in places.

The stream sets strongly through the narrows between Ile aux Moines and the mainland, and Les Réchauds rocks, marked by two beacons (stbd), are left to starboard. Thence the channel is straightforward, the critical points being well marked. Leave

Ile d'Irus to port,
Two beacons (stbd) on Pointe de Drec'h to starboard,
A tower (port) and a beacon (port) on La Truie to port,
A buoy (stbd) off Pointe d'Arradon to starboard,
The yachting centre of Arradon to port,
Ile de Logoden and Le Petit Logoden to starboard,
A buoy (stbd) to starboard.

An alternative and rather shorter channel carries 1.8m (6 ft). After passing Pointe de Drec'h leave Holavre tower (stbd) to starboard and pass S of Ile de Logoden, rejoining the other channel N of the next buoy (stbd).

After leaving Penbock pier to port there is a shoal in the centre of the channel carrying only 0.7m (2 ft) in places. There is a very narrow deep channel north of it, and a wider but tortuous channel south of it. However even extreme tides here never fall to within 0.5m (2 ft) of datum and one will usually be sailing here near high water, having come up on the flood or being bound down on the ebb. So this shoal is not usually anything to worry about.

Port Blanc, opposite Ille aux Moines. The ferry runs from here to Pointe des Réchauds.

The little chapel on Ile de Boëdic, looking W. There is an anchorage here, but not quite so close inshore as this picture indicates.

The channel continues leaving card W buoy to starboard and Roguedas tower (stbd) to starboard. The continuation of the channel, N of Ile de Boëdic, is not conspicuous from a distance. As one passes north of Ile de Boëdic the narrow gap opens up dramatically. When it is fully open turn sharply to port and steer through it. Coming out from this narrow passage the yachting centre of Conleau is to port and a wide expanse of shallow water lies ahead. The channel through this is marked by beacons; at the far end it takes a very sharp turn to port, and its bottom is only just above datum. Thence the channel is very narrow, though well marked by beacons, and there is only just room to pass oncoming traffic. The channel gets progressively shallower and is about 1.2m (4 ft) above datum when it reaches the vedette quay, above which is the dock gate admitting to the Vannes marina.

Anchorages
With the large scale chart many anchorages can be found; some of the better known ones are:
Larmor Baden, see page 179.
Ile ar Gazek (Ile de la Jument on chart 2358). On the east of the island, out of the tide. A good place to wait for a fair tide.
Ile Berder. To the SE of the island, NW of the BW buoy, or farther north in the Mouillage de Kerdelan. A good anchorage with little stream. Yachts on moorings indicate the best areas.
Ile aux Moines. There is a marina on the NW corner of the island, with some berths for visitors. It is also possible to anchor to the NE of the moorings. It is worth working out the depths carefully, because the bottom slopes very gently for a long way before suddenly dropping into deep water. To have more than just enough water one has to go a long way out, and tends to get more in the tide, though the tides are not too strong if one gets well into the bay. There is no official information about tidal constants for this point. If the tide tables in this book are used take high water as +0100 Brest, Index 0 at neaps, −1 at springs, MTL 2.9m; these constants are only estimates and some margin should be allowed.

It is also possible to anchor in the bay south of Pointe des Réchauds, but this is a fine weather anchorage, very exposed to the S and W.
Anse de Moustran. This is the bay just north of Port Blanc on the opposite side of the narrows to Ile aux Moines. The best spots are occupied by moorings, so that one is pushed out into deeper water where the tide is strong. If the wind comes against the tide the yacht

184

East of Ile de Boëdic the channel turns N, through the narrows, shown here, which open up suddenly.

sheers about and as the bottom is sharp sand *Black Jack* lost all the galvanising on 10 fathoms of chain in one night in this anchorage.

Arradon. A popular yachting centre. Moorings for visitors or anchor outside the moorings. Rather exposed in southerly weather near high water.

Penbock. Anchor east of the jetty. Again rather exposed.

Ile de Boëdic. There is a pleasant, secluded wee sheltered anchorage in the bight at the NW end of the island. The island is private and there is no landing.

Conleau. The inlet to the SW of the peninsula is full of moorings. The best available anchorage is in the bight on the port side just before the far end of the narrows. There are usually some fishing boats here.

Vannes. The basin formerly dried out before LW, but the provision of a dock gate has converted this into a convenient wet dock 6 cables long. At the town end there are pontoons accessible from both sides; below these there is a pontoon bridge for pedestrians, which is broken when the dock gate is open. The gate is worked between 0800 and 2200, opening $\frac{1}{2}$ hour before HW Brest, or 0800, whichever is later. Closing time is regulated to maintain a depth of 2.4m at the pontoons.

The anchorage off Conleau, at the north end of the narrows.

Vannes, looking N at the marina and Cathedral. The pontoon Bridge is open for entry.

As this is close to MTL, it makes little difference to the total daily opening period whether it is springs or neaps. At springs, the lock might open at 0800 for about 3 hours, and again in the evening; at neaps, there would be a midday period of about 5 hours. Timetable at the marina office, phone 54.16.08. Quieter pontoons on the W bank below the pontoon bridge; mooring buoys outside the lock for yachts awaiting opening, but yachts should not be left on them unattended.

Facilities
There are no facilities at all at Iles ar Gazek, Berder and Boëdic. Facilities are very limited at Port Blanc (Anse de Moustran), Arradon, Penbock and Conleau. At Ile aux Moines there are all the usual shops in the village and hotels and restaurants near the quay. At Vannes there are all the facilities of a cathedral city including chandlers. It is an attractive town with much of historical interest. Water on the pontoons, fuel outside the lock. Vannes is a main rail centre and communications by rail and bus are good. Buses from Conleau and Vannes marina pass Vannes R.S. There is a regular service of ferries from Vannes lock to Conleau, Ile au Moines, Port Navalo, Auray and other points in the Morbihan.

Southern and Eastern Morbihan

Tides: There is a lack of official information. Tidal heights can probably be calculated approximately, using the tables in this book and taking high water as +0100 Brest (later at Ile du Passage), Index 0 (neaps) or − 1 (springs), MTL 2.9m, but these figures are guesses and a margin should be allowed.

An interesting alternative after passing between Iles Berder and ar Gazek is to proceed south of Ile aux Moines. Ile aux Moines is joined to the mainland by an overhead cable with a least clearance above high water of 24m (78 ft). Beyond the narrows the channels, though fairly well marked, wind between mudflats and are probably best taken by a stranger on a rising tide. The tidal streams are not so fierce as in other parts of the Morbihan. Between Ile aux Moines and Ile d'Arz the flood runs to the S.

Anchorages
Anse de Kerners. Anchor outside the local boats. Water, showers and provisions in season.
Anse de Pencastel. Anchor outside the moorings.
Between Ile aux Moines and Ile d'Arz, landing at Pointe de Brouhel and at the slip N of Pointe de Brouel respectively. Anchor N of the line joining these points, or south of Ile Piren to the north. All shops on Ile aux Moines in the Bourg, 1 mile walk. Ile d'Arz is more primitive, but has all shops.
Ile du Passage. This is the last anchorage where one can lie afloat. Anchor midstream in the narrows to the north of the island in 4m (13 ft); the tide is strong. Quiet and rural, it has no supplies. This used to be the base for the Sinagots, fishermen living at Séné, who sailed an individual type of brown-sailed lug-rigged schooner with conspicuous skill. A few of these survive, sailed as yachts.

A casual anchorage for lunch and a swim at one of the islets is typical of the scores of anchorages to be found in the Morbihan.

187

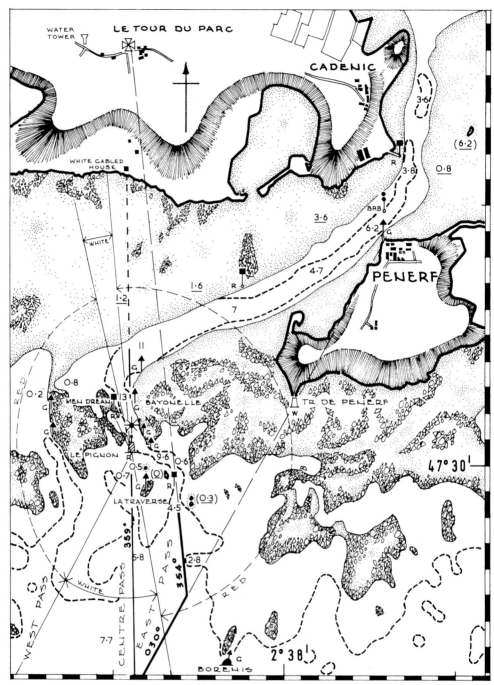

PENERF MLWS 0.6m; MLWN 1.9m; —0010 Brest, Index 2, MTL 3.0m
Based on French Chart No. 5418 with corrections   Depths in metres; right hand margin in cables

188

Charts: 2353, 2646
High water: −0010 Brest, Index 2, MTL 3.0m
MHWS 5.5m; MLWS 0.6m; MHWN 4.2m; MLWN 1.9m
Tidal streams: Between Pointe du Grand Mont and the river mouth the flood has a spring rate of 1 knot, the ebb 1½ knots. In the passes the streams run 3 knots springs when the rocks are uncovered, but only 2 knots ENE and WSW when the rocks are covered.
Depths: In the central pass 0.5m (1 ft), in the east pass 4.5m (15 ft). Inside, the river is deep as far as Cadenic.

This quiet and unspoilt river, 6 miles west of the entrance to La Vilaine, is sheltered from the Atlantic swell by groups of rocks and the peninsula on which Penerf is situated. The village is small, combining oyster culture with being a minor holiday centre. A fair number of yachts and fishing boats are moored off the village of Penerf and others off Cadenic on the other side of the river ½ mile further up. There is still plenty of room for visitors.

There are many rocky ledges near the entrance. They are well marked with beacons, but the channels are very narrow in a wide expanse of water; it is not safe for the stranger in bad weather or bad visibility as an error could have serious consequences.

Approach
Pointe de Penvins, 1½ miles SW of the entrance, is easy to identify. It is low, with a conspicuous mosque-like chapel on it. Half a mile SSE of Penvins chapel is the Penvins buoy (R, topmark cylinder and double cross), which is left to port. To the ENE of Penvins chapel are Le Pignon tower (red) and the Tour de Penerf, looking like a chess castle and painted white.

Enter the bay with the Tour de Penerf roughly in transit with the left hand side of the village of Penerf, bearing about 030°.

The white-gabled house, and other E pass marks.

Entrance

There are three passes into Penerf. The west pass may be disposed of by saying that, although it is preferred by the local fishermen in strong westerly winds, it is not well enough marked for strangers, who anyway have no business to be entering this port in strong westerly winds. The central pass is the easiest, but is not deep enough to use at low water. The east pass is less easy to follow but is deep.

Central pass. This pass carries a least depth of 0.5m (1 ft). Identify a prominent white house with a single gable (see photo) on the shore a little to the right of the conspicuous water tower, and bring Le Pignon tower (red) into line with it, bearing 359°: alter course to maintain this transit.

This transit leaves Borenis spar buoy (stbd) 4 cables to starboard and La Traverse beacon $\frac{3}{4}$ cable to starboard, with a port hand beacon beyond it.

If the prominent white house cannot be identified, an alternative transit is with the water tower open to the left of Le Pignon tower by about 3 times the height of the latter, bearing 354°, until La Traverse is passed.

On close approach to Le Pignon tower, bear to starboard and leave the tower 40m to port. Thence steer to leave the Bayonelle beacon (stbd) 20m to starboard; this course leaves to starboard two beacons (stbd) on the south end of the Petite Bayonelle rocks and Men Drean beacon (port) to port.

After passing between the Bayonelle beacon and Men Drean beacon hold the same course for nearly 1 cable, until another starboard hand beacon has come in transit with Penerf village. Then alter course to steer ENE for the boats on moorings off the village over 1 mile away. Leave the beacon (stbd) $\frac{1}{2}$ cable to starboard, and a beacon (port) half way to the village about 1 cable to port, as it is well up on the mud.

East pass. This pass carries 4.5m (15 ft) if the directions are followed, but the pass is narrow and there are rocky shoals to the east of it which it is essential to avoid. Before finally committing the yacht to the pass, that is to say before passing the outer port hand beacon, the following marks should be positively identified:

The port hand beacon on the east side of La Traverse, and the Men Drean beacon (port) beyond Le Pignon tower; the starboard beacon replacing the former Bayonelle tower east of Men Drean, and the 2 starboard beacons opposite Le Pignon.

Approaching on the transit (030°) of the Tour de Penerf with the left hand edge of the village of Penerf, identify Le Tour du Parc church steeple. This steeple is difficult to see as it is almost obscured by trees, but it is in the clump of trees close to the leading line for the central pass (Le Pignon and the conspicuous white house in transit bearing 359°) and may be identified as this line is crossed. Continue on the 030° transit. If La Traverse (port) beacon has not been identified by the time Borenis spindle buoy (stbd) is abeam, distant about 3 cables, go back.

When La Traverse port hand beacon comes in transit with Le Tour du Parc church bearing 354°, steer on this transit. If the church is still not visible, its position may be established as follows: to the right of the conspicuous white house which is the rear mark for the central pass are two smaller houses, one with a red roof, the other black, all equally spaced. Imagine a fourth

Penerf slip. Anchor just this side of the moorings.

house in this row: Le Tour du Parc church would be in the high clump of trees immediately behind this imaginary house.

The transit leaves very close to starboard a rock with 2.8m (9 ft) over it. When within 100m of La Traverse beacon alter course to leave it 20m to port. After passing it continue to steer about 355° for another 50m until Men Drean beacon (port) has come open to the right of both the starboard beacons on La Petite Bayonelle, bearing about 320°. Steer on this alignment for about 1 cable and then alter course as necessary to leave the two starboard beacons 30m to starboard and Le Pignon tower to port. Thence follow the directions given above for the central pass.

When leaving by the east pass it is important to bring La Traverse beacon in transit with Le Tour du Parc church quickly in order to avoid getting on to the eastern rocks.

By night : Le Pignon is lit, with white sectors covering the central channel. But a fair amount of light would be needed to go up the river and strangers are not recommended to attempt a night entry. The light is:
Le Pignon; Fl (3) WR 12s, 6m, 9M.

Anchorage
The most convenient anchorage is off Penerf slip, just below the local boats on moorings. There is about 6m (20 ft) here. The end of the slip is marked by a beacon (stbd). About 1 cable upstream there is another BRB (isolated danger) beacon. This had one of its two spheres missing in 1981; it should be regarded as a port hand mark, and given a reasonable berth: local boats use the channel on the other side but it is neither wide nor deep. In this anchorage the holding is indifferent and the tides are strong; it would be very uncomfortable indeed in strong westerly winds on the ebb. But in normal conditions it is convenient and comfortable.

There is also anchorage in 3.5m (11 ft) 4 cables up river, off Cadenic; this is sheltered from the west and the tides are not so strong. There is a slip here marked by a beacon (port).

Facilities
All shops, cafés and restaurant at Penerf. Café but no shops at Cadenic, but a travelling shop calls daily; orders for it could, no doubt, be left at the café.

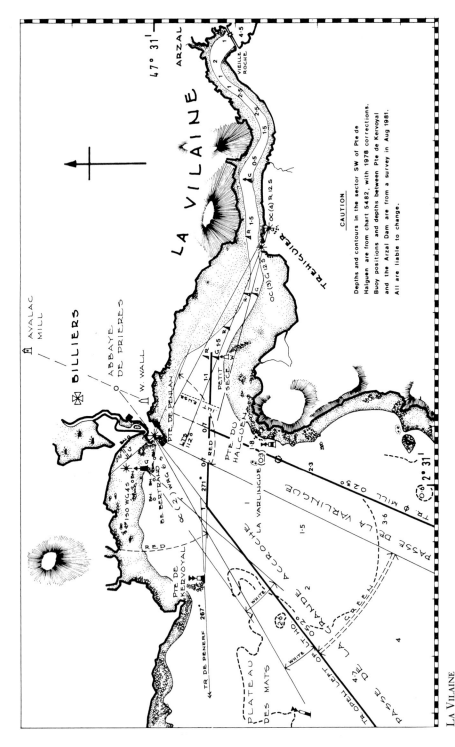

La Vilaine

MLWS 0.6m; MLWN 1.9m; −0010 Brest, Index 2, MTL 3.0m

Based on French Chart No. 5482 with corrections

Depths in metres; right hand margin in cables

Charts: 2353, 2646
High water: −0010 Brest, Index 2, MTL 3.0m
MHWS 5.4m (17.5 ft); MLWS 0.6m (2 ft); MHWN 4.2m (14 ft); MLWN 1.9m (6 ft)
Tidal streams. Not very strong but no official information.
Depths: Since the closure of the Arzal Dam, all charted depths have become unreliable due to silting. The outer passes have so far been little affected, but S of Pte de Penlan and thence to the dam depths have decreased so significantly as to necessitate buoying a new channel; depths and buoy positions are likely to change further from those surveyed in 1981.

On a summer's day few places are prettier than La Vilaine, running between meadows where cows ruminate, or between rush-covered banks or rocky cliffs.

Above the Arzal dam there is a tideless lake. This is not a tidal power scheme like that on the Rance, in north Brittany, with its rapid changes of level. The intention is to improve the river for drainage and navigation and to reactivate the port of Redon. So far no commercial traffic to Redon has developed.

At Redon the river connects with the Breton canal system, by which shallow draft yachts can travel between the Bay of Biscay and St Malo.

Approach and entrance
In the approach to La Vilaine the depths on the outer bar are not less than 1m (3 ft), except for La Varlingue, a rock drying 0.3m (1 ft), situated only ½ mile off Pointe du Halguen, which marks the SE side of the entrance. In good weather, with a sufficient rise of tide, it is only necessary to steer a mid-channel course.

With any sea or swell conditions are rough on the bar, especially on the ebb, and it is better to enter or leave on the last of the flood. Directions for the two recommended passes across the bar are given below, for use when the conditions call for them.

Passe de la Grande Accroche, the western pass, carries 1.5m (5 ft) least water and is lit, but the sea breaks heavily in it in strong onshore winds. Passe de la Varlingue, the eastern one, carries 1.3m (4 ft) and is not lit, but is preferable in heavy W or SW weather as the shallow part is inshore and gets some protection from the Grande Accroche bank to seaward. For both passes the principal landmark is the ancient abbey of Prières, a square tower inland to the NE of Penlan lighthouse on the prominent Pte de Penlan; it is too low to be visible when leaving the Vilaine. Also conspicuous is Billiers church, NE of Pte de Penlan.

Passe de la Grande Accroche. Approach with the tower of the Abbaye de Prières just open to the left of Penlan lighthouse, bearing 052°. This line leaves Plateau des Mâts buoy (card S) 6 cables to port and Basse de Kervoyal tower (card S) 6 cables to port. Shortly before the latter comes in transit with Penerf tower (white) bearing 267°, turn to starboard to make good 091°, with Basse de Kervoyal astern on 271°. This leads in 0.7m to the outer pair of small port and starboard spar

Tréhiguier, looking SW.   *Photo : D. Bremridge*

buoys north of the Petit Secé white tower. Follow the narrow channel defined by Nos 2, 4, 6, 8 port buoys, with starboard buoys Nos 1 and 5 opposite Nos 2 and 6. Note that the Tréhiguier lighthouses in transit define a line which now dries. East of Tréhiguier there is one starboard buoy with only 0.5m above it; thereafter the channel is narrow and unmarked, tending towards the outside of the bends.

By night : Approach in the white sector of Penlan light, between 052° and 060°. The sectors of Basse Bertrand light can be disregarded. When the intensified sector of the rear light at Tréhiguier opens red, at 106°, steer E to pass between the first pair of red/green channel buoys. Disregard the Tréhiguier light transit line, and follow the channel buoys to Tréhiguier, beyond which the channel is unlit. Due to channel changes a night entry should only be attempted when weather and tide conditions are very favourable. The lights are :
Penlan; Oc (2) WRG 6s, 25m, 16M.
Basse Bertrand; Iso WG 4s, 7m, 8M.
Tréhiguier, front; Oc (3) G 12s, 8m, 6M.

Arzal Dam: awaiting the bridge and lock, from upstream.

Tréhiguier, rear; Sync Dir Oc (4) R 12s, 21m, 11M.
Channel buoys; No. 1: Fl G 2s   No. 2: Fl R 2s
                                    No. 4: Fl (2) R 5s
           No. 5: Fl (3) G 6s No. 6: Fl (3) R 6s
                                    No. 8: Fl (4) R 7s

Passe de la Varlingue. This pass leads through a narrow channel between the shore and La Varlingue; the transit must be closely held. The leading marks are the tower of Abbaye de Prières in transit with a white wall beacon (in front) and Avalec Mill (1½ miles behind), bearing 023°; the wall beacon is not easy to locate. Follow this transit until the Petit Secé tower (white) bears 105°, then steer to make good 090° until Nos 1 and 2 starboard/port buoys N of Petit Secé are picked up.

The river
The lock is on the N side of the river, adjacent to the conspicuous control tower. The approach channels from above and below are marked by starboard hand buoys. The lock is worked on the hour during normal hours (0700–2100); it is not worked on public holidays, e.g. 14 July, 15 August. The sill level is 2m (6 ft) below datum, but there is only 1m just outside, preventing use close to LW; the level above the lock is maintained at 4.5m (15 ft) above datum (3.5m (11 ft) during floods). At high water springs there may, therefore, be a small drop on passing through the lock into the river. The road bridge over the lock is raised as necessary to allow masted vessels to pass. Securing in the lock is awkward, but the yacht should be properly secured and the ropes tended as the water level changes; there can be substantial turbulence. Do not be in a hurry to unmoor, because there will be further turbulence when the gates open and salt and fresh water mix.

The river is very beautiful for some distance above La Roche Bernard; farther up the hills draw away and the scenery is less interesting. Masted vessels can go all the way to Redon, which is a town of some character. There is a swing bridge at Cran, which is often slow to open, and has been known to stick altogether in very hot weather.

La Roche Bernard. Village and river marina, from the Bridge.

La Roche Bernard, looking downstream from the rock above St Antoine creek marina.

Above the dam a mid-channel course should be followed. Be careful not to cut corners, rather tend to keep to the outside. A few special dangers are marked on the lateral system.

Anchorages and facilities
Tréhiguier. A convenient anchorage near the entrance; it is exposed to W and NW winds. Anchor outside the moorings of local craft in soft mud. Land at the slip; restaurant.

Vieille Roche. An excellent anchorage, completely sheltered, on the starboard bank just below the dam. Anchor outside the moorings. There is a landing slip, but it is about a 2 mile walk to the shops.

Arzal. A marina with 6 pontoons off the south bank, and many moorings above the dam. Much development in hand on the north bank.

La Roche Bernard. Excellent anchorage and several moorings in the river. There is a marina in the small inlet on the starboard side, but the berths are often all reserved. There is another marina in the river below the bridge, and many mooring buoys. All shops in the town, $\frac{1}{4}$ mile walk up the hill; water and fuel by hose at the quay. Hot showers can be had, and there are facilities for washing clothes at the 'camping' near the marina. There is a yacht chandlery and marine engineer. There are a number of excellent restaurants in the town.

196

La Roche Bernard: the bridge, with abutments of earlier bridges.

Redon. A small marina has been built in the old dock, surrounded by picturesque old warehouses. There is little commercial traffic, though a few barges use the dock. There are all shops in the town, which is a major rail centre, offering good communications.

The Breton Canals. The canals offer a convenient route for shallow draught yachts which do not relish the long haul round the western end of France, where the seas can be rough. Any yacht which can safely reach the Channel Islands can easily get from there to St Malo and thence have a rural passage to the interesting and relatively sheltered waters of Quiberon Bay. The passage is especially attractive to motor yachts, but there are cranes at each end which the crew can use to lay the mast of a sailing yacht on deck; the crew should be sufficiently experienced to do this without calling on outside help. For limits of size, width must not exceed 4.5m (14 ft 9 ins) and headroom above waterline 2.4m (7 ft 10 ins). Permissible draught varies, but will never be more than 1.3m (4 ft 3 ins), 1.2m or 1.1m are more usual official limts, and if rainfall has been low, 1m may be difficult.

The normal, and quickest, route is from St Malo to Redon and thence to the sea via the Vilaine, about 130 nautical miles with 62 locks. The locks are worked from 0630 till 1930, with a short lunch break. There are speed limits of 6 km/h ($3\frac{1}{4}$ knots) in the canal north of Rennes, and 10 km/h ($5\frac{1}{4}$ knots) in the river between Rennes and Redon. By keeping going reasonably hard the passage can be made in five days. It is also possible to turn aside at Redon and go up to Josselin; from there 'over the hill' to Lorient the draught limit is 0.8m (2 ft 9 in). For Nantes, leave the Vilaine at Bellions lock; the canal from Redon is now closed.

No permit is now required, nor is any charge made for a single return journey, but enquiry should be made from the French Government Tourist Office, 179 Piccadilly, London, W1V 0AL for a list of the dates when the canals will be closed for maintenance. This period normally begins about September and lasts up to one month. There is little or no commercial traffic except for about 20 km to the S of Rennes: it is an advantage to plan to pass this section on a Sunday.

The lock keepers are careful in letting in the water, and with ordinary care no damage is to be

197

Haute Roche has the gayest garden on the Canal.

expected, but plenty of good fenders should be carried. There are strong currents as a lock fills and the yacht must be securely moored and the lines tended as the water rises; moor near the lower gates if possible, but somebody has to be in front if two or three yachts share a lock. It is a help to fit blocks at bow and stern so that the mooring lines can be led to the cockpit and tended by one person; on sailing yachts they will most easily be led round the sheet winches. Officially the lock keepers are not required to help with mooring lines and a crew member should go ashore to handle the lines; help with the gates is appreciated and will speed the passage. N of Rennes there are ladders in many locks and there is little difficulty in getting ashore. S of Rennes the gates are more difficult to climb and the lock keepers will usually help willingly by taking shore lines.

An invaluable canal guide with 1/25000 strip maps is published by ECM, obtainable from McCarta Ltd, 122 King's Cross Rd, London WC1 9DS.

There are cranes to help in masting at Dinan and Redon, the limits which can be reached by masted vessels; there are cranes at St Malo and La Roche Bernard, but these deprive one of some pleasant sailing; there are also cranes at Nantes and Lorient for those using these variants.

The Route

St Malo–Dinan. Accessible to masted vessels. The lock at Le Châtelier is only available for about 4 hours during the high water period in the Rance. The upper reaches are shallow out of the channel, but this is clearly marked.

Dinan–Rennes. Ille et Rance Canal. A straightforward canal section, with 47 locks, of which 11

198

A peaceful scene on the Ille et Rance Canal.

Boel lock, where the Vilaine has cut through a hill range. Note the unguarded weir.

in quick succession climb to the summit. Yachts of draught near the maximum will have trouble with soft mud in places. This mud is carried in by water courses joining the canal. If you begin to drag try to see which side the flow has come in; the best water will be near the opposite bank. Having found it, open up the engine and force a way through; the bad patches are not very long.

Rennes–Redon. Canalised portion of the River Vilaine. There are 12 locks. This river is wider and the best water is usually about one third of the way from the towpath bank (left bank to Pont Réan, right bank thereafter). There is a channel of the requisite depth all the way, but it is easy to get out of it and go aground. In some places the distance of the channel from the bank is indicated by notices on the towing path with an arrow head and a figure indicating the distance in metres. But there are other shallows, and if an echo sounder is available it is well to use it regularly between Boel and Mâlon. Do not trust the advice of fishermen; they have seen shallow draught hire boats travelling in parts of the river outside the proper channel and imagine that all boats can take the same course. Beware of fishermen, who tend to leave their rods and lines *in situ* while lunching elsewhere, and expect yachts to see and avoid them.

Redon. The normal route to the sea is straight ahead through the sluice. In flood turn right and pass through two locks into the dock. Having passed the sluice, turn sharp right at the junction if you want to enter the dock, straight on and then turn left for the sea.

Facilities

Nearly all the villages on the route have a café-restaurant which can supply a very adequate meal at a reasonable price; one is off the tourist route and does not have to pay tourist prices. They also have food shops. A number of the lock keepers are pleased to sell farm and garden produce. Water can be had at the 'campings' at Tinteniac (where it sometimes tastes of chlorine) and Pont Réan, the quays at Guipry, Port Roche and Redon and by hose at Beslé. There are hot showers at Pont Réan, cold at Tinteniac. There is a launderette near the yacht berths at Rennes and clothes washing facilities at Tinteniac and Pont Réan.

Charts: 2353, 3216, 2646
High water: −0020 Brest, Index 1, MTL 3.2m
MHWS 5.6m; MLWS 0.6m; MHWN 4.3m; MLWN 2.0m
Tidal streams: In the middle of the Baie du Croisic the streams are rotatory clockwise and weak, at HW Brest the direction is SE and at LW Brest it is N, spring rates 1 knot. Between the Pointe du Croisic and the Plateau du Four the pattern is similar, but the rates are greater, the greatest rate being $2\frac{3}{4}$ knots SW at +0250 Brest. The streams in the entrance to the harbour are very strong; west of the Mahon rocks they exceed the reputed 4 knots at springs.
Depths: On the leading line the channel is dredged to 1.2m (4 ft) as far as the 'zeroth entrance' (see below), to 0.5m (1 ft) as far as the second entrance, and dries 0.3m (1 ft) as far as the fifth entrance. Depths in the pool run up to 2.5m (8 ft), but the best spots are occupied by moorings. Inside the harbour, depths vary from drying 1.3m (5 ft) in the first *chambre* to drying 1 to 3.5m (7 to 12 ft) in the last.

The harbour of Le Croisic is situated in the SE corner of the Rade du Croisic. The town is a popular holiday resort with a fishing harbour, and is associated with Batz and La Baule to the eastward to form a district which is noted for its bathing sands and holiday amenities. There is a yacht builder and substantial yachting activity.

The harbour dries out, but there are good sheltered anchorages off it, though the best spots are now taken by permanent moorings. The entrance channel is shallow and is exposed to the W and NW and in fresh onshore winds is rough, owing to the shallow and irregular bottom. If approached on the flood with sufficient rise of tide it presents no difficulty.

Approach
The streams are strong and for this reason the best time for entry at springs is within the last hour of the flood, when the streams are weakening. It is difficult to enter against the ebb. At neaps there is more latitude, and by following all the transits a yacht can use the channel at any state of the tide.

Approaching from the south the extensive Plateau du Four with its conspicuous lighthouse lies on the west side and the Pointe du Croisic with off-lying rocks to the E. Near the eastern side of the passage is the Basse Castouillet, with a least depth of 0.3m (1 ft). This shoal is marked on its western side by a buoy (card W). After leaving this buoy to starboard steer about 045° towards La Turballe, which lies ahead conspicuously, until the leading marks for Le Croisic are in line. A short cut may, however, be made in reasonable weather by passing nearly midway between the Basse Castouillet buoy and the Pointe du Croisic. The leading marks for this approach are a white beacon on the shore to the northward of Le Croisic jetty in transit with the mill of Trévaly, bearing 058°. The mill is a stone mill tower with a conical top; there are some white houses on the hill behind it, with which it must not be confused. These marks are quite clear in a good afternoon light. The passage carries 1.5m (5 ft) least water; it leaves the Hergo tower (stbd) off the entrance, 2 cables to starboard.

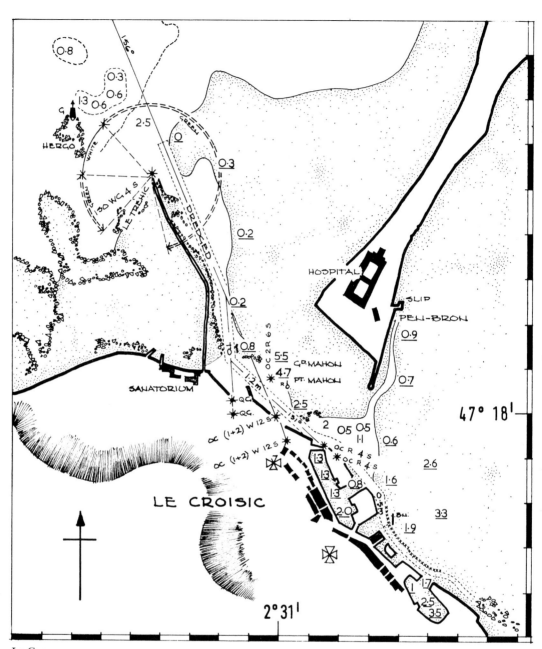

LE CROISIC
MLWS 0.6m; MLWN 2.0m; −0020 Brest, Index 1, MTL 3.2m
Based on French Chart No. 139 with corrections
Depths in metres; right hand margin in cables

On the left, the leading marks for the first line are indicated; from this viewpoint the rear mark is almost hidden by trees. On the right the marks for the intermediate line are indicated.

Approaching from the west or north west steer into the bay until the leading marks are identified.

Entrance
The prominent features of Le Croisic are the hospital on Pen Bron peninsula on the NE side of the harbour, the sanatorium on the SW side and the big church with a high belfry immediately behind the harbour. Steer in with the church bearing 157°. The leading light structures are close below the church. They are white pylons; the front has a GW check topmark, the rear a rectangular board painted with dark green and yellow chevrons. As soon as they are identified bring them in transit, bearing 156°.

On close approach the Hergo tower (stbd) will be left nearly 2 cables to starboard and the transit leads in about 100m E of the end of Le Tréhic breakwater. To port the sands dry. Proceed up the channel inside the breakwater on the transit of the leading lights. The inshore end of this line leads across rocks drying 0.8m (3 ft), which can be safely crossed if entry is made near high water. If they cannot be crossed safely the intermediate transit must be followed.

The intermediate transit, bearing 174°, consists of two rectangular white boards, with a thin black vertical stripe, situated at the left hand end of a line of trees, whose right hand end is behind the lifeboat house. These come in transit when the vessel is about opposite the sharp bend in the breakwater.

At sufficient rise of tide the intermediate transit is disregarded, and the vessel continues on the main transit, bearing 156°, leaving to port the red tower on the Grand Mahon rock. When this tower is abeam the leading marks for the final line will come in transit, bearing 134°; the marks are RW tanks with RW cheq openwork topmarks, situated on the outside edge of the first *jonchère*. Follow this transit until well past the front main leading mark pylon; then steer to leave the quays about 50m to starboard.

If the intermediate transit has been followed, leave it when the marks for the final line come

Red and white chequered boards, indicated here, are the marks for the final leading line.

in transit, bearing 134°, as above. If one is late on the tide one meets an ebb which runs like a torrent off the Grand Mahon at springs.

By night : Follow the transits as by day. Notice particularly that the white sector of Le Tréhic light, which leads clear of the distant dangers, such as Le Four and Ile Dumet, leads right onto the nearby rocks, and the close approach must be made in the green sector. The street lighting on the quays is good, and there is no difficulty once they are reached. The lights are:

Tréhic jetty; Iso WG 4s, 12m, 13M, Reed 15s.

Main leading light, front; Oc (––·) W 12s, 10m, 18M.

Main leading light, rear; Sync Oc (–––·) W 12s, 14m, 18M.

Intermediate transit; Q G (both).

Final transit; Dir Oc R 4s (both sync), 134°.

Grand Mahon; Oc (2) R 6s, 6m, 4M.

The pool, with Pen Bron hospital in the background.

Black Jack is aground just inside the first *chambre*. Pen Bron hospital and the rear leading mark for the final line in the background.

Mooring and anchorage

There is a fair sized pool, which provides good anchorage, though much of it is occupied by yachts on moorings. The position is shown approximately on the plan, and it will be necessary to take soundings to find where there is enough water clear of the moorings. There is an inlet to the east of the jetty on Pen Bron, the peninsula opposite the town, on which the hospital stands. This inlet has a fair depth of water, but is very narrow and steep-sided and well occupied by moorings. The ebb runs very hard in the inlet and even in the anchorage the streams are strong.

The harbour has a curious pattern of islands called *jonchères*, with backwaters behind them called *chambres*, in which vessels lie. The original character has been changed by the building of bridges to the islands, so that now only one remains in its original isolated state. The original first entrance is now blocked, so that it is convenient to call it the 'zeroth' entrance: when first seen it looks as though it is going to be an entrance; it is only as it opens up that it is seen to be blocked. Scouring sluices have been left in the base of the block, so be ready for a set in or out.

The fifth *chambre*, almost exclusively used by yachts, now developed as a yacht harbour. Yachts now berth end on to pontoons.

The channel leading to the fifth *chambre*, about half tide. The training wall extends some way seaward of the first beacon. The white roof is the yacht yard at the far side of the fifth *chambre*. The photograph was taken from the second *jonchère*.

The first entrance gives on to the first, largest and most popular *chambre*. To port there is a patent slip and scrubbing hard. A good place to try for a berth is just inside to starboard, where the bottom dries about 1.3m (4 ft), see photograph. Here one is away from the bustle of the quay and there is room to set up a line to hold the yacht against the wall. Fishing vessels occupy most of the town side of this *chambre*.

The second entrance gives on to a short *chambre*; to port is the fish market, and the quays must be left for fishing vessels. There might be a place on the starboard side, though it also is used by fishing boats.

The third and fourth entrances give on to a small *chambre*, which is shallower than the previous ones. Between them is the only remaining island *jonchère*. The quay by the fish market must be left. It might be possible to find a berth to starboard of the fourth entrance, but when the tide is out there is no way of getting ashore.

The fifth entrance leads to a *chambre* which is the principal yacht harbour. There are pontoons for small craft and elsewhere yachts lie bows to the wall with a stern line to moorings. Visitors are usually directed to starboard on entering. The *chambre* dries at low water.

If proceeding above the second entrance, notice that there is a training wall marked by red beacons. The training wall extends some distance seaward of the first beacon, as indicated on the plan. There are proposals to make a deep-water quay for yachts.

Facilities
The facilities are those of a fishing and yachting port. All shops, many restaurants and hotels, sea food sold on the quay. Yacht yard, marine engineer. Water, petrol and diesel by hose on the port side of the fifth entrance; water also on the quay in the first *chambre*, near the seaward end. Railway station and buses to La Baule, where there is an airport.

206

Charts: 3216, 2646
High water: —0035 Brest springs, —0020 Brest neaps, Index 1, MTL 2.9m
MHWS 5.4m; MLWS 0.5m; MHWN 4.1m; MLWN 1.7m
Tidal streams: The tidal streams in the offing are irregular in direction, the flood running generally in the easterly quadrant, and the ebb in the westerly quadrant, rates up to about 1½ knots. In the north of the bay itself the tide runs always westerly. In the river the tidal streams are strong.
Depths: The Le Pouliguen entrance dries nearly 1.5m (5 ft). In the pool in the outer part of the harbour there is water to float yachts up to 1.8m (6 ft) draft. The marina at Pornichet has 2.8m in the main berths.

La Baule is a sophisticated international beach resort with a casino and innumerable hotels and restaurants of all grades. It may be reached by train and by air to St Nazaire or its own smaller airport. There are two harbours, Le Pouliguen and Pornichet. The approach to the former dries out and it is essential for strangers to enter around high water. Pornichet is a modern, marina type yacht harbour providing 1,100 berths for yachts of all sizes. It is available at all states of the tide. The bay is sheltered from northerly and westerly winds and is often smooth in summer. Both harbours are very crowded in the high season and vessels over 10m long are frequently turned away from Le Pouliguen.

Approach to Le Pouliguen
Le Pouliguen is situated in the NW corner of the bay of the same name, and is some 6 miles E of Le Croisic. The best approach from any direction is the western passage between the Pointe de Penchâteau on the west side of the bay and the ledges and rocks to the SE which extend nearly 4 miles to the Grand Charpentier lighthouse. Even from the east it is easier to approach south of the Grand Charpentier along the Chenal du Nord in the entry to the Loire. There is an inshore passage from the east which can be followed, using chart No. 3216; this channel joins the western channel south of the Vieille beacon.

The approach is sheltered from the N, through W to SW, but southerly swell breaks in the shallow water, and it is fully exposed to the SE. The sands shift and if the available margin of depth is very small it is worth seeking advice from local yachtsmen or the club boatman.

Leave the Penchâteau red pillar buoy 100m to port. Thence steer NNE to leave the Basse Martineau buoy (port) also 100m to port. There is an anchorage about 2 cables NNW of this buoy where a yacht may await the tide in good weather.

Entrance
Shortly before HW proceed towards the entrance, leaving La Vieille beacon (stbd) and Les Petits Impairs tower (stbd) well to starboard, and two red beacons well to port. Close to the harbour entrance there are five black beacons to be left to starboard, and one red beacon to be left to port. The channel usually lies closer to the red beacons than to the black ones.

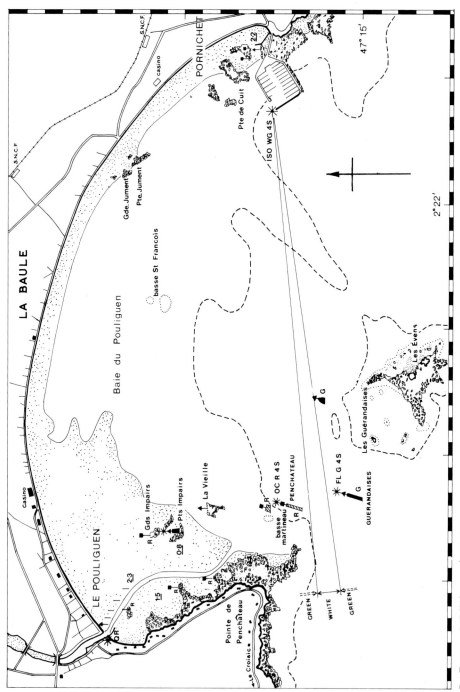

LA BAULE

LE POULIGUEN

PORNICHET

Baie du Pouliguen

Gde. Jument

Pte. Jument

basse St Francois

Pte de Cuit

ISO WG 4S

47° 15'

2° 22'

Gds Impairs

Pts Impairs

La Vieille

R

0.8

2.3

1.5

R

R

R

OR

Casino

Pointe de Penchâteau

Le Croisic

basse
martineau

PENCHATEAU

OC R 4S

2.2 R

R

FL G 4S

G

G

GUERANDAISES

Les Guérandaises

Les Evens

GREEN

WHITE

GREEN

casino

S.N.C.F.

S.N.C.F.

LA BAULE   MLWS 0.5m; MLWN 1.7m; −0035 (sp), −0020 (np) Brest, Index 1, MTL 2.9m
Based on ECM Chart No. 547   Depths in metres; right hand margin in cables

208

The approach to Le Pouliguen, with beacons on each side. The slender white lighthouse is left to port.

Approach the entrance with the church spire open between the pier heads. The lighthouse on the west pier head is a very slender white structure. This should be left to port and the vessel then proceeds between stone embankments. Special care must be taken on near approach to the entrance as the channel is narrow between high sands on either side. On the starboard side a slender wooden beacon marks the end of a training wall; it lies well inside the line of rather thicker iron beacons marking the approach and must not be overlooked.

By night: The lights are few in number, and some local knowledge is desirable for a night entry. The lights are:
Les Guérandaises by; Fl G 4s.
Penchâteau by; Oc R 4s, 4m, 5M.
Les Petits Impairs; Fl (2) G 6s.
Le Pouliguen, S Jetty; Q R, 13m, 9M.
Pornichet, W breakwater head; Iso WG 4s, 9m, 10M.

Mooring
Deeper draft yachts moor fore and aft to buoys on the La Baule (east) side near the entrance. Shallower drafts and those which can take the ground moor and warp to pontoons farther up. Berths are allocated by the club boatman. Visitors should moor temporarily to the first quay on the starboard hand (where the fuel pumps are) and ask for a berth to be allocated.

Facilities

The Yacht Club is a large and clearly labelled building on the La Baule side above the first road bridge. It is hospitable to visitors and its boatman acts as harbour master. There are all shops handy in Le Pouliguen, yacht yards, chandlers and marine engineers are all close at hand. There are many hotels and restaurants. All the facilities of a sophisticated sailing centre. Water by hose at the pontoons; petrol and diesel by hose on quay to starboard entering.

The first quay to starboard, showing the moorings.

Approach to Pornichet
From the Penchateau and Guérandaises light buoys the white lighthouse at the end of the outer mole can be made out amongst the buildings at the eastern end of La Baule, bearing 083°, and course should be altered towards it. An unlit green conical buoy marking the northern extremity of the Guérandaises shoal is left to starboard.

Entrance. The entrance faces N, and it is not till close approach that the red and green beacons marking the underwater projections from the pierheads will become clear, and course must be altered to pass between them.

By night. The approach is covered by the White sector of Pornichet pierhead light, which can be seen from 081° to 084°. This sector just excludes the Penchateau light buoy and the Guérandaises unlit starboard hand buoy; the Guérandaises light buoy lies 2 cables S of this white sector. The beacons in the entrance show flashing red and green lights. The lights are:
Penchateau by; Oc R 4s. 4m, 5M.
Les Guérandaises by; Fl G 4s.
Pornichet pierhead light; Iso WG 4s.
Pornichet entrance West; Fl G 2s.
Pornichet entrance East: Fl R 2s.

Mooring There are 10 pontoons, A–J on the southern side of the harbour and 4, K–N on the northern. The heads of all of these are allocated to visitors, together with the whole of pontoon J and the west side of pontoon I, although these are both suitable only for boats under 6m length. All the main berths carry a depth of 2.80m and as the bottom is soft mud, vessels of deeper draft will sink their keels into it and remain upright. Charges are substantial.

Facilities
VHF Channel 9. Fuel barge immediately to port on entry. Water and electricity are laid onto the pontoons. Yacht yard with travel lift of 24 tonnes capacity. Ice, showers, restaurant and chandlery shop (chart agent) in marina, with groceries and a good wine merchant.
   Across the bridge to the mainland there are many shops, hotels and restaurants.

Pornichet marina: the entrance, looking E.

Charts: 3216, 2646
High water: −0035 Brest springs, −0010 Breast neaps, Index 2, MTL 3.0m
MHWS 5.4m; MLWS 0.7m; MHWN 4.1m; MLWN 1.7m
Tidal streams: Outside the flood runs E, the ebb W, spring rates 1¾ knots. The streams in the harbour are weak.
Depths: Off the yacht harbour there is 2m (6 ft). Inside this the depths shoal rapidly. The channel dries 1m (3 ft) as far as the entrance to the inner harbour. Inside the inner harbour the north quays dry about 1.3m (4 ft), the south quays about 1·8m (6 ft).

The Baie de Bourgneuf is a big wide bay east of the Loire, formed between the mainland to the north and east and the Ile de Noirmoutier on the south. The bay is exposed to the W and shallows progressively. There is plenty of water for yachts and although there are many shoals and rocks, they are, with the exception of the Kerouars bank in the northern part, well marked, so that there are few navigational difficulties except in thick weather. There is no exit from the bay to the south between Ile de Noirmoutier and the mainland, as there is a causeway drying at low water, across which there is insufficient depth at any state of the tide.

The harbours, however, are poor except for Pornic and L'Herbaudière. Those on Ile de Noirmoutier are described in the next chapter. Pornic harbour, situated half way along the northern shore of the Baie de Bourgneuf, is rather off the usual route for foreign yachts. The harbour is easy of access in reasonable weather and supports considerable local yachting activity. It is a pretty little place which is well worth a visit. Bluebeard's castle overlooks the harbour just seaward of the quays.

Approach
In the outer approach from the SW the outlying dangers to the north of Ile de Noirmoutier are well marked by a series of buoys and towers, but from the NW care must be taken to avoid the Banc de Kerouars, which is unmarked except for a buoy (stbd) 1 mile off its western end and a buoy N of La Couronnée, a rock near the western end which dries 1.9m (6 ft). The least depth near the eastern end is 1m (3 ft). To the north of the bank there is a passage, which is over ½ mile wide and ¾ mile off the land, or entry can be made south of the bank, if it is not safely covered.

Leave the tower on Notre Dame (BRB, topmark two spheres) about ½ mile to starboard and the marina to port with the lighthouse behind it. The lighthouse is not very conspicuous.

Entrance
The inner harbour dries about 1.3m (4 ft) and it is assumed that no attempt will be made to go up the harbour unless the tide has risen sufficiently to float the yacht there. On this basis

Pornic marina.

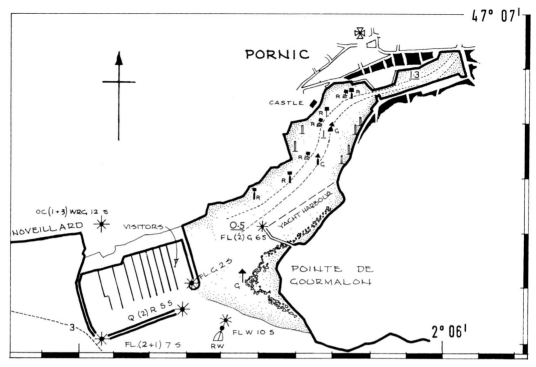

PORNIC   LWS 0.7m; MLWN 1.7m; −0030 (sp), −0027 (np) Brest, Index 2, MTL 3.0m
Based on French Chart No. 5039, and *Instructions Nautiques*, Planche No. 60
Depths in metres; right hand margin in cables

there is sufficient water in the outer part of the harbour provided that course is set roughly near the centre. Just beyond the marina a beacon marks a rock to starboard. The breakwater, which extends from the E side of the entrance (Pointe de Gourmalon), is marked at its end by a GW beacon.

About half way up the harbour the narrow dredged channel begins. It is marked by port and starboard buoys and posts, as shown on the plan. The posts should not be confused with various other posts, mostly white, erected for swimmers to dive from. There is a silting problem in the harbour east of the marina entrance, and entry should not be attempted near LW.

The approach to Pornic inner harbour; buoys, beacons and a bathing pole can be seen.

Pornic harbour, looking downstream past Bluebeard's Castle to the marina in the distance.

By night: The white sector of the main light clears the Banc de Kerouars. The marina and Gourmalon yacht harbour can be reached, but strangers should not attempt to go up the harbour. The lights are:

Pointe de Noveillard; Oc (— — · ·) WRG 12s, 22m, 14M.
Marina elbow; Fl (2 + 1) W 7s.
Marina SW breakwater head; Q (2) R 5s, 4m, 2M.
Marina E breakwater head; Fl G 2 sec, 4m, 2M.
Gourmalon breakwater head: Fl (2) G 6s.
Fairway buoy; Fl W 10s.

Anchorage and mooring

Berth in the marina; visitors use the eastern pontoon. Yachts which can take the ground can use the Gourmalon yacht harbour.

Yachts can also berth alongside the quays in the inner harbour. The quay on the north side in the entrance to the inner harbour is prohibited, and immediately inside the entrance to port is the berth reserved for the Noirmoutier ferry. The north side is the best, though it is principally used by fishing vessels. Not only is the water deeper here (dries 1.3m, 4 ft), but the quay is stone faced with many recessed ladders. On the south side, where the local yachts mostly berth, the mud dries about 1.8m (6 ft), and the quay is faced with vertical wooden rubbing piles, though there are again plenty of ladders.

Facilities

The facilities of a small holiday town. All shops and several restaurants and hotels. Marine engineer. Diesel by hose at the south quay; petrol close by. Communications by bus and branch railway line. All facilities at the marina. Club house with showers at Gourmalon yacht harbour.

213

Charts: 2646, 2647
Tidal information is given below for the NE side of the island; for Fromentine see page 215.
High water: −0020 Brest, Index 2, MTL 2.8m
MHWS 5.4m; MLWS 0.3m; MHWN 4.0m; MLWN 1.6m
Tidal streams: In the middle of the entrance to the Baie de Bourgneuf the tide is rotatory clockwise: at +0450 Brest N, ½ knot springs; at −0300 Brest E, 1 knot; at −0100 Brest S, ½ knot; at +0250 Brest W, 1½ knots springs. In Chenal de la Grise, at the NW end of the island NE begins −0615 Brest, 2 knots springs; SW begins −0145 Brest, 3 knots springs. Off Bois de la Chaise SE begins −0545 Brest, NW begins −0040 Brest, spring rates 2 knots.
Depths: L'Herbaudière has about 2m; less in the entrance channel. Bois de la Chaise has about 1.5m (5 ft). Noirmoutier dries about 2.5m (8 ft).

The Ile de Noirmoutier is a long, narrow, sandy island measuring about 9 miles from NW to SE. It is separated from the mainland by the narrow Goulet de Fromentine. North of Fromentine is a road from the mainland to the island over a causeway which covers, but is so high that it is not safe for a keelboat to attempt the crossing even at high water. A bridge has been built across the Goulet.

The island, which was invaded by the English in 1388, by the Spanish in 1524 and by the Dutch in 1674, is now invaded only by crowds of summer holiday makers. L'Herbaudière in the north has a marina in rather a bleak spot. It is, however, a convenient passage anchorage. Bois de la Chaise is an open anchorage, though with enough shelter to be the summer base of many yachts. Noirmoutier town dries and can only be reached near high water (high water springs for deep draft yachts) and Fromentine is approached over a shallow bar exposed to westerly winds and swell, though it is easily accessible at high water in offshore winds.

There are shoals and rocks extending a long way off the island; they are adequately marked, but call for care in the approach.

Approach
The approach is not simplified by the fact that the island lies on the overlap of two charts, both of scale about ½ in to the mile. The French chart 5039, which covers it and the approaches on a scale of 1½ in to the mile, is to be preferred.

The approach from the N or NW is straightforward on chart 2646. A useful lead is to keep La Blanche Abbey, on the shoreline, in transit with Noirmoutier church spire, bearing 142°. Although there are a number of shoals—le Four, la Banche, Kerouars—to be avoided, they lie in the approaches to St Nazaire and the Loire and are consequently very well marked.

From the S or SE, unless going to Fromentine, it will be necessary to clear Les Boeufs, after which one can pass through the Chenal de la Grise. This channel carries 3.3m (11 ft). It is marked on its NW side by a buoy (card S), and on its SE side by a beacon (card W) off Pointe de l'Herbaudière, which should be given a berth of at least 1 cable. Basse du Martroger

L'Herbaudière harbour near LW. Yachts berth right, fishing boats left, of this centre channel.

tower (card N), in transit with the Pte de l'Herbaudière beacon, bearing 050°, clears all the dangers of Les Boeufs. A mid-channel lead is the tower of Ste Marie Church, on the mainland, in transit with Martroger tower, bearing 058°. On close approach pass rather closer to the buoy than the beacon, and steer to leave the Basse du Martroger tower 1 cable to starboard. There are shoals to the E and ENE of Basse du Martroger; although there is a beacon on these shoals it is $\frac{1}{2}$ mile inside the northern edge. A safe course is to keep the Pte de l'Herbaudière beacon in transit with Basse du Martroger tower, bearing 230° astern, until the Basse des Pères buoy (card E) bears 090°, when alter course to pass 1 cable south of it. Thence steer to give the Pointe des Dames a reasonable berth. The Pointe des Dames is a steep headland, heavily wooded; only the top of the lighthouse shows above the trees. A wooden pier projects from the headland. At low water it will be necessary to keep clear of the Banc de la Chaise, with a least depth of 1.4m (4 ft).

By night: The following directions lead to L'Herbaudière.

From the north west. Approach in the white sector of Basse du Martroger light, bearing 124° to 153°, and thence in the white sector of L'Herbaudière light. Finally, leave the Fl G light buoy close to starboard.

From the south. Go through the Chenal de la Grise in the white sector of Basse du Martroger light, bearing between 055° and 060°. When l'Herbaudière light turns white steer in this sector for the harbour leaving the Fl G light buoy close to starboard. The lights are:
Point de St Gildas; Q WRG, 23m, 15M.
    Radiobeacon, call NZ, 289.6 kHz, 1/6 min, begins H + 1 min.
Ile du Pilier; Fl (3) W 20s, 33m, 29M, Horn (3) 1 min.
    also aux light (covers Les Boeufs); Q R, 10m, 12M.
    Radiobeacon, call PR, 298.8 kHz, continuous, 10M.

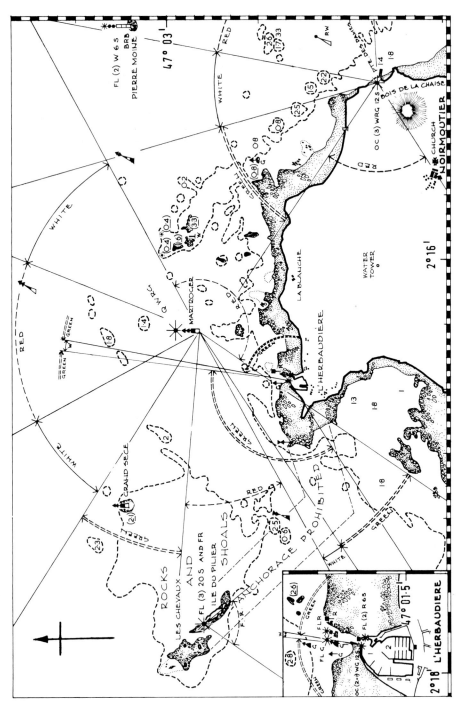

L'HERBAUDIÈRE   MLWS 0.3m; MLWN 1.6m; −0020 Brest, Index 2, MTL 2.8m
Based on French Chart No. 5039 with corrections   Depths in metres; right hand margin in cables

216

Bois de la Chaise. *Black Jack* is lying on a mooring, but later in the season there might be no mooring free. Pointe des Dames lighthouse just shows over the treetops.

Basse du Martroger; Q WRG 10m, 12M.
L'Herbaudière West mole; Oc (––·) WG 12s, 9m, 10M, Reed 30 sec.
L'Herbaudière, East mole; Fl (2) R 6s.
L'Herbaudière by; Fl G.
Pointe des Dames; Oc (3) WRG 12s, 34m, 17M.
La Pierre Moine; Fl (2) W 6s, 14m, 8M.

L'Herbaudière

No special directions are needed. Make a point W of Basse du Martroger tower, as described in the approach, and steer for the harbour entrance in transit with L'Herbaudière church, bearing 185°. There are two starboard buoys and one port in the near approach, and a port hand beacon at the foot of the new east side spur, which gives added protection to the harbour. The west side is a busy fishing port. The entrance to the marina is said to be dredged to 1.3m (4 ft), the berths to 2m (6 ft), but in 1980 an obstruction was reported with only 0.8m in the entrance. It is possible to anchor outside, keeping clear of the fairway, but the bottom is rocky in places. The anchorage is exposed to most winds.

There are all the facilities of a marina, and all shops near the harbour. The pontoon immediately to port in the marina is reserved for visitors.

There is an open anchorage in the bay to the south of L'Herbaudière in 1.5m (5 ft), sand, sheltered from all easterly winds. There are rocks in the approach and French chart 5039 is needed. With this there should be no difficulty in approach.

Bois de la Chaise

This open anchorage is sheltered from the W and S. It is exposed to the N and E, but the fetch is not more than 5 miles, and in summer many yachts lie on moorings here. It is an attractive situation though the facilities are limited.

Approach and anchorage
Keep Pointe des Dames lighthouse bearing more than 165°, and less than 191° if it is necessary to clear Banc de la Chaise, which has 1.4m (4 ft) over it. On close approach steer parallel

with the shore, leaving the wooden pier to starboard, and the buoys marking a wreck to port.

There are four lines of private moorings. Unless permission can be obtained to use one it will be necessary to anchor outside. Land at the steps halfway along the pier; the end must be left clear for the ferries. There are some moorings for visitors.

Facilities
Two restaurants, a paper shop and a patisserie (which does not sell bread). Good shops in Noirmoutier, 1½ miles walk. There is a big camp site behind the beach to the south. In the summer a general shop opens there to serve the camp and there is also a butcher (July and August only). To reach them it is easier to land on the beach to the south of the anchorage than to land at the pier and walk round.

Noirmoutier
This port is approached by a circuitous route through the rocks, and thence up a long, straight, narrow channel. It should be regarded as drying 2.5m (8 ft), and is therefore not accessible to deep draft yachts at neaps, but more water can be found by close attention to the following directions.

The channel swings steadily to starboard, leaving a succession of port hand beacons about 1 cable to port. It is assumed that entry will not be made until there is water farther in, and at such times there is considerable latitude near the outer beacons. Pass the third last beacon, Goemonhour, at a distance of 50m and steer for the second last beacon, Atelier, bearing about 260°; the channel now becomes narrow. As a check, the prolongation of the line of the inner training wall will be crossed about halfway between these two beacons.

Pass the Atelier beacon at a distance of 10m, do not steer straight from it to the last beacon, Mariolle, but borrow about 30m to starboard, returning to leave the Mariolle 10m to port. After passing the beacon borrow sharply to port before returning to leave the breakwater head, with the light structure, 10 m to port. Follow the breakwater round at a distance of 10m until it comes

Noirmoutier harbour at low water. The quay on the right is the best place to moor.

218

to an end. Thence steer to enter the main channel (just beyond the quay to starboard) midway between the first two port hand beacons and the training wall to starboard. Thence keep about 10m from the line of port hand beacons, until the striped beacon is passed half way to the town. After that keep only 5m from the line of beacons. Moor to the first quay on the starboard hand, before the crane is reached. Farther up the quays are shallower. The mud is very soft so that the keel will probably sink in, leaving the yacht upright.

Facilities
All shops; restaurants and hotels. Shipyard and marine engineer. A pleasant town.

Fromentine

High water: −0020 Brest, Index 1, MTL 2.9m
MHWS 5.3m (17.5 ft); MLWS 0.5m (1.5 ft); MHWN 4.0m (13 ft); MLWN 1.8m (6 ft)
Tidal streams: In-going stream begins +0600 Brest, 4 knots springs, outgoing begins −0220 Brest, 5½ knots springs.
Depths: The bar varies in position and depth; it dries about 1½m (5 ft)

The Goulet de Fromentine, between the south of Ile de Noirmoutier and the mainland, has not a very good reputation among yachtsmen, as the entrance is on a lee shore if the wind is in any westerly direction and the bar of sand dries and shifts position. The streams are very strong in the narrows and run seaward for nearly 9 hours, from about 1¾ hr before high water to 1 hr after low water. The channel is, however, well buoyed and as it is used by the Ile d'Yeu motor ferry all the year round, it may be regarded as fit for navigation in reasonable weather conditions.

The channel shifts greatly. A bridge across the narrows has been built. On arrival there are tolerable anchorages and the town of Fromentine is a pleasant little holiday resort.

Approach and entrance
On no account approach from the Baie de Bourgneuf as there is a causeway which dries 3m (10 ft) with guide posts and raised refuges between the island and the mainland.

The coast of Noirmoutier and the mainland south of it merge together into a line of sand dunes when viewed from seaward. There are several windmills painted white with black tops on the Noirmoutier side, and a very conspicuous water tower. The bridge is the most conspicuous landmark. At Fromentine there is the Notre Dame des Monts lighthouse and in the background a water tower. Half a mile seaward of the bridge are two towers, the northern one red, and the southern one white.

The sea shoals some 6 miles west of the entrance, before the landmarks can be located if the weather is at all thick. Accordingly it is best to fix the vessel's position precisely on Les Boeufs buoy or beacons if approaching from the NW or L'Aigle buoy if coming from the SW.

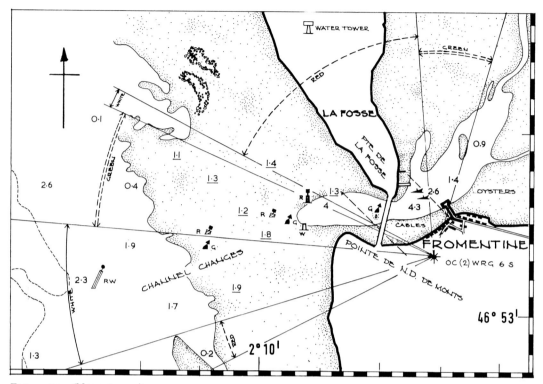

FROMENTINE (NOIRMOUTIER)
MLWS 0.5m; MLWN 1.8m; −0020 Brest, Index 1, MTL 2.9m
Based on French Chart No. 147 with buoy positions corrected to 1980
Depths in metres; right hand margin in cables

Although the Ile d'Yeu ferry uses the port near HW, strangers would be unwise to attempt it in a strong onshore wind, or if there is a swell high enough to break on the shoals. If it is not rough and the approach is made during the last two hours of the flood there will be plenty of water over the outer shoals, the shallowest being Basse de l'Aigle with 2.9m (9 ft) over it.

The landfall buoy (RW, Bell) is situated 1.95 miles at 264° from Fromentine lighthouse. The channel in 1980 ran between 2 pairs of port and starboard buoys, the positions of which are changed as required; then it left the red tower close to port, and rounded a starboard hand buoy west of the bridge centre. Two port hand buoys lie between the bridge and Fromentine ferry jetty.

In passing the narrows, go through the main navigation arch of the bridge. The clearance, at high water, under the bridge is 27m (88 ft), and the navigation arch is clearly marked.

By night : No stranger should attempt the entry at night.

Anchorage
The usual anchorage is about 1 cable west of the pier, just east of the cable area. The streams

220

Cohoe III indicates the best anchorage, just eastward of the cable area, looking E.

in the fairway are very strong, but they moderate towards the shore. Anchor as far in as draft and tide will allow. Owing to the strength of the tide it is said to be unwise to leave a yacht unattended while at anchor, and this would certainly be true at the top of spring tides.

Anchorage with less tidal stream can be found on the Noirmoutier side in a pool north of the pier on that side. It is not practical to row across the stream to Fromentine in the dinghy and the bridge is a very long way round.

Facilities
A small holiday resort with hotels, restaurants and small shops. Ferry to Ile d'Yeu.

Chart: 2647
High water: −0050 Brest, springs, −0020 Brest, neaps, Index 0, MTL 3.0m
MHWS 5.2m; MLWS 0.8m; MHWN 4.1m; MLWN 2m
Tidal streams: There is considerable variation in the directions and rates of the streams round the island and tidal charts should be consulted. There are local variations close inshore.
Depths: The principal harbour, Port Joinville, has been dredged and a new marina excavated. Port de la Meule dries, but there is an anchorage outside which can be used in offshore winds, as can also that further east at Anse des Vieilles.

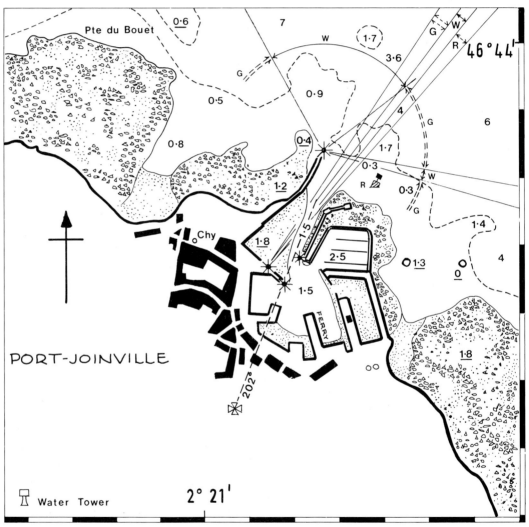

PORT JOINVILLE (ILE D'YEU)   MLWS 0.8m; MLWN 2.1m; −0050 (sp), −0020 (np) Brest, Index 0, MTL 3.0m
Based on French Chart No. 6613   Depths in metres; right hand margin in cables

The Ile d'Yeu, situated about halfway between Belle Ile and La Rochelle, is the furthest from the mainland of the outlying islands off the coast of the Bay of Biscay. It measures about 5 miles long and 2 miles across. The only deep harbour, Port Joinville, is an important fishing port, especially for tunny, with good berths at the quays and an anchorage outside sheltered from prevailing winds. The town is a pleasant one with excellent facilities as the island is a popular one for visitors.

The south coast of the island is very rocky and deeply indented by the action of the Atlantic seas. There are two bays which can be used as temporary anchorages in offshore winds. In one of these is the narrow winding inlet which forms Port de la Meule which, although Lilliputian, is the only other harbour in the island. The other is the Anse des Vieilles, near the SW corner of the island.

Despite its lack of good harbours Ile d'Yeu appears very prosperous, perhaps because the fishing industry is so active. The houses are whitewashed with brightly painted doors and shutters. The whole island seems trim and well cared for; it is high, wind-swept and bracing.

The coastline is magnificent, especially on the southern side where, overlooking a rock-studded bay, there are the ruins of an eleventh-century castle, complete with dungeons and moats. In recent history Marshal Pétain was imprisoned near Port Joinville, and his simple tomb is to be seen in the cemetery there. The island is well worth a visit and provides a convenient port of call when bound for La Rochelle.

Port Joinville

This harbour, on the north side of the Ile d'Yeu, is exposed to N and E winds, though the extension to the NW mole, now completed, has improved the shelter. Swell enters in strong winds from these directions, and there is sometimes a surge during gales from other directions; none of this however affects the new yacht marina, in which there is complete shelter. It is the only safe harbour on the island.

Approach and entrance

The high water tower will be seen just behind the town; in the distance this is more conspicuous than the island's main lighthouse. The town and breakwaters at the harbour entrance are easy to locate from seaward; an approach with the water tower bearing 224° will lead in. The light on the extended NW breakwater should be left 1 cable to starboard, and a can buoy ½ cable to port. The entrance lies between a stone breakwater on the NW side and an open pier on concrete pillars on the SE. An approach midway between the breakwaters on the same bearing 224° carries 1.4m. Apparently blocking the way will be seen the mole of the old Gare Maritime, with a green-topped white lighthouse at its left hand (E) end. When this lighthouse comes in transit with the church on the hill (photo page 224), steer on this line until the harbour opens up to port. This transit line was formerly used for the distant approach to the harbour and was lit, but must now only be used within the harbour; the rear lighthouse shown in the 1980 photograph is disused.

The ferry boats from Fromentine now berth at a new mole on the S side of the harbour.

The entry to Port Joinville, with church and lighthouses indicated. The rear lighthouse which appears in this 1980 photograph is now unlit and may be removed. The building on the extreme right of the photo is part of the old Gare Maritime.

By night

Approach in the white sector (218°–220°) of the new WRG light. When the R light on the W corner of the E breakwater bears 190°, steer on 200° to pass midway between it and the G light on the old Gare Maritime mole. The lights are:

Main island light; Fl W 5s, 56m, 24 19M. Horn, 1 min, sounded $\frac{3}{4}$M to NW.

      Radiobeacon, call YE, 312.6 kHz 1/6 min, begins H + 2 min.

Old Gare Maritime W side; Dir Q WRG. G 215°–218°, W 218°–220°, R 220°–223°.

Old Gare Maritime E side mole head; Iso G 4s, 6M.

NW Jetty head; Oc (3) WG 12s, 6m, 11M.

E side breakwater W corner; Fl R 5s.

Anchorage and mooring

The harbour has a history of continued development. It is not many years since it was considered a drying harbour, where a yacht which could take the ground might dry out among fishing boats, or be fortunate in finding a suitable vacant quay. The eastern basin was then formed, at first only quayed on the west side, with bottom at chart datum. When the rest of the harbour too was dredged, this became available for yachts, with fishing craft using the western

224

Port Joinville: the marina; looking SW.

basins. The next step was the improvement of the east basin with quays on all sides; it has now reverted to use by all craft. A new mole has been recently added for the ferries, parallel to that on which the high ice factory stands; it accommodates a new Gare Maritime. For yachts, a new marina is now available, excavated from the rocky ground on the east side of the entrance breakwater. Since thick surrounding embankments enclose it on all sides with complete shelter, its area is limited and there are only 3 pontoons, with shore access from the east side. The limited area has made it necessary to rule that visiting yachts may be required to move on after one night; it is not known how often this has to be enforced. Unless the dinghy is used, one must walk right round the harbour to reach the town; the marina charges are above average. If the marina is full, it may be possible to lie to anchors fore and aft in the basin just E of the new Gare Maritime.

There is a good anchorage in southerly winds in the Anse de Ker Chalon, 6 cables to the SE of the harbour entrance. Anchor in about 3.5m (12 ft) sand and mud; farther in there are some rocks in the sand.

Facilities

There are all the facilities of a town; shops of all kinds, banks, hotels, restaurants, chandler, shipyard, marine engineer, sailmaker (who is, however, more used to trawlers' riding sails than yacht work). Water from a tap at the head of the steamer pier. Showers at the municipal baths, near the church, on Saturdays. There is a regular ferry service to Fromentine on the mainland and also, in summer, to St Gilles sur Vie and less frequently to Les Sables d'Olonne.

Port de la Meule, showing the entrance, lighthouse (with square white panel) and chapel. The quay is round the corner, behind the lighthouse. See photo on opposite page.

Port de la Meule

A picturesque but tiny fishing harbour on the south side of Ile d'Yeu, which is rewarding to visit if one is lucky enough to get the right conditions of offshore wind, but is to be avoided in unsettled weather. In suitable weather it tends to be crowded (three yachts make a crowd!), especially at weekends.

Approach and entrance

The entrance is not conspicuous, but lies between two fairly prominent headlands, La Panrée, $1\frac{1}{2}$ miles to the W, and Pointe de le Tranche, $\frac{3}{4}$ mile to the SE, behind which there is, on high ground, a conspicuous Semaphore tower, the upper part of which is painted red. Another landmark is the ruined castle 1 mile to the W. The ruins are of similar rock to the cliffs behind them, but can be distinguished on a clear day.

From seaward the entrance has little to distinguish it from the other inlets on this coast until it is opened up, when the white panel on the lighthouse on the W side, and the white chapel at the NE end of the inlet can be seen. The bay in which Port de la Meule is situated is clear of off-lying rocks, except for those off the headlands or in the immediate vicinity of the cliffs. Steer for the lighthouse, bearing 022°, allowing for any set of the tide.

On near approach a headland on the west side of the entrance will lie to port. This has rocks off the south end which are well off the line of approach, but there is also a reef projecting eastward almost facing the headland on the opposite side. These rocks can usually be seen as the swell breaks on them, but an incoming vessel should borrow to starboard to give them an offing.

The headland on the east side, which is an island (Tête Jaune) at high water, does not project seawards so far as does the west headland. There are rocks off its southern extremity, which it is convenient to regard as a short underwater continuation of the headland.

226

Port de la Meule; the anchorage, looking SSW.

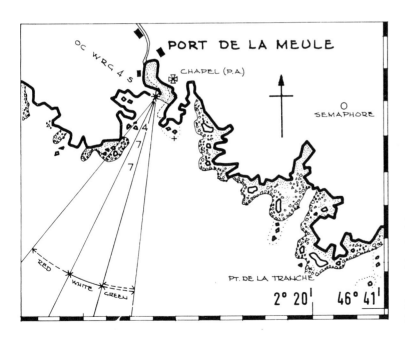

Port de la Meule (Ile d'Yeu)
MLWS 0.8m; MLWN 2.1m;
—0050 (sp), —0020 (np)
Brest, Index 0, MTL 3.0m
Based on French Chart No.
147, much enlarged
Depths in metres; right hand
margin in cables

Thus, in the near approach, first give reasonable clearance to the reef of rocks to port, then keep the inlet between the lighthouse and the cliff on the east side open, steering parallel with the eastern side of the inlet. When within the entrance, where there is 4m (13 ft), lobster pot buoys will be seen on the west side, which are an aid to navigation, as the outer ones are normally laid where they may be treated as port hand marks, to be left close to port. On the opposite (east) side there are a few rocks at the foot of the cliffs, one of which lies close to the channel. Hence, if proceeding to the quay, a vessel should now keep rather W of the centre of the channel and turn sharp round the end of the point on which the lighthouse stands.

There is shelter at the quay in normal conditions with the wind from W through N to E, but if the wind goes into a southerly quarter the swell will surge right in and the harbour is untenable. In southerly gales even the local boats move round to Port Joinville.

Anchorage and mooring

In settled offshore winds it is practicable to anchor in the entrance, though some swell comes in even in NE winds. There is very little swinging room so it is necessary to moor to two anchors.

It is also possible to enter the harbour and lie against the quay. There are three slips and the best walls to lie against are between the first and second (although there are said to be some stones on the bottom here) or between the second and third, where it will be necessary to keep clear of the chain moorings for fishermen's dinghies. The bottom is rocky off the first slip and above the third. The local fishermen are helpful and say there is always room for a yacht; it would be wise to seek their advice on exactly where to lie.

By night : Night entry cannot be recommended to a stranger. The light is:
Oc WRG 4s, 9m, 12M.

Facilities

There are two restaurants, but almost no other facilities. There are paths over the hills and cliffs to the east and west. The ruined castle 1 mile to the west is interesting.

Port de la Meule, the quay.

45 Saint Gilles sur Vie

Chart: 2647
High water: −0020 Brest, Index 1, MTL 3.1m
MHWS 5.3m; MLWS 0.8m; MHWN 4.1m; MLWN 2.1m
Tidal streams: The streams are weak in the offing, but strong in the harbour itself, the ebb reaching nearly 6 knots in the narrow parts. The ebb is increased and the flood reduced (or even fails to occur) after heavy rain.
Depths: The channel is said to be dredged to 1.5m, so that both fishing harbours and the yacht marina should be accessible at all states of the tide. There is however a serious silting problem, with continuous dredging necessary to prevent two sand bars forming.

This harbour is formed by La Vie river; the entrance is protected by moles on either hand. The entrance faces SW, and is therefore unsuitable for entry during strong onshore winds or if there is a swell. As the ebb tide can reach 6 knots at springs, conditions for entry are impossible when a strong wind opposes this; and it is safer to make both entry and exit before high water.

Within the river there are two enclosed basins for the fishing fleet on the north side; above this lie the pontoons of the yacht marina. There are also quays below the bridge further up the river at St Gilles sur Vie on the southeast side. Croix de Vie is larger than a stranger might expect and the fish quays near the railway station are very busy. There is substantial yachting activity in the port, with pontoon berths for 530 in the marina and a long waiting list. There is also a pontoon for local boats behind the Grand Mole, and moorings opposite the marina and between the marina and bridge.

Approach

In a rather featureless sandy coastline, with churches and three water towers in the background, the entrance may be located by the low rocky headland of Grosse Terre on the north side, with many houses and a lighthouse, the two church spires and the high lighthouse at Croix de Vie. On nearer approach the Pilours, a low reef of rocks like a small island, will be seen, marked by a pillar light buoy (card S), with the entrance and the lighthouses beyond.

The leading lighthouses for St Gilles sur Vie are indicated. Grand Môle on the left.

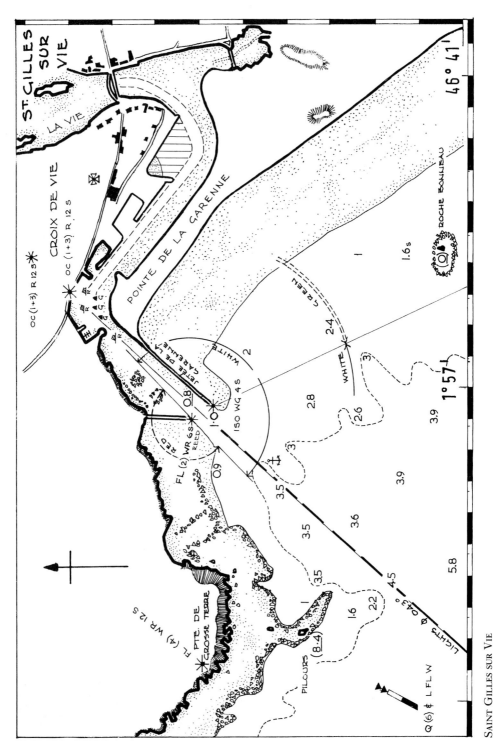

SAINT GILLES SUR VIE
MLWS 0.8m; MLWN 2.1m; −0020 Brest, Index 1, MTL 3.1m
Based on French Chart No. 6613 with corrections
Depths in metres; right hand margin in cables

Approach should be made, preferably shortly before high water, with the leading light-houses in transit, bearing 043°; the front is a short square tower with red framing and a red door, the rear a tower with a black top. The front lighthouse is not very easy to see, and should not be confused with a battlemented stone tower on the head of the Grand Môle.

This approach leaves the bell buoy (card S) 2 cables to port and Les Pilours rocks $2\frac{1}{2}$ cables to port. Soundings fall gradually from 6m (20 ft) opposite the buoy to 1m (3 ft) 1 cable off the pier head. Thence the channel dries 1m (4 ft). A more direct approach from the north or west is to leave the bell buoy close to port and then keep the west mole head, the tower on the Grand Môle and the rear leading lighthouse in transit, bearing 045°; this line carries 2m (6 ft) least water, until the harbour is close at hand.

Entrance

The entrance lies between the two outer breakwater heads, and the transit leads on the SE side of the entrance, so that an incoming vessel follows up parallel and very close to the SE mole (Jetée de la Garenne). The channel dries 1m (4 ft).

At the inner end of the entrance channel there is another short breakwater on the NW side. This is the Grand Môle, with a small stone tower at its end. A red buoy marks a spit off the end of the Grand Môle, the buoy is left to port. Having left the Grand Môle to port course is shaped to pass fairly between three black conical buoys to starboard and two red conical buoys to port. All these buoys are moored on the high ground beside the channel and should be given a good berth. The stream runs very hard about here.

The channel now swings to starboard leaving the quay on the south side of l'Adon harbour

The inner fishing harbour, with the marina beyond.

to port. The dredged channel, some 30m wide and marked by port and starboard buoys, runs straight past the entrance to the second fishing harbour to a small jetty which marks the beginning of the yacht harbour. The channel curves to port close to the ends of the yacht pontoons, then tends to cross towards the quays of St Gilles sur Vie on the E bank.

Departure should be made before high water, as the strong ebb quickly raises a sea at the entrance.

By night
Provided weather conditions are suitable, entry is easy at night. The lights are:
Pointe de Grosse Terre; Fl (4) WR 12s, 25m, 19M.
Rochers Pilours by; Q (6) + L Fl W, 15s.
Leading lights, front; Dir Oc (−−··) R 12s, 7m, 15M.
Leading lights, rear; Sync Dir Oc (−−··) R 12s, 28m, 15M.
SE mole head: (Jetée de la Garenne); Iso WG 4s, 7m, 8M.
NW mole head: (Jetée de Boisvinet); Fl (2) WR 6s, 8m, 9M. Reed (2), 20 sec.
Many buoys inside the harbour are lit.

Anchorage and mooring
Anchorage in the channel is prohibited. The berths near the shore ends of the western marina pontoons may dry out, but the mud appears to be soft and boats remain upright. If no marina berths are available in this popular harbour, there are mooring buoys on the south side of the channel opposite the marina; it may also be possible to berth at the quay to starboard at St Gilles sur Vie, where the streams are not so strong.

The quay and bridge, St Gilles Sur Vie.

Yachts which can take the ground could enquire if a berth is available at, or just off, the pontoons of the sailing club just inside the Grand Môle.

There is an anchorage outside in offshore winds, about 2 cables off the pierheads, keeping well clear of the leading line. There is no convenient landing place for dinghies except at the harbour moles. The ebb could set up a nasty sea for dinghy work.

Facilities

All shops, banks, hotels and restaurants, the best of which will be found at Boisvinet, to the west of Croix de Vie. There are shipbuilders, a marine engineer and chandlery. There is a railway station just by the harbour. Croix de Vie is an important fishing port with all facilities for fishing vessels.

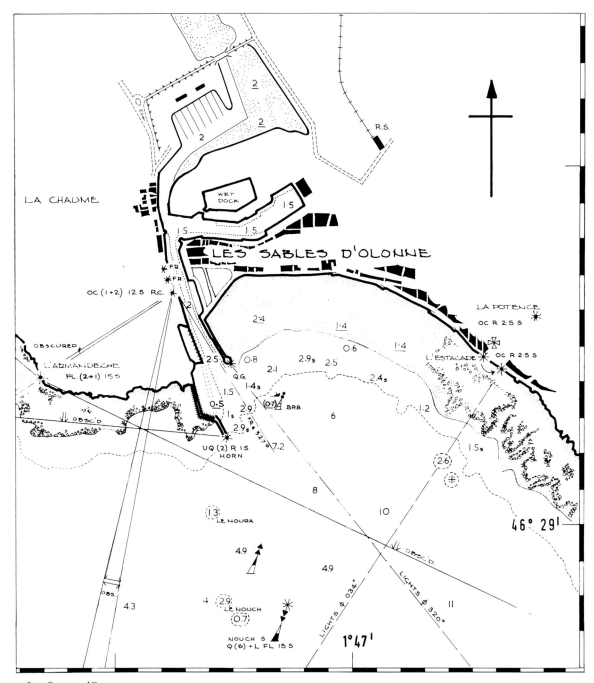

LES SABLES D'OLONNE
MLWS 0.8m; MLWN 2.1m; −0020 (sp), +0015 (np) Brest, Index 0, MTL 3.1m
Based on French Chart No. 5611 with corrections
Depths in metres; right hand margin in cables

46 Les Sables d'Olonne

Charts: 2648, 2647
High water: −0020 Brest, springs, +0015 Brest, neaps, Index 0, MTL 3.1m
MHWS 5.3m; MLWS 0.8m; MHWN 4.2m; MLWN 2.1m
Tidal streams: In the offing the streams are weak, rarely exceeding ½ knot; they are rotatory clockwise, N at LW Brest, S at HW Brest. In the Rade the streams are negligible and in the harbour itself the streams are weak, except on the rare occasions when it is scoured from the scouring basin, when there is a very fast ebb stream.
Depths: The harbour is dredged to 1.5m (5 ft).

Yachts bound south for La Rochelle pass within sight of Les Sables d'Olonne, which is situated some 35 miles NW of their destination. It is a convenient staging point, although on a small scale chart the entrance appears shallow, beset by rocks, and a lee shore to the prevailing winds. With the aid of a large scale chart, however, the approach is found to be easy and the harbour and town provide excellent facilities. The approach is rough in strong SE, S or SW winds, especially if there is a swell, owing to the shoals. In bad weather the SE approach is the safer, and given plenty of rise of tide, fishing vessels approach and enter the harbour in severe weather.

The town of Les Sables d'Olonne on the east side of the entrance is a large sophisticated holiday resort with a casino, many hotels and restaurants facing the sands. A narrow peninsula separates this from the fishing port with its market and cafes. Visiting yachts can no longer lie here, and a large new marina has been set up in the dredged scouring basin further inland. This is now a long way from the town by the ring road, and the west bank shops of La Chaume are more easily accessible.

Approach and entrance
The harbour lies about 1 mile to the SE of the Pointe de l'Aiguille, SE of which is the tall lighthouse of l'Armandèche. The hotels and other large buildings on the front are conspicuous from seaward. Les Barges lighthouse, 1 mile offshore, makes the entry easy to locate.

Les Sables d'Olonne, viewed along the 051° pre-1984 leading line N of Le Nouch shoal; left to right are the prominent church, La Potence lighthouse, and the disused front one, now being moved to a position 1½ cables SE on the front.

The close approach is from a SW direction, about 2 miles S of l'Armandèche lighthouse. The principal landmark is the prominent church to the left of a group of water towers. Steer on the church bearing 034°, or on the lighthouses in transit on the same bearing, leaving the Nouch-S buoy 1½ cables to port.

As the entrance opens up to port the square La Chaume tower will be seen ½ mile up the entrance channel on the west side. When this tower comes in transit with the east mole head lighthouse, bearing 320°, alter course on to this transit. When the west mole head is abeam to port bear to port until the inside of the east mole is opened up. The transit of the inner leading light structures can be followed, but strict attention to this line is unnecessary, except near LW, when hold strictly to the inner line, leading close to the eastern side of the passage. The front light has a board striped WRW, the rear a similar board striped RWR vertically.

Approaching at half tide and over in ordinary weather, attention to the leading lines is unnecessary and yachts can easily cross over the rocks and shoals, and sail direct to the harbour entrance.

Approaching from the south, it is simpler to use the SE approach, sailing straight for the transit of the east mole head and La Chaume tower, bearing 320°. This leaves all the shoals to port, and the water is deep until within 2 cables of the harbour entrance; this approach should always be used in bad weather.

By night: Entry is as easy as by day in reasonable conditions. The lights are:
L'Armandèche; Fl (2 + 1) W 15s, 42m, **23**, 17M.
Nouch-S by; Q (6) + L Fl, 15s.
SW front, replacing L'Estacade; Oc R 2.5s, 12m, 20M.
SW rear, La Potence; Oc R 2.5s, 33m, 20M.
SE front, east mole head; Q G, 11m, 10M.
SE rear, La Chaume; Oc (– –·) W 12s, 33m, 13M.
    Radiobeacon, call SO, 291.9 kHz, continuous 5M.
West mole head; V Q (2) R 1s, 16m, 10M; Horn (2) 30s.

The leading line for the SE entrance; the lighthouses are indicated, bearing 320°.

236

The new marina, looking towards the entrance and La Chaume.

Inner leading line, front; Q R, 6m, 5M.
Inner leading line, rear; Dir Q R, 9m, 11M.

Anchorage and mooring
Enter under power (sailing forbidden) past the fishing harbour to starboard, being wary of fishing boats leaving it at speed, and proceed straight up the channel, now dredged to 2m. It swings to starboard and the large marina then opens up to port, with 7 pontoons for 600 yachts. Visitors should check in at the Capitainerie on the port side before entering the marina for allotment of a berth.

Visiting yachts may no longer use the convenient fishing harbour; the few pontoons remaining there are for local craft with rights acquired over many years.

The wet dock off the fishing harbour opens $1\frac{1}{2}$ hours from HW at neaps and 2 hours at springs, but it may only be entered with prior permission from the port authority.

Facilities
The marine ancillary buildings include shops, cafes, restaurants and full facilities, with more building in hand; the nearest outside shops are those of La Chaume. Excellent communications from Les Sables d'Olonne by train, bus and air.

Charts: 2641, 2648
High water : —0050 Brest, springs, +0010 Brest, neaps, Index 3, MTL 3.6m
MHWS 6.0m (19.5 ft); MLWS 0.8m (2.5 ft); MHWN 4.8m (15.5 ft); MLWN 2.4m (8 ft)
Tidal streams: The streams, which are weak offshore, increase as the island is approached. The streams south of the island, in the Pertuis d'Antioche, are given under La Rochelle on page 249. North of the island, in the Pertuis Breton, where the harbours are, they are as follows: Off Pointe de Lizay, at the north of the island, the flood runs ESE, the ebb WNW, spring rates 1½ knots. Off the mainland opposite, near Pointe du Grouin de Cou, the turn is about half an hour after high water and low water, and the rates about half a knot higher. Near the eastern end of the island the flood meets the north-going flood through the Rade de la Pallice, and the ebb splits similarly, leaving a zone of relatively weak streams off the NE of the island. The streams in the Rade de la Pallice do not exceed 1½ knots, springs.
Depths: See the individual ports.

This large island projects seaward west of La Rochelle. Yachtsmen who have approached this port through the Pertuis Breton on the north side or through the Pertuis d'Antioche on the south side of the island are familiar with its coastline. The ports, which are all in the Pertuis Breton, are a popular destination for a weekend sail from the mainland and support a substantial yachting activity of their own.

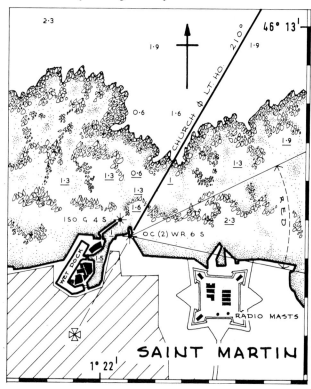

SAINT MARTIN, ILE DE RÉ
MLWS 0.8m; MLWN 2.4m; —0050 (sp), +0010 (np) Brest, Index 3, MTL 3.6m
Based on French Chart No. 157
Depths in metres; right hand margin in cables

In the prevailing winds from the S and W the harbours are situated on the sheltered side of the island. This is useful to the cruising man, who can, in these winds, anchor off them while waiting to enter.

The Ile de Ré is a sandy island fringed in many parts by rocks, of which the most notable are the Banc du Nord extending from Les Baleines in the NW, and those off the Pointe de Chanchardon on the S and the Pointe de Chauveau on the SE. These are marked by light towers. The island is low and the scenery is like Holland, where windmills (now mostly converted to dwellings) and tall church spires rise high over the land. The houses are as tidy as the Dutch ones. The island is a pleasant place in summer and an endless succession of box-like ferries carry holidaymakers from La Pallice to Sablanceaux at the extreme east.

Peaceful as it is today, the Ile de Ré has been the scene of much fighting and suffered greatly from the attacks of the English, and also during the religious wars. St Martin, the capital, is a fortified town with Vauban ramparts and a citadel, which was considerably damaged during the bombardment by the Anglo-Dutch fleet in 1696.

There are three harbours: St Martin, La Flotte and Fier d'Ars. All the harbours are tidal, but St Martin has a wet basin where yachts can lie afloat in complete shelter, in the centre of the old walled town with restaurants and shops close by.

Saint Martin

Depths: The near approach dries 1.6m (5 ft), the inner harbour dries 1.5m (5 ft). In the wet dock there is 3m (10 ft) at neaps, more at springs.

St Martin stands rather east of half way along the NE side of the Ile de Ré. The harbour consists of an Avant Port, not well sheltered by a mole and a jetty, connected with the drying harbour by a narrow entrance channel. From the drying harbour a channel to starboard leads through dock gates to the wet dock. There is active local yachting, as well as some fishing.

Approaching in the morning light the harbour is easily located, for the white lighthouse, the church tower and the citadel will be seen from afar. In the afternoon, with the sun in

This photograph of St Martin is taken from the final line of approach. The outer approach is conveniently made with the lighthouse and church tower, indicated here, in transit bearing 210°.

The Avant Port at St Martin, near LW.

one's eyes, the walls do not stand out against the dark background and trees and the first landmarks to be seen are the lighthouse and the church tower with ruined walls close to it, see photograph.

There are extensive ledges of rock in and especially E and W of the approach, where they extend over ½ mile seaward of the land. They are not so formidable as they appear at first glance on a chart, as the ones to the west farther offshore do not dry as much as the entrance channel, and the ones to the east are marked by a beacon (card N).

The approach should be timed according to the draft of the yacht; between 3 hr before and 2 hr after high water should give 2.2m (7 ft) of water in the entrance on all tides. Convenient leading marks are the church tower and the lighthouse in transit, bearing 210°, but it is not necessary to follow this line closely. When the church tower dips behind the trees, borrow to starboard and make the final approach with the church tower open of the trees and seen over the port hand side of the inner entrance, see photograph. Leave the mole head to starboard at a distance of less than 10m and steer straight for the centre of the channel leading to the drying harbour. Immediately after the vessel has entered the drying harbour, the channel to the dock gates will open up to starboard.

Approaching from the east, keep well to the north of the beacon (card N) on the Couronneau rocks unless the tide is well up, as rocks drying up to 1m (3 ft) lie to the north of the beacon, and the 3m (10 ft) contour passes nearly 3 cables to the north of it. Thence bring the lighthouse and church into transit and steer as described above.

240

The drying harbour; the entrance to the dock is on the left.

By night : Enter in the white sector of St Martin light, bearing 210°. Note that the white sector extends from 124° to 245° and crosses part of the outer ledges; it is not safe simply to enter in the white sector. On close approach bring the mole light to bear 210° and steer so, passing it close to starboard. The lights are:

St Martin de Ré; Oc (2) WR 6s, 18m, 9M.
Mole; Iso G 4s, 10m, 7M.

Mooring

There are quays in the drying harbour which dry 1.5m (5 ft); vessels should not berth at the west quay beyond the fuel pump as there is a grid. The swell gets into this harbour in onshore winds. It is better to moor either side of the entrance to the wet dock until the bridge is opened and go into the wet dock.

   The gates are open for about an hour or more at high water but the swing bridge is not necessarily opened for all this period, especially early in the morning or late at night. A clockface on the bridge shows the opening hours each tide. There is stated to be 4m (13 ft) of water in the dock on a mean tide, 1m (3 ft) less at neaps and more at springs. A map at the hut also shows the parts of the quay allotted to clubs, shipyard, etc. Visitors moor where they can on the W or S wall, alongside others if necessary. There is a pontoon alongside the SW end of the dock, to which yachts berth stern on.

Facilities

All shops, restaurants and hotels close by. Shipyard, chandler, marine engineer. Water taps at intervals round the dock. Petrol and diesel from the garage labelled 'Renault' on the east side of the drying harbour.

   St Martin is an historic town of moats, walls and gateways, with a large church which has been partly restored, though parts are still in ruins. At one period the Ile de Ré was in-

241

dependent for Customs purposes and St Martin was a prosperous port, carrying on a vigorous trade with America and distant parts; sailing ships loaded salt and wines and returned laden with woods, spices and other merchandise. It now has some signs of decay and is living on the past. The wet dock is now principally used by yachts, for which it is ideal, being clean and having every convenience at hand. The only disadvantage is that it is so attractive that it is overcrowded.

There is a recognised anchorage for big ships a mile seaward of the harbour, and in offshore winds yachts can get closer in to anchor rather less than $\frac{1}{2}$ mile off the entrance in 2m (6 ft), sand and mud.

La Flotte

Depths: The approach and harbour dry 2m (7 ft)

La Flotte lies about 2 miles SE of St Martin; it is easily identified and the tall square church tower is conspicuous. The harbour is formed by two jetties, protected by a long curved outer mole. The narrow entrance faces east, across the shallow bay. Although there is no wet basin as at St Martin, the harbour is well sheltered, and is uncomfortable only in strong onshore winds.

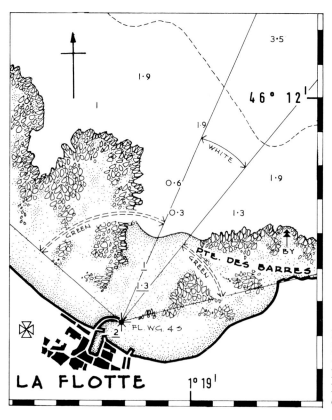

La Flotte is a fishing port, famous for lobsters, shrimps and sole. It is a compact town of short narrow streets and whitewashed houses with a beautiful church. It is less popular and more cheerful than St Martin. Except for the trouble of drying out, some yachtsmen may prefer it; yachts will be aground for long periods on each tide.

La Flotte, Ile de Ré
MLWS 0.8m; MLWN 2.4m; −0050 (sp), +0010 (np) Brest, Index 3, MTL 3.6m
Based on French Chart No. 157
Depths in metres; right hand margin in cables. Close approach line not shown.

242

The narrow entrance to La Flotte, between the jetty heads.

Facing NE across La Flotte harbour entrance. The motor boat is lying in the best place.

Approach and Entrance

La Flotte is easy to locate in the bay $\frac{1}{2}$ mile W of Pointe des Barres. It is approached by a channel with mud and sand bottom which dries 2m (7 ft) and lies between ledges of rock on either side which extend $\frac{1}{2}$ mile seawards.

Approach with the lighthouse bearing 215°. On this bearing (which it is not necessary to hold closely) the lighthouse will be in transit with a small belfry, not the main church tower. A beacon (card N) on the rocks off Pointe de Barres will be left about 3 cables to port. If approaching from the east, give a good berth to the beacon as the rocks extend outside it. Within 500m of the lighthouse, a vertical black and orange stripe will be visible day and night, defining the close approach on 212° 30′. A deviation to port from this bearing changes the coloured strip into an arrow pointing to the right, the direction to be taken to regain the course; similarly a left-pointing arrow will result from any deviation to starboard. Leave the breakwater head to starboard and steer for the narrow entrance between the jetty heads.

By night: As by day, the light is:
Mole; Fl WG 4s, 10m, 12M; Horn (3) 30 sec, by day, near HW.

Mooring

The inner harbour is rectangular and dries 2m (7 ft). The inner part is much used by fishing boats and the best berth for visitors is against the jetty immediately to starboard on entering. It would also be possible, in settled weather, to lie against parts of the inside of the outer breakwater, but the bottom is not all level and it would be necessary to keep clear of the moorings of local boats which moor and warp their sterns to the mole.

Facilities

All shops, hotels and restaurants. Water from a tap by the club on the east quay.

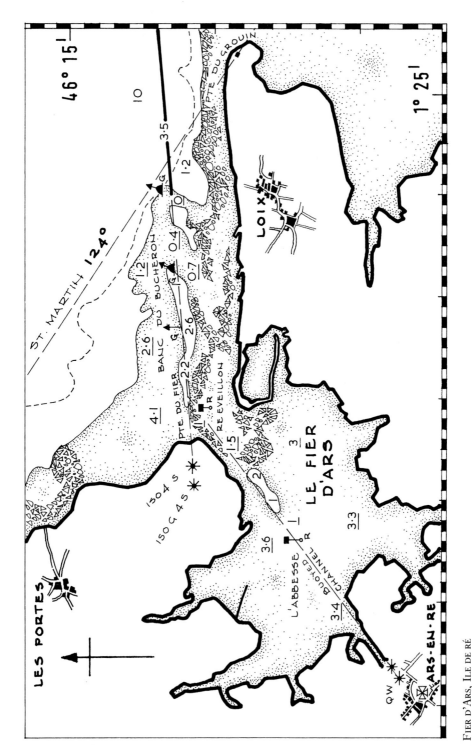

Fier d'Ars, Île de Ré
MLWS 0.8m; MLWN 2.4m; −0050 (sp), +0010 (np) Brest, Index 3, MTL 3.6m
Based on French Chart No. 6521 with corrections
Depths in metres; right hand margin in cables

Fier d'Ars

Depths: The outer bar dries 0.4m (2 ft), the outer anchorage has 2.6m. The second bar dries 1.5m, the main anchorage has 2m. The channel to the harbour dries out about 3m.

The Mer du Fier is a lake-like expanse of water, most of which dries at low tide. The word *Fier* is said to be derived from the Scandinavian *Fjord*, but the resemblance is remote. It is entered from the Pertuis Breton through a narrow entrance some 5 miles east of Les Baleines. Though shallow, it is well sheltered and is the principal yachting centre of the Ile de Ré. The local boats are dinghies or of shallow draft to suit local conditions. Deep-keel yachts can lie afloat in the main anchorage off the Pointe du Fier, a delightful spot, or further out in a more exposed anchorage. It is possible to go up the channel to the harbour at tide time, but it is so crowded that it would be difficult to find a quayside berth for a yacht that cannot take the ground. The town is an attractive one; the local industries are making salt by evaporating sea water in salt pans and cultivating oysters.

Approach and Entrance

The approach is from the eastward and the channel lies between the ledges of rock extending from the island shore and the Banc du Bûcheron (called La Sablière on chart 2641), a big sandbank extending 2 miles to the east of Pointe du Fier.

Close with the land ½ mile W of Pointe du Grouin (called Pointe de Loix on chart 2641). To the east will be seen Les Islattes tower (card N), to the west is the wooded Pointe du Fier and the shore north of it. The approach is with the two lighthouses on the Pointe du Fier in transit, bearing 265°. The lighthouses are not at all conspicuous and must not be confused with the high tower of Les Baleines lighthouse, which stands out more clearly; it is well to the right of the alignment. The lighthouses appear in a nick in the trees. The rear is a green turret on the top of a house. The front is a pylon with a square white board, which is on rails so that it can be moved when the channel shifts.

Approaching on the transit a buoy (stbd) marking the end of the Banc du Bûcheron will be left to starboard. The Banc is tending to move southwards, and a further starboard buoy and beacon close to the transit mark its present limit. The channel shoals midway between the buoys, where it dries 0.4m; it then deepens again, and just beyond the beacon is a narrow hole with up to 2.6m. This is the outer anchorage. Continuing on the transit for another ½ mile Roche Eveillon beacon (port) will be seen. Just before the yacht reaches this beacon the leading lights at Ars en Ré will come in transit, bearing 232°. They are not easy to see by day; it is easier to keep Ars en Ré church spire, with a conspicuous black top, bearing 231° and open to the left of l'Abbesse beacon (R). A conspicuous chimney will be seen to the right of the beacon, bearing 232°. Follow this alignment, leaving the Roche Eveillon beacon 1 cable to port, over a rocky bottom which dries 1.5m (5 ft). The alignment runs parallel to the shoreline of the Pointe du Fier, at the inshore end of which there is a landing slip. At this point begins the second deep pool forming the main anchorage; it has 2m (6 ft) and there are usually some boats anchored there.

If proceeding to the harbour keep the chimney open to the right of l'Abbesse beacon, passing the latter close to port. Thence the channel is marked by black and red buoys, to starboard and port, until it enters the canalised portion leading to the harbour itself. The channel and harbour dry 3m (10 ft), and the latter is very crowded with local boats.

By night : Make the initial approach with St Martin light showing white, bearing more than 124°. Enter as by day; both leading lines are lit, but the pools will have to be found by sounding. The harbour is not accessible to strangers by night. The lights are:
Les Baleines; Fl (4) W 15s, 53m, **27**, *20*M.
        Radiobeacon, call BN, 303.4 kHz, 1/6 min, starts H + 5 min.
St Martin; Oc (2) WR 6s, 18m, 9M.
Pointe du Fier, front; Iso W 4s, 8m, 10M.
Pointe du Fier, rear; Sync Dir Iso G 4s, 12m, **13**, *11*M.
Ars en Ré, front; QW 5m, 9M.
Ars en Ré, rear; QW 13m, 11M.

Anchorages
The outer anchorage is exposed to the N and E, but is sheltered from S and W. Being outside the inner, shallower, bar there is more freedom to come and go, but it is a long way to go to the landing, with very strong tides.

    The main anchorage has much better shelter, though it is somewhat exposed to the NE at high water. The tides also run hard here and the bottom is weedy. Land at the Pointe du Fier, which is a delightful strip of sand backed by woods.

    The harbour is bordered by quays on each side, the width being 35m. It is shallow in the centre with deeper water along the quays. Hold well off the quays, since the foundations project. An inner harbour lies beyond a single dock gate, but this may be left open to help scour the channel.

Facilities
From the anchorages by Pointe du Fier it is necessary to walk 2 miles to Les Portes to reach the shops. Restaurant and shipyard at the harbour. All shops, restaurants and buses in Ars en Ré, ½ mile from the harbour.

The lighthouses at Pointe du Fier, bearing 265°; Les Baleines lighthouse is out of the picture, to the right.

48 L'Aiguillon and Marans

Charts: 2641, 2648

High water: −0050 Brest, springs, +0010 Brest, neaps, Index 3, MTL 3.6m
MHWS 6.0m (19.5 ft); MLWS 0.8m (2.5 ft); MHWN 4.8m (15.5 ft); MLWN 2.4m (8 ft)

Tidal streams: For the streams in the Pertuis Breton, see page 238. In Le Lay, leading to L'Aiguillon the currents are about 1.5 knots springs. In La Sèvre Niortaise, leading to Marans, the streams are about 4 knots springs.

Depths: Le Lay dries in parts; in 1958 there was about 1.8m (6 ft) at LW neaps. La Sèvre Niortaise dries 1m (3 ft); the port of Marans is deep.

Six miles north of La Pallice, and to the NE of the Ile de Ré, two rivers flow between mud flats into the Pertuis Breton. The westernmost is Le Lay, leading to the town of L'Aiguillon. The eastern is La Sèvre Niortaise which leads from the Anse de l'Aiguillon to a lock, from which a canal leads to Marans. It is perverse that the town of L'Aiguillon is on a river which does *not* flow into the Anse de l'Aiguillon.

The entrances to both these rivers, though sheltered at a distance by the Ile de Ré, are exposed to the S and W, and being shallow, are rough in winds from that quarter. Entry should only be attempted in fine weather or offshore winds. Neither river is much used by yachts and they provide an interesting excursion off the beaten track in suitable conditions. The scenery is similar to Holland or the Fens. The land is low and the rivers wind between training banks.

L'Aiguillon

Caution. The coast outside and the river banks are devoted to the culture of mussels. These are grown on substantial timber piles which cover at HW and are very dangerous. The areas are marked by a line of yellow buoys (outside the river) and withies with branching tops (inside). Withies with plain tops mark oyster beds.

The entrance of Le Lay river is not easy to locate from seaward. The low Pointe d'Arçay merges with the low shore NW of Pointe de l'Aiguillon and it is not until an incoming vessel closes with the land that the course of the river opens up. Pointe de l'Aiguillon is a long finger of sand which may be seen from a considerable distance if the sun is on it. There is a large black beacon on the extremity. Pointe d'Arçay is low, but may be identified by the belt of low

L'Aiguillon; the jetty with a beacon on the end, and another beacon on the sands. Many oyster stakes are left close to starboard.

247

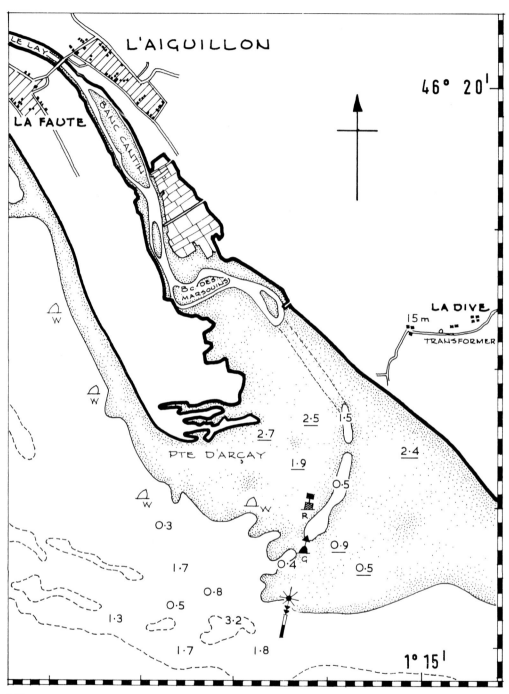

L'Aiguillon

MLWS 0.8m; MLWN 2.4m; −0050 (sp), +0010 (np) Brest, Index 3, MTL 3.6m
Based on French Chart No. 6521   Depths in metres; right hand margin in cables

This picture shows where the channel crosses over to the west side of the river towards the port hand beacon, before Banc Cantin is reached. The second beacon can be seen just to the left of the trees.

trees growing on it. Some 3 miles NW of Pointe de l'Aiguillon there is a curious land formation which looks like an inland island, and is conspicuous in the absence of any other break in the low coastline. This formation is named La Dive. It is now a farm, and has an electric transformer by it, adjacent to a conspicuous barn, but the buildings are erected on the site of a pre-Christian sanctuary.

The entrance to the river is with the transformer on La Dive bearing 033°. This course leaves the card S buoy (YB) about 3 cables to starboard, No. 1 buoy (stbd) 1 cable to starboard and No. 2 buoy (port) 1 cable to port. Thence the channel swings steadily about 60° to port, until the river opens up and the distant town, with a prominent church tower, is seen ahead. The channel is marked by beacons; keep closer to those on the SW side, keep 10m away from beacons and withies throughout.

A low stone jetty will be passed and there are a few buildings on the starboard bank, $\frac{1}{2}$ mile beyond the jetty. Here the channel swings round S of W and becomes very narrow so that it is better to proceed under power. There is a middle ground, the Banc de Marsouins, marked by beacons; the southern channel is very narrow and the northern one is to be preferred, though the deepest water is close to the middle ground and is also narrow.

Keep to the E side of the next reach until opposite the last starboard hand mark before Banc Cantin, when cross to the W bank; pass two port hand beacons and then cross back to the E bank at the last starboard hand beacon on Banc Cantin. The yacht is then in the anchorage. The position of the best water changes from time to time, but the key to pilotage is to keep very close to one edge or the other of the channel, not midstream.

Anchorage and Facilities
Anchor in the pool below the bridge. There was about 2m (6 ft), mud, at neap tides. All shops, restaurants, hotels, bus service. A short walk across the peninsula leads to good bathing at La Faute.

Marans
The tides run very hard in La Sèvre Niortaise, but it is desirable to enter well before high

The fishing boat shows where the channel crossed again to run close to Banc Cantin.

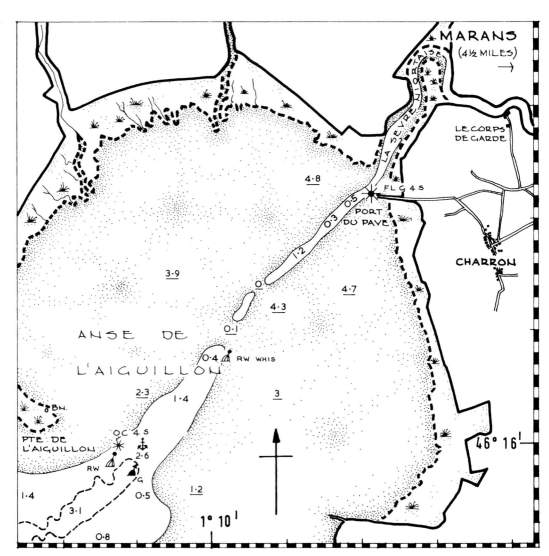

La Sevre Niortaise (Marans)   MLWS 0.8m; MLWN 2.4m; −0050 (sp), +0010 (np) Brest, Index 3, MTL 3.6m
Based on French Chart No. 6521 with corrections   Depths in metres; right hand margin in cables

The anchorage and town of L'Aiguillon. The best water lay near the moorings.

water, to ensure reaching the lock in time. On the Pointe de l'Aiguillon there is a large black beacon, with a topmark. Some $\frac{3}{4}$ mile to the SE of the beacon is L'Aiguillon RW fairway buoy, with a small buoy (stbd) close SE of it. Make L'Aiguillon buoy, and pass between the two buoys. Thence steer about 040° for a large whistle buoy (RW vert. stripes), and leave this buoy to starboard. After this the channel is obvious, being marked by port and starboard buoys numbered up to 10, and leads into the river. There are beacons on the river banks, but these are not channel marks. The Port du Pavé jetty, with a pylon on the end, is left to starboard. This is the shallowest part of the river and dries 1m (4 ft).

In the first reach after entering the river the flats cover at high water springs, but the plan shows where the channel lies in relation to the training banks. After this there are a few buoys marking shoals on the bends, otherwise keep in the middle. About $1\frac{1}{2}$ miles further up there is a landing on the starboard bank at Le Corps de Garde.

About 3 miles from the river entrance the yacht will reach the lifting bridge and lock giving access to the canal leading to Marans. This lock is on the starboard hand and is worked once only 2 hr each side of HW at springs and 1 hr each side of HW at neaps. The lock is enormous, being 104m long and 45m wide with gently sloping banks. It is not easy to make fast as there is no wall to secure to; the simplest thing is to remain under way, using the engine to keep in the middle while the lock is being filled. At the upper end of the lock a swing bridge carries a disused road across the canal.

The vast lock is full and the swing bridge opens on to the Canal de Marans.

The pretty tree-lined canal leads straight, for a distance of about 3 miles, to the port of Marans. Towards the end of the canal it appears as if there is a dead end, but a channel opens up to starboard, through a pair of permanently open lock gates, into the port of Marans.

By night : Although the L'Aiguillon buoy and the jetty at Port du Pavé have lights strangers should not attempt a night entry.

Anchorage and Mooring

By far the best place is the port of Marans. Go past the berth used by the coasters, and moor on the starboard side, just beyond a barrage to port.

It is possible to anchor at Le Corps de Garde, where some fishing boats lie, and there is a landing with access to Charron, $1\frac{1}{2}$ miles away. This is quite sheltered but the tides run hard. Since one would only enter the river on the tide there does not seem to be much reason for stopping here rather than going on to Marans.

It is also possible to land at the jetty at Port du Pavé, whence Charron is a walk of $1\frac{1}{2}$ miles. This anchorage is apparently exposed to the SW at high water. However at neaps the extensive mud flats are only just covered at high water, leaving a narrow channel between them. At neaps, therefore, the shelter is better than it looks. The depth is only 0.5m (1 ft) in the channel here, but at LW neaps there will be nearly 3m (9 ft). So this anchorage is possible in settled weather at neap tides.

Facilities

All shops, restaurants and hotels at Marans. The facilities at Charron have not been sampled, but there must be at least simple shops. A few yachts berth at Marans.

Marans: the port.

49 La Rochelle

Charts: 2746, 2641, 2648
High water: −0035 Brest, springs, 0000 Brest, neaps, Index 3, MTL 3.7m
MHWS 6.1m; MLWS 1.0m; MHWN 4.9m; MLWN 2.5m
Tidal streams: for the Pertuis Breton, see under Ile de Ré, page 238. In the narrows off La Pallice the flood runs N, the ebb S, spring rates 1½ knots. In the entrance to the Pertuis d'Antioche, north of Pointe de Chassiron, the flood runs E, the ebb W, spring rates 2¼ knots; south of the Ile de Ré the streams turn about ½ hr after HW and LW and are slightly weaker. The streams are weak in the harbour and its near approaches.
Depths: The approach carries 1.0m (3 ft) as far as Tour Richelieu; the buoyed channel has 0.2m (less than 1 ft) as far as the towers. There is a berth in the harbour just outside the dock, with 1.3m (4 ft), and there is ample water for yachts in the wet dock.

La Rochelle, half way down the coastline of the Bay of Biscay, may be a convenient port of call for yachts bound to or from Spain or the Mediterranean via the Midi canal, or it may mark the farthest port in a cruise from England. There are few yachting centres south of it until the Gironde is entered, and beyond the Gironde, Arcachon is the only port in a long sandy featureless coastline, and it is not accessible in strong onshore weather.

Thus the geographical position of La Rochelle makes it important to yachtsmen, and it also offers all facilities. There is a large modern marina at Port des Minimes, with pontoon berths for 2,200. This has eased the congestion, but it is a long way from the shops and sights of the town. The entrance to the town harbour is shallow; once inside there is a wet dock where all can lie afloat and shallow draft yachts can lie in the Avant Port. The entrance, between the two towers of St Nicholas on the east and La Chaine on the west, is impressive, and the historical old town is most attractive.

The entry into the old harbour is between Tour St Nicholas, seen here, to starboard and Tour de la Chaine to port.

253

The Tour Richelieu; the towers of La Rochelle are in the distance. The lighthouses, bearing 059°, are indicated. The tide gauge shows the depth in the channel.

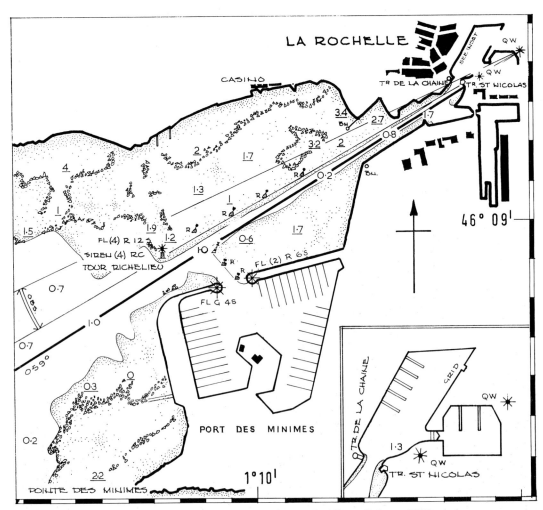

LA ROCHELLE   MLWS 1.0m; MLWN 2.5m; −0035 (sp), 0000 (np) Brest, Index 3, MTL 3.7m
Based on French Chart No. 6468 with corrections   Depths in metres; right hand margin in cables

Approach and entrance

The distant approach is either through the Pertuis Breton, on the north side of the Ile de Ré, and thence through the Rade de la Pallice, or through the Pertuis d'Antioche on the south side. *Caution.* A firing danger area exists to the S of the entrance, marked by Bl W buoys. This area is prohibited during working hours on weekdays, except public holidays.

The near approach lies from a position about 1 mile S of Le Lavardin lighthouse. The towers and church of La Rochelle will be seen bearing about 060°; steer on these until the leading lighthouses can be made out. This course will leave the Pointe de Chef de Baie, with a radar tower, about $\frac{3}{4}$ mile to port, and then the Pointe des Minimes, with off-lying rocks, about $\frac{1}{2}$ mile to starboard; it leads close southward of the red Tour Richelieu.

The leading lighthouses are: front, a white tower with three red horizontal bands and a red top; rear, a taller white tower with a green top. They should be seen just to the right of the two towers guarding the entrance to the harbour. Steer on the transit of these lighthouses, bearing 059°, leaving to port the Tour Richelieu, with a tide gauge, and the four red buoys

Port des Minimes: pontoons not yet complete.   *Photo: Régie du Port de Plaisance.*

marking the edge of the channel. When close to the towers, bear to port and enter the harbour, leaving to starboard the entrance to the commercial harbour. If going to Les Minimes yacht harbour turn to starboard about 1 cable beyond the Tour Richelieu.

By night: Entry by night is easy. The lights are:
Le Lavardin; Fl (2) WG 6s, 14m, 11M.
Richelieu; Fl (4) R 12s, 10m, 9M. Siren (4) 1 min, near HW.
　　　Radiobeacon, call RE, 291.9 kHz, continuous, 5M.
Front leading light; Dir QW (Fl W 4s by day), 15m, **13**, *12*M.
Rear leading light; Sync QW (Fl W 4s by day), 25m, 12M.
Les Minimes W breakwater head; Fl G 4s, 9m, 6M.
Les Minimes E breakwater head; Fl (2) R 6s, 6m, 5M.

Mooring
In Port les Minimes, turn sharp to starboard on entering the marina; the 2 north pontoons are for visitors, but the depth should be checked. In the old port, visiting yachts can usually enter the wet dock, but with shallow draught or neap tides there may be room to berth at the visitors'

The wet dock, in empty condition. The vessels in the foreground show the best berth in which to lie until the dock gates open.

pontoon in the outer harbour, where they will lie afloat, or at worst take the ground upright in soft mud. The gates of the wet dock are open from 2 hours before to one hour after HW. It is necessary to contact the Bureau du Port, by the commercial harbour, to arrange to have the dock gates opened.

Yachts which arrive, or intend to leave, when the dock gates are closed should berth against the quay between the dock and Tour St Nicholas. The berth here with the deepest water is on the straight section between the curves leading to Tour St Nicholas (to the SW) and to the dock (to the NE). There are usually some fishing vessels berthed here as well. The first part of the quay beyond the dock entrance is reserved for the ferries to the islands. Beyond that is the scrubbing berth (see below).

Facilities
Every imaginable facility is available. All kinds of shop, hotels and restaurants of every grade, yacht builders, chandlers, sailmakers. Bonded stores are available. French charts can be bought at a bookshop up the street under the old clock tower. There is a long scrubbing berth on the eastern side of the Avant Port. Most of it is gridded; in part the grid is widely spaced and unsuitable for most yachts, but in part the grid is closely spaced and could be used by a yacht with a long straight keel. In part the grid stops short of the wall, so that a yacht of sufficiently narrow beam can lie on level ground between the wall and the grid. Anyone intending to use the grid should see it at low water to select a suitable point.

Port des Minimes has marina berths for 2500, to increase to 3000 in 1985. Restaurants, cafés, chandlery, sailmakers are available on the W side of the site, avoiding the need for the long journey to the town. Except at lowest tides, a 'bus de mer' runs approximately hourly to the Avant Port from the SW corner of the marina.

The town is very attractive and historically interesting. There is a good train service.

La Pallice. This is the large modern commercial port of La Rochelle. It has no facility for yachts, which are not welcome; nor has it any attractions for the yachtsman. The outer harbour is fully occupied by the comings and goings of the ferries to Ile de Ré, and the business of the port. No doubt it would be possible to use the port in emergency, but no directions are given as the entry is obvious from charts 2746 or 2641 (2648 is on too small a scale).

Charts: 2746, 2648
High water: −0050 Brest, springs, +0010 Brest, neaps, Index 3, MTL3.6m
MHWS 6.1m (20 ft); MLWS 0.8m (2.5 ft); MHWN 4.9m (16 ft); MLWN 2.4m (8 ft)
Tidal streams: 3 miles NW of the island the SE stream begins −0520 Brest, the NW begins +0040 Brest, spring rates 1 knot. 1 mile SW of the island the SE stream begins −0530 Brest, the NW begins +0140 Brest, spring rates 2 knots.
Depths: An open roadstead, depths as required.

The Ile d'Aix lies about 8 miles from La Rochelle and is a popular objective for a day sail, though the anchorage is sufficiently sheltered for a night stop in fine weather. It is pleasanter in the evening, after the day trippers have gone. The island is horse-shoe shaped and measures about a mile at its maximum. Within this area is built a walled and moated village where Napoleon was imprisoned before he was taken to St Helena in HMS *Bellerophon*.

At the east side of the island a prison still exists, but there are no restrictions elsewhere. A

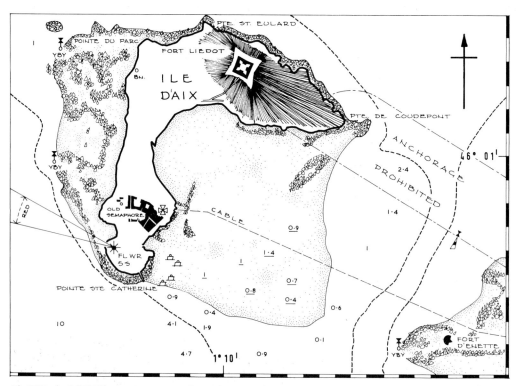

ILE D'AIX   MLWS 0.8m; MLWN 2.4m; −0050 (sp), +0010 (np) Brest, Index 3, MTL 3.6m
Based on French Chart No. 3711 with corrections   Depths in metres; right hand margin in cables

few fishermen live on Ile d'Aix, together with people who seek the peace of an island, free of convention and so small that all parts are within hearing distance of the sea.

Approach

The approach is straightforward from any direction, but probably easiest from the NW. Two beacons (card W) mark the outlying rocks on the west side. The northern one should be given a berth of at least ¼ mile, the southern one at least 1 cable. When the two white towers, one carrying the light and the other the screen for the red sector, come in transit, bearing 110°, the island can be approached. The SW side of the island is fairly clean and can be passed at a distance of 1 cable.

There is a narrow, deep channel to the E of the island which can be followed by keeping the beacon (card W) off Fort d'Enette bearing 197°, leaving to port the card W buoy off Pte de L'Epée and altering course to round the beacon at a distance of 2 cables. But when the tide is up and the flats to the SE of Ile d'Aix are well covered there is plenty of room.

By night : From the W keep in the white sector of Ile d'Aix light until Chauveau light turns from red to white, bearing 342°; steer 162° down this boundary, passing through the red sector of Ile d'Aix light. When this turns white again, steer on the leading lights for the Charente, bearing 115°. When Ile d'Aix light bears N steer 020° and anchor in 3m (10 ft). There are many lights; the significant ones are:

Ile d'Aix; Fl WR 5s, 24m, **23**, 13M.

(on the sector limits each flash shows successively white and red)

Chauveau; Oc (−−·) WR 12s, 23m, **17**, *14*M.

Charente leading lights; Dir Q R, **18**, *10*M.

Anchorage

Anchor 50m to 100m off the jetty and landing slip at Pointe Sainte Catherine, the south point of the island, going as far in as draft, tide, and the need to keep clear of moorings allow. This anchorage is really sheltered only from N and NE, but is partially sheltered from other directions by the mainland and Ile d'Oléron, so that it can be used in fine summer weather. The approaches are so well lit that there would be no difficulty in running for shelter to La Rochelle or elsewhere. The mud is very soft and the holding consequently poor.

Facilities

Those of a village, shops and a restaurant. Interesting Napoleonic museum.

The anchorage to the SE of Ile d'Aix.

Charts: 2746, 2748, 2648
High water : −0050 Brest, springs, +0010 Brest, neaps, Index 3, MTL 3.0m
MHWS 5.6m (18.5 ft); MLWS 0.3m (1.0 ft); MHWN 4.4m (14.5 ft); MLWN 1.7m (5.5 ft)
Tidal streams: Off the entrance the SE stream starts −0530 Brest, the NW starts +0130 Brest, spring rates 2 knots. In general streams in the river are about 2 knots, but where the river is narrowed they run up to 4 knots; they are affected by flood water. There is a bore on big spring tides; at such times the river should be avoided at all costs. At Rochefort the streams begin about 1 hr after HW and LW.
Depths: The approach is shallow, 0.5m (1 ft), but there is more water in the river. Without the large scale chart it should be treated as having 1m (3 ft). Off Soubise there is 4m (13 ft) or more.

Important note. No plan of the river is given in this book; anybody wishing to enter it should have No. 2746, which will tell him all he needs to know.

La Charente is an interesting river, away from the crowds, with a lot of bird life. The river lies between reedy banks, which have been reported to harbour mosquitoes on occasion. Rochefort is a historical town; a naval base well up the river for security from the British fleets. The remaining naval activity is all in 'stone frigates'. It is practicable to anchor off Soubise. A few miles above Soubise there is a lift bridge. This bridge opens for yachts only at set times, for a period of about 10 minutes. The times should be checked, but are at present (based on tides at La Rochelle) at HW −2, HW +1 hr. Three fixed white lights indicate that the passage is open. A yacht harbour has been developed at Rochefort. Masted vessels can go up to Tonnay, and the river is navigable for motor yachts, and said to be very attractive, for a considerable distance upstream to Saintes.

Approach and entrance
Straightforward, see chart No. 2746, at sufficient rise of tide. There are two pairs of leading

The anchorage at Soubise, looking upstream. The towers of the lift bridge and the old transporter bridge are seen in the background.

lights to follow through the outer shoals. When the river is entered it is sufficient to keep in midstream. There are beacons on the shore defining a succession of leading lines for the steamers. Many of the lines are marked at both ends, and the beacons for each line carry the same letter. It is better not to rely on them as the large scale chart shows that in some cases the intersection is in shallow water, so that it is necessary to turn off one line before the next is reached. Entrance and exit should be made on the flood or at the high water slack. As soon as the ebb starts any sea outside produces breakers on the bar.

Anchorage
At Soubise anchor on the S side of the river, as near to the bank as possible. There is a disused ferry slip at which it is possible to land, but it is silted up with soft mud. At Rochefort No. 1 dock is developed as a yacht harbour. The gates only open near HW. The docks farther up are strictly commercial.

Facilities
At Soubise all shops and hotel in the village, 5 minutes walk. There are no specifically yachting facilities. At Rochefort all the resources of a substantial town.

Rochefort yacht harbour: entry through gate and swing bridge off right hand edge.

Charts: 2746, 2648
Tides and depths: see under the ports.

This island, formerly somewhat of a backwater, looking back to the days when it was part of the realm of the kings of England, has now been connected to the mainland by a bridge. Consequently it is developing many of the characteristics of a standard French summer resort. The *quichenotte*, a starched bonnet designed to resist the attentions of the licentious British soldiery, is not now much worn. The name is a corruption of 'kiss–not'.

There are three main harbours, for two of which descriptions follow. The third, La Cotinière, is on the west side of the island; there is a substantial fishing fleet based there on heavy moorings against the Atlantic swell, though a new mole has improved the shelter. The other two harbours have rather different characteristics. Le Château d'Oléron was at one time the terminal of the car ferry; it is now wholly devoted to oyster culture. It is very crowded, but it has considerable character. The entrance is easy and the depths are such that a yacht will spend a substantial period afloat. La Perrotine has less character; there is a crowded

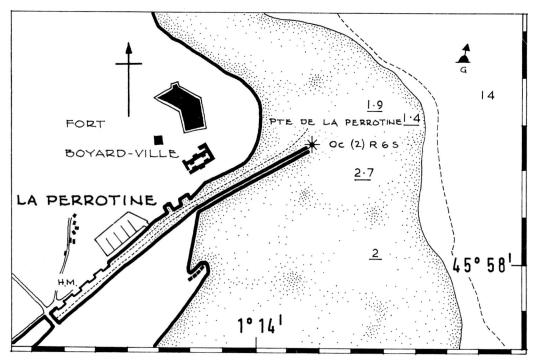

BOYARDVILLE, ILE D'OLÉRON   MLWS 0.8m; MLWN 2.5m; −0050 (sp), +0010 (np) Brest, Index 3, MTL 3.6m
Based on French Chart No. 3711 with corrections   Depths in metres; right hand margin in cables

Boyardville marina in a wet dock; apart from this, the available berths for a yacht which cannot take the ground are few. There is less water in the approach; there is some local yachting activity.

The Coureau d'Oléron is an interesting place to explore, rather off the beaten track. The large scale French charts 6335 and 6037 are recommended for exploration, but the ports can be reached with the English charts and the plans in this book.

Boyardville (La Perrotine)

High water: −0050 Brest, springs, +0010 Brest, neaps, Index 3, MTL 3.6m
MHWS 6.1m (20 ft); MLWS 0.8m (2.5 ft); MHWN 4.9m (16 ft); MLWN 2.3m (7.5 ft)
Tidal streams: Outside SE begins −0600 Brest, NW begins +0030 Brest, spring rates 1½ knots. There is some stream in the harbour, but it is not excessive.
Depths: The bar dries about 2m (7 ft). Yachts take the ground inside, but the channel does not completely dry. There is a marina in a wet dock.

The small port consists of a tidal river with a bar at the entrance, which dries. There is a long stone jetty on the SE side of the entrance. Outside the dock there are only a few berths suitable for yachts which cannot take the ground.

Approach
The entrance lies about 2 miles, 200°, from the conspicuous Fort Boyard. Leave the buoy (stbd) off the end of the jetty well to port and approach the end of the jetty, keeping the NW side open. Give the end a fairly wide berth, say 40m, and close with the jetty about 50m from its end. Thence keep close to the jetty, say 10m off, until the side begins to slope as the river is entered. Thence steer mid-channel, or rather to starboard of mid-channel.

By night: It is not very practical for a stranger to enter by night, unless there is very bright moonlight. The only light is:
Jetty head; Oc (2) R 6s, 8m, 9M.

The river quays at La Perrotine.

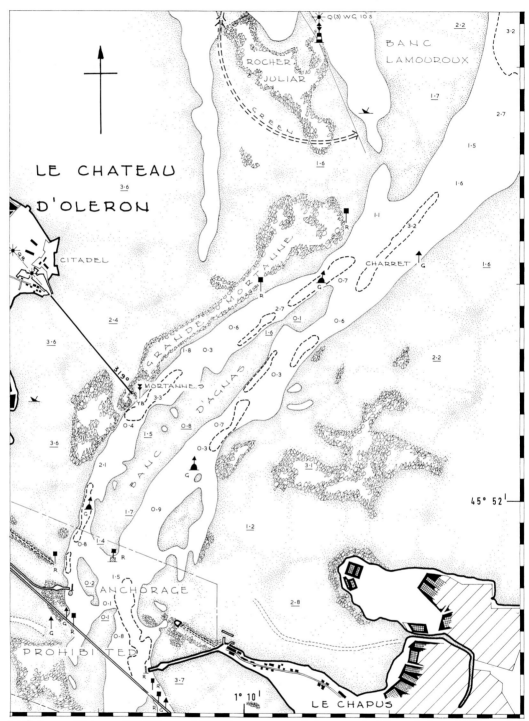

Le Château d'Oléron   MLWS 1.0m; MLWN 2.4m; −0040 (sp), +0015 (np) Brest, Index 2, MTL 3.5m
Based on French Chart No. 6037 with corrections   Depths in metres; right hand margin in cables

Boyardville marina entrance.

Mooring

The entrance to the wet dock (depth 2m) is at its E corner; the gates open and close automatically about 2 hours either side of HW, a warning light indicating their movement. Visitors berth against the NE wall of the dock, which is piled so that a plank is useful. The 5 pontoons are generally full. Yachts can lie in the river against quays above the marina entrance, the second from the sea end being recommended, or they can take the ground between the last quay and the bridge. The harbour master's office is on the quay, and his help should be sought. Yachts take the ground but do not dry completely. The bottom is not level everywhere so care is needed.

Facilities

Small supermarket and restaurants on the quay side. Yacht yard, chandlery and fuel on the port hand entering. Good bathing beaches within easy reach. There is not much of a village, but it has a certain simple attraction.

La Château d'Oléron

High water : −0040 Brest, springs, +0015 Brest, neaps, Index 2, MTL 3.5m
MHWS 6.0m; MLWS 1.0m; MHWN 4.7m; MLWN 2.4m
Tidal streams : Off the entrance the SSW stream begins −0500 Brest, the NNE at +0100 Brest. Spring rates about 1¼ knots. There is no stream in the harbour.
Depths: The approach has a depth of 0.6m (2 ft), the harbour dries 1.6m (5 ft).

Le Château d'Oléron is a small port wholly occupied with oysters; there is no yachting activity. The large number of fishing boats backed by the walls of the old fortifications which overlook the harbour make a picturesque scene. Le Château has the facilities of a holiday town, with the historical interest of the old fortifications.

Approach
The approach is made in the Coureau d'Oléron.

From the north. After clearing the dangers off La Charente and passing through the Rade des Trousses, leave to port the buoy (card W) off Les Ormeaux. Then leave to starboard the buoy (card E) off Banc Lamoreux; this buoy lies on the western side of the channel.

After this point the channel is marked on the lateral system, as an entrance to Rochefort, so that red marks will be to starboard, black to port. The marks are rather far apart, considering the complexity of the channels. Swing slowly round to leave a beacon (stbd) 2 cables to port, and then leave the buoy (stbd) on the north end of Banc d'Agnas close to port. Two beacons on the Grande Mortanne are left to starboard; the first is a port hand beacon, to be left at least 1 cable to starboard, the second marks the entrance, see below.

From the south. The channels look rather intricate, and at low water the chart is the best guide.

The harbour of Le Château. The leading light structures are indicated. This side of the harbour is very busy; yachts should berth to starboard.

But if the rise of tide is sufficient to enter the harbour, it will be possible to pass safely over the shoals in midstream; note that the Banc d'Agnas dries 1.4m (5 ft) and 1.7m (6 ft) in places.

Entrance

Keep the Mortanne Sud beacon card S close aboard to starboard. Steer straight for the leading light structures. The front mark is a tubby white cylindrical tank with a red board above it, the rear mark is an ordinary light tower. The starboard side of the entrance channel is marked by a line of withies; leave these about 10m to starboard. The channel is 10m wide, and is dredged to a depth of 0.8m (2 ft).

By night: A stranger would not be able to navigate the Coureau d'Oléron by night. If he has reached the entrance by nightfall there are leading lights to take him up to the harbour. They are:

Front; Q R 11m, 7M.
Rear; Q R 24m, 7M.

Harbour

The best water is at the quay on the port side of the outer harbour, drying 1.6m (5 ft). The bottom is soft mud. Here a yacht will be very much in the way of fishing vessels and must take advice. The quay on the starboard side dries about 3m (9 ft), bottom soft mud, near the seaward end, getting shallower near the shore. Here the yacht will be out of the way and this is the place to go. There are plenty of ladders and mooring rings.

There is an inner harbour. It has a serviceable dock gate, but this is not used. The inner harbour is therefore shallower and it is absolutely packed with fishing boats.

Facilities

Petrol and diesel available on the quay. No visible signs of water. Chandlers near the harbour. All shops and restaurants in the town, about 10 minutes walk. Municipal showers at the far end of the town. This is an interesting little harbour; the only difficulty is to find enough space clear of all the fishing boats.

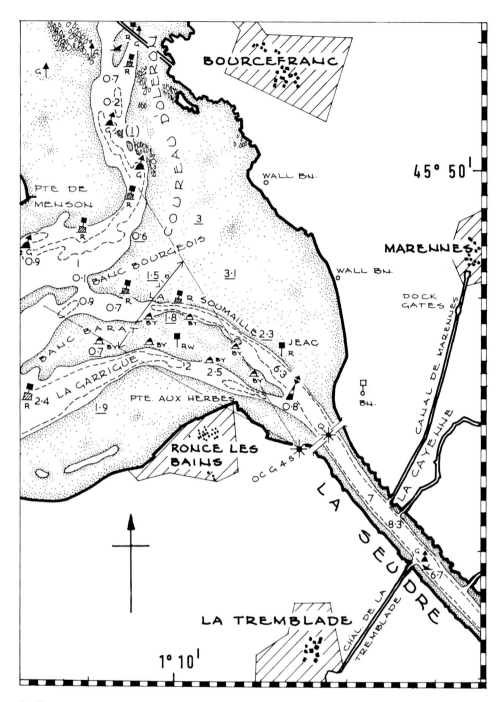

LA SEUDRE
MLWS 1.2m; MLWN 2.4m; −0030 (sp), +0020 (np) Brest, Index 1, MTL 3.5m
Based on French Charts Nos. 6335 and 6037 with corrections Depths in metres; right hand margin in cables

268

53 La Seudre

Charts: 2648, 2910
High water : −0030 Brest, springs, +0020 Brest, neaps, Index 1, MTL 3.5m
MHWS 5.8m (19 ft); MLWS 1.2m (4 ft); MHWN 4.7m (15.5 ft); MLWN 2.4m (8 ft)
Tidal streams: In the Coureau d'Oléron the tides vary considerably from point to point, but typically run up to 2½ knots springs. In the River Seudre the currents run up to 3 knots springs.
Depths: The channels of approach are shallow, one carrying 0.3m (1 ft) and the other drying 0.7m (3 ft). The river is deep, typically about 7m (24 ft).

La Seudre offers a secure anchorage near the southern end of the Coureau d'Oléron. The entrance is shallow and cannot be taken near low water, but once inside there is plenty of water. The scenery is not exciting, as salt pans lie for some distance behind either bank; in these an extensive and intensive oyster culture is carried on. Both La Tremblade and Marennes are pleasant towns in the season; the latter is farther both from the main river and the inner end of its canal.

Approach and entrance
There are two entrance channels, La Soumaille to the north and La Garrigue to the south. Both channels are narrow and the stranger should take frequent soundings to ensure that he is keeping in the deep water.
Chenal de la Soumaille. This channel carries 0.1m (0 ft) in theory, but it is better to treat it as drying 0.7m (3 ft). From the Coureau d'Oléron, bring the Pointe de Menson (the eastern point of the island, with a sanatorium on it) to bear 335° astern, and steer so. When the first of the buoys marking the channel, Soumaille NW (port), bears 090°, distant about 4 cables, alter course to pass about 1 cable S of it. Thence steer to leave the second buoy, Soumaille

The bridge over the Coureau d'Oléron.

The dock at Marennes, 1980.

SE (port), about 50m to port. From this point the channel is deep and swings gently round to pass to the south of the Jéac beacon (port), about 1 mile away to the ESE. The channel is narrow and very steep-to on the northern side. Three small BY buoys mark the northern side of Banc Barat. A good guide is to follow the 3m (10 ft) contour on the southern side of the channel. On reaching Jéac beacon steer to leave Saut de Barat buoy (card E) to starboard. Thence steer up the centre of the river. The river is crossed by a bridge with a clearance of 15m (49 ft) at high water.

Chenal de la Garrigue. The outer part of this channel is well buoyed on the port side; the first buoy is Galon d'Or (RW fairway spar) and it is followed by three port buoys. From the last of these, Barat, the channel continues towards the Barat beacon, 1½ miles away to the ENE. The small BY buoys marking the oyster beds help to define the channel. Keep a wall beacon on the shore in transit with the Barat beacon, bearing 068°. About 2 cables from the Barat beacon the channel turns to starboard. Steer to keep the Saut de Barat buoy (card E) bearing 108°. The channel shoals to about 2.5m (8 ft), then deepens again. Finally, as the Saut de Barat buoy is passed, the shallowest point, 0.8m (2 ft), is reached. Thence steer up the centre of the river.

Anchorage and mooring
The best anchorages are near the disused ferry slips for Marennes (north bank) and La Tremblade (south bank). The former is called La Cayenne and is about ½ mile downstream of the latter. Anchor near the side of the river and land on the ferry slip, carrying the dinghy ashore clear of the slip.

There are canals, which dry, going to the villages of Marennes and La Tremblade. That to La Tremblade should be treated as drying 2.5m (8 ft); to get this depth it will be necessary to stay close to the centre of the canal. The canal is lined on each side by the boats and other apparatus of oyster culture. It is possible to berth alongside the stone quay to starboard just round the bend at the top end of the canal. Once round the bend the best water is on the starboard side; the bottom is soft mud. The water shoals rapidly once the far end of the quay is reached. There is not much room, but visitors are helped to find a berth. Although some yachts are based at the top of the canal, the canal is really better for a dinghy excursion, which is worth while if only to have it brought home how many oysters there are.

The canal to Marennes should also be considered as drying 2.5m (8 ft); again it is necessary to keep exactly to the centre for the best water. At the entrance, which lies to the west of the ferry pier, there is a slight bend to starboard—the perches are high on the mud, but the best water lies roughly midway between them. At the upper end of the canal is a wet dock, the gates of which are opened about 1 hr each side of high water. This dock is used by some 70 yachts, and provides a convenient and pleasant berth if there is room. The oyster culture, though notable, is not quite on the scale of that at La Tremblade.

Facilities

At La Tremblade all shops and restaurants. Marine engineer and outboard specialist. At Marennes there are all shops, reached by a few minutes walk through pretty municipal gardens. There is a yacht builder at the wet dock.

Canal de Marennes, looking up from its mouth.

Chart: 2910
High water: as Brest, Index 1, MTL 3.5m
MHWS 5.8m (19 ft); MLWS 1.2m (4 ft); MHWN 4.7m (15.5 ft); MLWN 2.4m (8 ft)
Tidal streams: The E stream begins about +0600 Brest, spring rate 3 knots, the W stream begins about −0100 Brest, spring rate 4 knots.
Depths: Variable, but sufficient for yachts near high water.

Note: The information for this chapter comes principally from Mrs Tew, Mr Ian Tew and Mr P. C. Hordern.

The Pertuis de Maumusson, between the southern end of Ile d'Oléron and the mainland, has such a bad reputation that many people say that it cannot be used by yachts in any circumstances. Discussions with local fishermen and yachtsmen, and the experience of at least one yachtsman who has used it, suggest that this is not true. The passage is, however, undoubtedly very SEVERE (see page 25), and those who intend to use it should, if possible, seek local advice.

The passage is completely exposed to the Atlantic, and if there is any onshore wind or swell the shallow and uneven bottom causes breakers to form right across as soon as the flood tide stops. The passage must, therefore, be made on the last of the flood, and at that only in calm weather or with an offshore wind, and in the absence of swell.

The bottom is sand, so that the channel shifts and is said to be tending to get shallower. The buoys are not moved to follow all these shifts, though normally they indicate a line which will give enough water for a yacht at high water in smooth conditions. Only the local people know the current position of the deepest water in relation to the buoys; hence the need for local advice.

For the outward passage there is the opportunity to inspect the channel near low water if one arrives in good time, to see the state of the sea, and if necessary, to turn back with a favourable tide, since the passage should be taken before high water.

The inward passage must contain an unacceptable element of risk except in very good weather. The breakers, if they exist, cannot always be seen clearly from seaward, it is more difficult to identify the run of the channel, and if one gets into difficulty, it will be hard to retreat to sea with the tide carrying one in. This makes it essential to seek local advice at La Cotinière, or the Yacht Club at Royan, before attempting the inward passage.

Finally, it must be emphasised again that this passage is very SEVERE, only to be attempted in very good weather by those who have experience of tidal race conditions. Adequate and reliable power is essential. The speed with which the breakers begin near high water is dramatic.

55 Royan and the Gironde

Charts: 2910, 2916, 2664
High water: +0010 Brest, Index 0, MTL 3.0m
MHWS 5.2m; MLWS 0.9m; MHWN 4.1m; MLWN 1.9m
Tidal streams: In the main entrance channel the flood begins E about −0500 Brest, spring rate about 2½ knots, the ebb W about +0130 Brest, spring rate 4 knots. Off Royan the flood begins SE at −0530 Brest, the ebb NW at +0130 Brest, spring rates 3¾ knots. In the bay close to the port there is an eddy; the stream runs continuously southward, 1 knot during the flood, 3 knots during the ebb.
Depths: The approach and harbour were dredged to give a depth of 1.5m but in 1980 the harbour was about datum level.

The church of Notre Dame at Royan is conspicuous. On the right is the south jetty.

Royan was a German base during the war and was consequently heavily damaged; the buildings are all new. The unsymmetrical spire of the modern church of Notre Dame stands up above the town and is a landmark. The town is a holiday centre with a yacht harbour; it is twinned with Gosport. It is an excellent staging point for those entering or leaving the Gironde on the way to or from the Midi canal, but it is so busy that the visitor's welcome will fade after a day or two.

Approach
Entry to the Gironde should not be attempted in heavy weather. A recently corrected chart is essential; the banks shift and not only does this entail frequent movement of the buoys, but also of the leading lights. The Palmyre front lighthouse has recently been moved southwards to cover a new deep water channel on 081½°; the BXA light buoy lies very close to this alignment, about 2 miles south of its old location. Coming from the N, it is only necessary to keep 4 or 5 miles offshore to avoid Banc de la Mauvaise and Grand Banc, joining the Palmyre lighthouses alignment at the outer channel buoys. The new deep water channel is narrow for 3 miles, and it may be preferred to sail a parallel course; after 7 (card N) buoy the channel is wide; 7, 7a and 9 starboard buoys are all just N of the leading line, and there is no problem in following the buoyed channel for Royan.

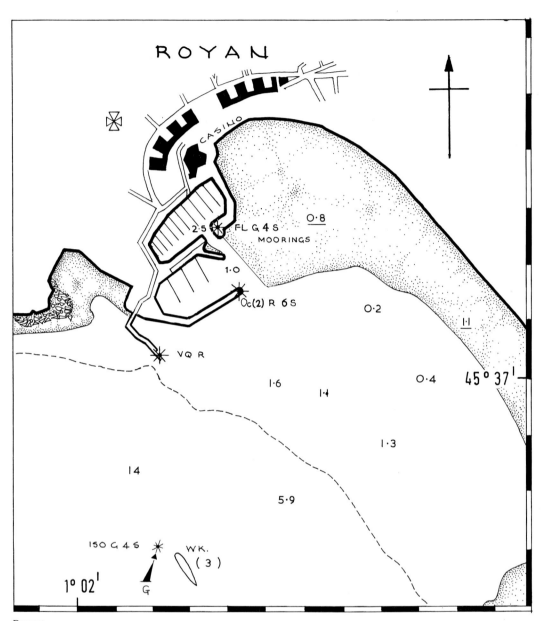

ROYAN
MLWS 0.9m; MLWN 1.9m; +0010 Brest, Index 0, MTL 3.0m
Based on French Chart No. 6141 with corrections
Depths in metres; right hand margin in cables

The town of Royan, with its white buildings and modern church, will be easily identified. The shore should be given a berth of two cables; on reaching Pointe du Chay, steer for the red and white light tower on the south jetty head, where the ferry berths.

From the SE, pass outside Banc de St. Georges, leaving to starboard 12 (port hand) buoy at its NW end, or cutting the corner if tide height and conditions allow. An alternative daylight course inside the Banc passes 2 or 3 cables off Pointe de Susac and Pointe de Vallières; thence on 330° for the south jetty head, avoiding wrecks over which there is 3m, marked by a starboard buoy.

By night : The outer approach is as by day. The lights are:
BXA light buoy; Iso W 4s, 8m, 10M, Whis.
     Radiobeacon, call BX, 291.9 kHz, continuous, 5M.
La Coubre; Fl (2) W 10s, 64m, **31**, *21*M.
     also FRG, 42m, 12M.
     Radiobeacon, call LK, 303.4 kHz, 1/6 min, begins H + 3 min.
Cordouan; Oc (−−·) WRG 12s, 60m, 23M.
La Palmyre, front; Oc W 4s, 21m, 22M.
La Palmyre, rear; Q W 57m, 27M.
     also rear; Dir FR, 57m, 17M.
with Terre Nègre, front; Oc (3) WRG 12s 39m, 17M.
The channel buoys are:
Port; red, flashing or occulting.
Starboard; green, flashing or occulting or isophase except for No. 7 (card N), white.

Entrance
On close approach leave to port the south jetty and the outer harbour mole. The harbour entrance then opens up, the straight approach on a NW course leaving 3 mole heads to port and one to starboard.

By night : The lights are:
South jetty; VQ R 11m, 13M.
Outer mole; Oc (2) R 6s, 8m, 6M.
Entrance, E side; Fl G 4s, 4m, 2M.
Starboard buoy marking wreck; Iso G 4s.

Mooring
The outer mole encloses the new fishing harbour; the inner harbour, formerly shared between yachts and fishing boats, is now exclusively pleasure; 10 pontoons, accessible from the NW end, accommodate 620 boats with 3.5m, though the access channel has only 1.0m. On entry, secure to the pontoon to port, and report to the port office on the jetty above for a berth to be allotted.

Royan yacht harbour, at LW springs, 1980. It has since been dredged to 2.5m.

There are about 30 mooring buoys on the NE side of the entrance channel, somewhat exposed except in northerly winds.

Facilities
All the facilities of a sophisticated holiday town. All shops, chandlers, restaurants, banks, close by, many in the arcade overlooking the marina. Water by hose at the pontoons, petrol and diesel from pumps on the port side mole head by the harbour office. There is a scrubbing hard at the SE corner, and a crane on the east mole which could be used for dismasting by anyone who preferred to do this here rather than at Bordeaux. A ferry runs from the south jetty to Port Bloc.

The Gironde
Although outside the scope of this book, the following notes may be helpful. There is a well marked ship channel up to Bordeaux. The tide runs so hard that with a reasonable turn of speed a yacht can make Bordeaux on a single tide. It is also possible to stop at a number of places, such as Pauillac and Blaye, on the way up. At Bordeaux there is a marina to starboard just above the suspension bridge, and it is also possible to enter the docks, a little further up to starboard, from 2 hr before HW until HW. There are cranes for dismasting both at the marina and at the docks.

56 Port Bloc

Charts: 2910, 2916, 2664
High water: +0010 Brest, Index 0, MTL 3.1m
MHWS 5.3m (17.5 ft); MLWS 1.0m (3.5 ft); MHWN 4.2m (14 ft); MLWN 2.0m (6.5 ft)
Tidal streams: The SE stream begins at −0530 Brest, the NW at +0130 Brest, spring rates 3¾ knots.
Depths: The approaches are deep. There is 2 to 2.5m (6 to 8 ft) in the harbour.

Port Bloc, a small harbour just behind Pointe de Grave, is a convenient passage harbour. It is used by the ferries to Royan and by the buoy maintenance vessels, but is otherwise a long way from anywhere. Pleasantly situated among the pine trees, it is reasonably sheltered, though some swell is said to enter in bad weather. Verdon, to the SE, is being developed as a major port; this may affect facilities here.

Approach and entrance
For the outer approach, and notes on the Gironde, see the previous chapter. By night the final entry to the river can be made with La Palmyre red light in transit with Terre Nègre, astern, bearing 327°.

The main problem in the final approach is not to be set on to the mole off Pointe de Grave or swept up the river, depending on the tide. The harbour entrance faces NE, nearly parallel with the shore. The entrance is not very easily made out until it is close to, but it is only about 3 cables to the south of the extreme tip of the Pointe de Grave.

Approach on a SW course, from buoy No. 13B, and enter between the light structures, white with red top to port, white with green top to starboard. The ferries occupy the whole of the entrance, so if one is on the move stand off until the entrance is clear.

Port Bloc. The ferries at the left are parked; the ferry landing is to starboard on entering.

Port Bloc, looking N. The ferries would be strong competitors if a cup were offered for the world's ugliest ship.

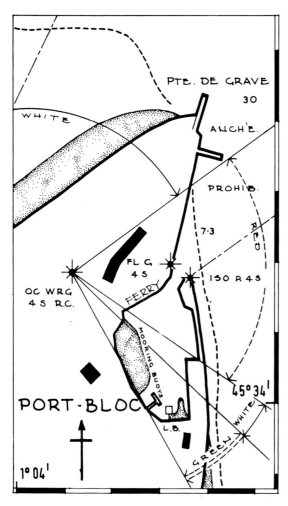

PORT BLOC
MLWS 1.0m; MLWN 2.0m
+0010 Brest, Index 0, MTL 3.1m
Based on French Chart No. 6141
Depths in metres; right hand margin in cables

278

By night: The lights are:
Pointe de Grave; Oc WRG 4s, 26m, 18, *14*M.
      Radiobeacon, call VR, 308 kHz, 10 sec, continuous by day.
Buoy 13B; FG, 7m, 5M.
Entrance, west side; Fl G 4 sec, 8m, 7M.
Entrance, east side; Iso W 4 sec, 8m, 8M.

Anchorage and Mooring
There is a line of white mooring buoys running down the centre of the harbour in a north-south direction. The eastern or seaward side of the harbour is for the use of the ferries, the buoy vessels and the lifeboat. Yachts berth between the mooring buoys in 2 to 2.5m (6 to 8 ft), or if a berth is available, at the pontoon at the top of the harbour. It is possible, but uncomfortable, to anchor west of the white buoys, but the bottom shoals towards the shore, especially in the bay near the ferry slip.

Facilities
Virtually none; only a kiosk and a café. There is a railway, with train services to Bordeaux.

Port Bloc, looking S from the ferry slip in 1980. These moorings are shallow and crowded.

Tide Tables

From the Nautical Almanac take the time and height of HW Brest. From the chapter heading for the port (or the caption to the plan of the port) take the time of local high water as compared with Brest, the Port Index, and the mean tide level (MTL).

1. Calculate the time of local high water (HW Brest ± difference for the port).
2. Calculate the interval between local HW and the time when the height is required.
3. Along the top of the tide table, below, find the column with the nearest height of HW Brest (in feet or metres).

Brest HW {ft / {m; Tide index	18.2 / 5.5 / 0	18.5 / 5.6 / 1	18.8 / 5.7 / 2	19.0 / 5.8 / 3	19.3 / 5.9 / 4	19.6 / 6.0 / 5	20.0 / 6.1 / 6	20.4 / 6.2 / 7	20.8 / 6.3 / 8	21.2 / 6.5 / 9	21.7 / 6.6 / 10
Total index	0	1	2 (add)	3	4	5	6	7 (port)	8	9	10
oh 00	0.8	0.9	0.9	1.0	1.1	1.1	1.2	1.3	1.4	1.5	1.6
20	0.8	0.8	0.9	1.0	1.0	1.1	1.2	1.3	1.3	1.4	1.5
40	0.8	0.8	0.9	0.9	1.0	1.1	1.1	1.2	1.3	1.4	1.5
1h 00	0.7	0.8	0.8	0.9	0.9	1.0	1.1	1.1	1.2	1.3	1.4
10	0.7	0.7	0.8	0.8	0.9	0.9	1.0	1.1	1.2	1.2	1.3
20	0.6	0.7	0.7	0.8	0.8	0.9	1.0	1.0	1.1	1.2	1.3
30	0.6	0.6	0.7	0.7	0.8	0.8	0.9	1.0	1.0	1.1	1.2
40	0.5	0.6	0.6	0.7	0.7	0.8	0.8	0.9	0.9	1.0	1.1
50	0.5	0.5	0.6	0.6	0.7	0.7	0.7	0.8	0.9	0.9	1.0
2h 00	0.4	0.5	0.5	0.5	0.6	0.6	0.7	0.7	0.8	0.8	0.9
10	0.4	0.4	0.5	0.5	0.5	0.6	0.6	0.6	0.7	0.7	0.8
20	0.3	0.4	0.4	0.4	0.4	0.5	0.5	0.5	0.6	0.6	0.7
30	0.3	0.3	0.3	0.3	0.4	0.4	0.4	0.4	0.5	0.5	0.5
40	0.2	0.2	0.2	0.3	0.3	0.3	0.3	0.3	0.4	0.4	0.4
50	0.1	0.2	0.2	0.2	0.2	0.2	0.2	0.2	0.2	0.3	0.3
3h 00	0.1	0.1	0.1	0.1	0.1	0.1	0.1	0.1	0.1	0.1	0.1
10											
20	0.1	0.1	0.1	0.1	0.1	0.1	0.1	0.1	0.1	0.1	0.1
30	0.1	0.1	0.1	0.2	0.2	0.2	0.2	0.2	0.2	0.2	0.3
40	0.2	0.2	0.2	0.2	0.3	0.3	0.3	0.3	0.3	0.4	0.4
50	0.3	0.3	0.3	0.3	0.3	0.4	0.4	0.4	0.4	0.5	0.5
4h 00	0.3	0.3	0.4	0.4	0.4	0.5	0.5	0.5	0.5	0.6	0.6
10	0.4	0.4	0.4	0.5	0.5	0.5	0.6	0.6	0.6	0.7	0.7
20	0.4	0.5	0.5	0.5	0.6	0.6	0.6	0.7	0.7	0.8	0.8
30	0.5	0.5	0.5	0.6	0.6	0.7	0.7	0.7	0.8	0.8	0.9
40	0.5	0.6	0.6	0.6	0.7	0.7	0.8	0.8	0.9	0.9	1.0
50	0.6	0.6	0.7	0.7	0.8	0.8	0.9	0.9	1.0	1.0	1.1
5h 00	0.6	0.7	0.7	0.8	0.8	0.9	0.9	1.0	1.1	1.1	1.2
20	0.7	0.7	0.8	0.8	0.9	1.0	1.0	1.1	1.2	1.3	1.4
40	0.8	0.8	0.9	0.9	1.0	1.1	1.2	1.2	1.3	1.4	1.5
6h 00	0.8	0.9	0.9	1.0	1.1	1.1	1.2	1.3	1.4	1.5	1.6

Left-side labels: Interval from local HW; Add to MTL (m) (upper portion); Subtract from MTL (m) (lower portion).

4. Note the corresponding Tide Index, add the Port Index (see opposite), and locate the column headed by the total.

5. Run down this column to the correct interval from local HW, calculated in (2) opposite, and read off the correction to the MTL. The answer will be in metres, even if you started with Brest HW in feet.

6. Add or subtract this to or from the MTL (opposite), as indicated in the margin, to obtain the rise of the tide above chart datum.

22.7	23.3	23.9	24.5	25.2	25.9						
6.9	7.1	7.3	7.5	7.7	7.9						
12	13	14	15	16	17						

index 12	13	14	15	16	17	18	19	20	21	22		
1.8	1.9	2.1	2.2	2.3	2.5	2.7	2.9	3.1	3.3	3.5	oh oo	
1.8	1.9	2.0	2.2	2.3	2.5	2.6	2.8	3.0	3.2	3.4	20	
1.7	1.8	1.9	2.1	2.2	2.4	2.5	2.7	2.9	3.1	3.3	40	
1.6	1.7	1.8	1.9	2.1	2.2	2.3	2.5	2.7	2.9	3.1	1h oo	
1.5	1.6	1.7	1.8	2.0	2.1	2.2	2.4	2.6	2.7	2.9	10	
1.4	1.5	1.6	1.8	1.9	2.0	2.1	2.3	2.4	2.6	2.8	20	
1.3	1.4	1.5	1.6	1.7	1.9	2.0	2.1	2.3	2.4	2.6	30	Add to MTL (m)
1.2	1.3	1.4	1.5	1.6	1.7	1.8	2.0	2.1	2.2	2.4	40	
1.1	1.2	1.3	1.4	1.5	1.6	1.7	1.8	1.9	2.0	2.2	50	
1.0	1.1	1.1	1.2	1.3	1.4	1.5	1.6	1.7	1.8	1.9	2h oo	
0.9	1.0	1.0	1.1	1.2	1.3	1.3	1.4	1.5	1.6	1.7	10	
0.8	0.8	0.9	0.9	1.0	1.1	1.1	1.2	1.3	1.4	1.5	20	
0.6	0.7	0.7	0.7	0.8	0.9	0.9	1.0	1.0	1.1	1.2	30	
0.4	0.5	0.5	0.6	0.6	0.7	0.7	0.7	0.8	0.9	0.9	40	
0.3	0.3	0.4	0.4	0.4	0.5	0.5	0.5	0.5	0.6	0.6	50	
0.1	0.2	0.2	0.2	0.2	0.2	0.2	0.2	0.2	0.3	0.3	3h oo	
											10	
0.1	0.2	0.2	0.2	0.2	0.2	0.2	0.2	0.2	0.3	0.3	20	
0.3	0.3	0.3	0.4	0.4	0.4	0.4	0.5	0.5	0.5	0.6	30	
0.4	0.5	0.5	0.5	0.6	0.6	0.6	0.7	0.7	0.8	0.8	40	
0.6	0.6	0.7	0.7	0.7	0.8	0.9	0.9	1.0	1.0	1.1	50	
0.7	0.8	0.8	0.9	0.9	1.0	1.1	1.1	1.2	1.3	1.4	4h oo	
0.8	0.9	0.9	1.0	1.1	1.2	1.2	1.3	1.4	1.5	1.6	10	
0.9	1.0	1.1	1.1	1.2	1.3	1.4	1.5	1.6	1.7	1.8	20	
1.0	1.1	1.2	1.3	1.4	1.5	1.6	1.7	1.8	1.9	2.0	30	
1.2	1.2	1.3	1.4	1.5	1.6	1.7	1.8	2.0	2.1	2.2	40	Subtract from MTL (m)
1.3	1.4	1.5	1.6	1.7	1.8	1.9	2.1	2.2	2.3	2.5	50	
1.4	1.5	1.6	1.7	1.8	2.0	2.1	2.2	2.4	2.5	2.7	5h oo	
1.5	1.6	1.8	1.9	2.0	2.2	2.3	2.5	2.6	2.8	3.0	20	
1.7	1.8	2.0	2.1	2.2	2.4	2.6	2.8	2.9	3.1	3.3	40	
1.8	1.9	2.1	2.2	2.3	2.5	2.7	2.9	3.1	3.3	3.5	6h oo	

Index

282